Mercedes-Benz

W126 S-CLASS
1979-1991

Mercedes-Benz
W126 S-CLASS
1979-1991

Nik Greene

THE CROWOOD PRESS

First published in 2019 by
The Crowood Press Ltd
Ramsbury, Marlborough
Wiltshire SN8 2HR

www.crowood.com

British Library Cataloguing-in-Publication Data
A catalogue record for this book is available from the British Library.

ISBN 978 1 78500 541 1

Acknowledgements
The job of a writer is more often than not solitary, sitting at a screen, losing oneself in content. This often spills over into relaxation and sleep time when words, ideas, images and research get mulled over, cogitated and sometimes involuntarily spoken aloud in the small early hours. Not once did my wife Trudy complain at the loss of company or the glazed look she received upon my realization that she was actually talking to me. I thank her sincerely for her support from beginning to end.

I would like to thank all at The Crowood Press for once again having the faith in my enthusiasm for the 126.

I must give a massive thank you to those at the Daimler Archives in Stuttgart for the time, dedication and continued enthusiasm they have showed me. The Daimler Classic archives resource is an incredible place to be for an enthusiast, and never once did they take that for granted.

My special thanks go to my patient, enthusiastic friend, Bert van de Bovenkamp, who accompanied me without complaint on every research trip to Stuttgart, aided me with the German language and drove me around for no other reason than being supportive and sharing in my enthusiasm for the 126 and German beer; a true friend.

I would like to thank Ralf Weber for the photos of his beautiful 560SEL Station wagon, but more importantly for the assistance he gave with the introduction to and during the interview with Bruno Sacco; not only a Mercedes enthusiast to the core, but a rare philanthropist of his knowledge.
I wish to sincerely thank Bruno Sacco for not just agreeing to be interviewed by me but for really spending quality time with me. It was a day I shall remember fondly for as long as I live.

Thank you to all those who assisted me with photos and enthusiasm, especially: Bram Corts, author of the website resource www.1000sel.com; Allen Kroliczek for his beautiful AMG Engine pictures; and of course Philip and Les Kruger for the stunning photos of their 'limited edition' South African-built 126. Hopefully seeing your 'pride and joy' on the front cover will give you joy also.

Designed and typeset by Guy Croton Publishing Services,
West Malling, Kent

Printed and bound in India by Parksons Graphics

CONTENTS

INTRODUCTION: 'THE BEST OR NOTHING'

When writing a book such as this, the common practice is to write an introductory biography about the company itself; however, not wanting to make light of the contribution made by Gottlieb Daimler, Wilhelm Maybach and Karl Benz as the founders, what really set Mercedes-Benz, and latterly Daimler AG, apart as a company was not only the vision and ethic that they brought with them as individuals, but the fact they were willing to recognize the talent and abilities in others – never more so than in those early days, when the 'horseless carriage' transitioned into the motor car. A dizzying number of inventions from an equally dizzying number of inventors rushed to make a name for themselves and instead of competing against them, Daimler quickly realized that quality over quantity was what would really raise them above the rest and consequently 'cherry picked' these talented people.

Gottlieb Daimler's motto, '*Das Beste oder nichts*' ('Nothing but the best') was as much about the company as it was the product.

The story of Emil Jellinek giving the name of his daughter Mércédès Jellinek, to his line of racing engines and eventually, after merging with Daimler to become Daimler-Benz, giving the Mercedes name to the vehicles produced thereafter, is a story well told and, although this is of great importance to the company history, what is doubly important is the man himself. Apart from being a perfectionist, he expected nothing less from anyone else. His fiery temper and a willingness to speak his mind raised a few hackles at DMG (Daimler Motoren Gesellschaft), especially Gottlieb himself. 'Your engineers should be locked up in an insane asylum' and 'Your car is the chrysalis and I want the butterfly', were just two documented harangues.

Wilhelm Maybach, on the other hand, knew exactly where he was coming from; he could already see that the only thing

Emil Jellinek. BARON HENRI ROTHSCHILD

Emil Jellinek and his chauffeur Hermann Braun in Baden near Vienna. First Daimler vehicle (6-hp 'Double Phaeton' model) from 1898, which Emil Jellinek had purchased in Cannstatt.

holding back the development of better, faster and more efficient engines was the vehicle itself. They understood that making a better vehicle meant making it more capable of being better; the 'horseless carriage' could never progress without addressing stability and safety.

Emil Jellinek summed up what Daimler-Mercedes would become when he said, 'I don't want a car for today or tomorrow, it will be the car for the day after tomorrow'.

It is all too easy to look at big companies such as Daimler AG and just see a large, faceless corporation, and you may feel these early pioneers are a million miles from what has become the Daimler AG of today, but you would be wrong – these people were just the beginning of a string of individuals who 'stuck to their guns' and kept the integrity of their design intact. It is these individuals who would mould the company into what it is today.

The small 'bio' will give the reader some idea of the talent involved in creating every vehicle in the Daimler/Benz/Mercedes range, and on reading through the content of this book, hopefully it will bring alive the individuals, as opposed to just being faceless names.

WERNER BREITSCHWERDT (BORN 23 SEPTEMBER 1927)

Having been drafted to the eastern front at the age of sixteen, Werner Breitschwerdt's electrical engineering apprenticeship at the Technical University of Stuttgart had to be put on hold until his return and release from active duty and, even though he did everything in his power to 'catch up', it still put him back a couple of years by normal standards. After achieving physics to undergraduate level and gaining his diploma in electrical engineering, he continued to work at the same university as scientific assistant.

After joining Daimler-Benz AG in April of 1953 he was put in charge of a team to develop the industry's first CAD (computer-aided design) system and quickly made a name for himself as a very capable street-smart engineer; he was eventually asked to join the passenger car body division as experimental engineer.

Although not everyone took to his hands-on, outside-of-the-box, perfectionist way of working, within twenty years he was appointed director and head of develop-

Barényi (second from the left), Häcker (third from the left), Wilfert (third from the right) and Professor Breitschwerdt (far right) explaining the constructive details, 1960.

ment for this section, with styling (as the design division was then known) being added to his responsibilities one year later.

In 1977, Breitschwerdt joined the board of management of Daimler-Benz AG as a deputy member before being appointed a full member in 1979. In this capacity, he was once again responsible for research and development. Under his stewardship, he oversaw the development of the CIII range of research and experimental vehicles, which became a test bed for all future technologies that would play a definitive role in shaping the vision of accident-free driving by way of electronic assistance systems, alternative drive concepts and multilink suspension set-ups.

One particular milestone was the electronics side of the ABS anti-lock braking system alongside Professor Guntram Huber, which celebrated its worldwide series premiere in the S-Class (W 116) in 1978.

What Breitschwerdt's hands-on dogged pursuit of vehicle and occupant safety in all vehicles proved to Daimler was that it didn't have to be at the expense of their usual standards of quality, robustness, dynamic attributes and sporting elegance, and this went on to stand them in good stead as they entered a large, medium-range car segment that has continued today in the C Class range.

Professor Dr Werner Breitschwerdt.

Mercedes-Benz record car C III/III, 5-cylinder turbo-diesel in trial and record runs on the circuit in Nardo, April 1978. Standing in front of the record car, and sitting from left to right: driver Paul Frère (blue driver suit), driver Guido Moch, Professor Werner Breitschwerdt, Professor Hans Scherenberg, Rudolf Uhlenhaut, driver Rico Steinmann, driver Dr Hans Liebold, Friedrich van Winsen and Günther Molter.

From 1983 until 1987, Breitschwerdt was chairman of the board of management and CEO of Daimler-Benz AG, and during this time he initiated a joint research project called PROMETHEUS (Programme for European Traffic with Highest Efficiency and Unprecedented Safety). The result was the advancement of numerous technologies offering huge leaps forward in safety. At Mercedes-Benz, these were translated into specific technical products such as the DISTRONIC PLUS cruise control system and the automatic PRE-SAFE® brake system, which we now take for granted.

Although Breitschwerdt's manner and appearance made him an easy mark for detractors who thought he should be a little more polished, his achievements spoke for themselves. He summed himself up succinctly when he said, 'Top management should be able to create the right motivation that gets more ideas out of the organization than the company can use'.

He has been, and he was, the recipient of numerous awards culminating in receiving the 'Grand Order of Merit of the Federal Republic of Germany' and being inducted into the European Automotive Hall of Fame, Geneva, in 2009.

BÉLA VIKTOR KARL BARÉNYI (BORN 1 MARCH 1907)

Bela Barényi started life in Hirtenberg near Vienna. Being born into one of the wealthiest Austrian families in Austria–Hungary afforded him the privilege of witnessing, first hand, the early transitional growth of the automobile in a world of horse-drawn carriages, as his father owned an 'Austro-Daimler' motor car. Little did Bela Barényi know that it would be this very automobile that would not only shape 'his' future, but that of the automotive world also.

After his father was killed in action in the First World War, the following 'Great Depression' quickly brought the family business to financial ruin and great hardship ensued. Having little money to afford to pay his school fees, he had to rethink his future. It was only the fond memories of that first automobile that spurred him on to fight tooth and nail to find the means to enrol as an engineering student at the Viennese Technical College of Mechanical and Electrical Engineering.

As a young student he quickly developed an amazing 'vision' of design and problem-solving, which focused his attention not on current models and thinking, but of poten-

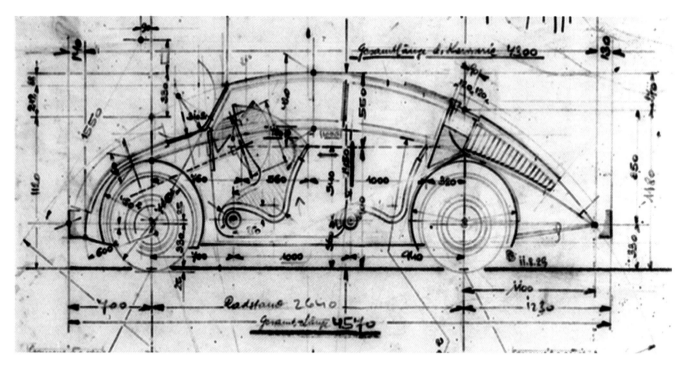

Barényi called his design for a people's car a Volks-wagen. This would become very significant twenty years later.

tial future enhancements. Within a year he had sketched his ideas of a future 'people's car'.

More struggling was yet to come; he graduated with excellent marks in 1926 just as the Great Depression was starting to bite. His aim was always to get into DMG (Daimler-Motoren-Gesellschaft) and, even though they had merged with Benz & Cie, the current economic climate had put a hold on recruitment.

It took almost a decade of surviving on temporary posts and a freelance draughtsmanship before finding himself a steady job at Gesellschaft für technischen Fortschritt (GETEFO, Society for Technical Progress) in Berlin; but, once again, at the beginning of 1939 he was made redundant.

Again he applied to what had now become Mercedes-Benz but was turned down. With nothing to lose, he approached Chairman Wilhelm Haspel directly and demanded a face to face interview to show him his abilities. His tenacity and determination won him over; Haspel recognized immediately his passion, not just for the motor car, but safety, 'You, Herr Barényi are twenty years ahead of your time, you will be put under a bell-jar at Sindelfingen and everything you invent will go directly to the patent department'. Barényi never had to fill out another job application again.

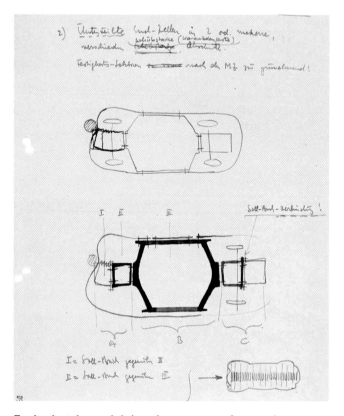

Early sketch, explaining the concept of crumple zones.

The first Mercedes-Benz vehicle with bodywork developed according to this patent was the 1959 W III series – better known as the 'Tailfin Mercedes'.

Particularly in the 'post-war era', no one really wanted to be reminded of the dangers of driving and, in essence, the topic was thought to be a sales killer; but, again, Barényi's passion forged onward. His biggest breakthrough came on the 23 January 1951 when he registered patent DBP 854.157 with the description, 'Motor vehicles especially for the transportation of people'; behind this austere description was no less than the description commonly referred to as the 'crumple zone'.

Béla Barényi was the first to recognize years before, in fact, that kinetic energy should be dissipated by deformation so as not to harm the occupants of the vehicle.

All in all, this discovery was to revolutionize the entire automotive industry and became the decisive factor in 'passive safety'. The ingenious mastermind of the idea knew that, contrary to the popular belief that 'a safe car must not yield but be stable', in a collision, kinetic energy must be absorbed through deformation in order for the occupants to be protected. He logically split the car body into three 'boxes': a soft front section, a rigid passenger cell and a soft rear section. The patent was granted on 28 August 1952.

Being an inventor through and through, and not one to rest on his laurels, Béla Barényi's considerations under the engine hood were equally revolutionary: the steering gear moved far to the rear and the auxiliary units were arranged in such a way so as not to form blocks with each other in

the event of a collision, but rather to slip past one another, permitting more effective crumpling of the bodywork.

The interior of the W III didn't escape his touch either: for the first time ever in any automobile, the interior was completely redesigned so as to reduce further injury hazard in an accident. Hard or sharp-edged controls were replaced by yielding, rounded or recessed units, combined with recessed door handles, a dashboard that yielded on impact, padded window ledges, window winders, armrests and sun visors, and a steering wheel that featured a large, padded boss. Under heavy impact, the rear-view mirror was released from its bracket. In 1961, anchorage points for seat belts were fitted as standard in the 'tail fin'. Lap belts were available from 1957 and the first diagonal shoulder belts appeared in 1962. Round-shoulder tyres also made their debut on this car.

More than 2,500 patents originated from him. Some of them have saved thousands of lives and still set the automotive standard today. He became known as 'The Life Saver'.

What of the sketch of the 'people's car'? Well, in a legal battle that lasted three years, he finally won his claim that the drafts he had made of the 'future people's car' as a student be recognized as the 'intellectual parent' of what became the Volkswagen Beetle.

In 1972 Barényi retired – but he was never forgotten. In 1994, he was received into the 'Automotive Hall of Fame' in

Béla Barényi.

In 1967, Béla Barényi received the Rudolf Diesel Gold Medal from the German Inventors' Association.

Detroit and welcomed into the circle of outstanding inventors and innovators. He died in Böblingen near Stuttgart in 1997.

Since 2005, the Béla Barényi Prize is awarded in Vienna to people who have made outstanding achievements in the field of traffic and automotive transport.

FRIEDRICH GEIGER (BORN 24 NOVEMBER 1907)

Freidrich Geiger was born in Süben in the south of Germany. He originally trained as a cartwright; however, his artistic nature soon drew him away from coach building and closer to coach and cart design. Although somewhat unusual for the time, he decided to give up his work as a cartwright to go to university to formally study as a design engineer. In hindsight, this turned out to be a logical and consistent career path, as, on graduation, he was lucky enough to fall straight into a position at the 'special coach-building depart-

ment' at the Sindelfingen factory of Daimler-Benz AG, led by Hermann Ahrens.

Geiger was able to convincingly demonstrate his double talents as a hands-on engineer and a person with a sense of aesthetics and proportion, and he was given a free hand to put this into practice when customers would request one-off creations to fit to a factory-made chassis. These models became known as 'Sindelfingen Coachwork'. Geiger's own stunningly beautiful Mercedes 500K (W 29) was one of his first full designs.

The stresses and losses of the Second World War seemed to break his spirit, so around April 1948 he decided to take a sabbatical to find his passion once more. In a very short while he had rekindled his love for watercolour painting and became a very accomplished artist.

Around June 1950, Karl Wilfert welcomed him back with open arms as a test engineer to the newly created styling department in Sindelfingen and within a couple of years he had been appointed head.

His quiet and unassuming manner, coupled with his iron discipline and rigour, would often be mistaken as aloof arrogance and this made him reticent to put himself in the lime-light, so he relied heavily upon his team, not just a stylists but as his mouthpiece.

To mark the designer's 100th anniversary, Günter Engelen summed him up in one sentence when he wrote: 'Friedrich Geiger was rather the type of reticent conductor who was capable of bringing out the very best from his chamber orchestra without being overly ostentatious.'

On 1 October 1969, Geiger was appointed senior manager within the styling directorate and there he remained until his retirement on 31 December 1973. Alongside designers such as Paul Bracq and Bruno Sacco he left behind a legacy of numerous outstanding saloons, coupés, convertibles and roadsters for Mercedes-Benz.

The range of model series for which he was responsible includes the Fintail cars (W 110 and W 111/112), the Pagoda (SL from the W 113 series) and the representative Mercedes-Benz 600 (W 100). These were followed by the luxury-class models from the W 108/109 and W 116 series, the SL (R 107) launched in 1971 and the famous cars from the mid-sized series W 114/115 and W 123.

His legacy of design integrity lived on in a long line of automotive designers. Bruno Sacco said of him, 'He created timeless designs.'

Friedrich Geiger (with a white coat) usually stayed in the background. Here (from left to right) with Karl Wilfert, Fritz Nallinger and Paul Bracq.

Sketches of the the 190 SL and 300 SL.

Friedrich Geiger.

Professor Guntram Huber joined the Daimler-Benz AG in 1959 as an experimental engineer and, in 1971, became head of department for the development of passenger car bodies. From 1977 until his retirement in 1997, Professor Huber headed this area as director.

GUNTRAM HUBER (BORN 20 MARCH 1935)

Having completed his formal education at a Landshut secondary school that specialized in classical studies, Guntram Huber went on to graduate with a degree in mechanical engineering at the Technical University in Munich.

Upon walking into a job at Daimler-Benz AG in 1959 as a test engineer in the Engineering Department for Passenger Car Bodies, he was thrown in at the deep-end, working alongside Daimler-Benz's safety guru Béla Barényi with what was referred to as the new 'shape-stable occupant cell and crumple zone' for the W 111 (commonly called the *Heckflosse* or Fintail). Although it was almost ready for production, proper verification crash tests were yet to have been carried out, so the young engineer became personally involved in the early crash test methods, using winches and steam-powered rockets.

Huber had found his niche and over the years became a fervent promoter and constant proponent of advances in active and passive safety measures, to the point of encourag-

ing Daimler AG to custom-design a new indoor crash test hall at Sindelfingen.

By 1971, he had been promoted director of development passenger car bodies and in March 1977, Huber succeeded Werner Breitschwerdt as head of engineering for passenger car bodies. During his tenure, numerous safety innovations developed under his direction made their way into the new range of S-Class vehicles. Major milestones such as the ABS system, which Mercedes-Benz presented as a world first in the 116 model series in August 1978, continuing with the first passenger car in the world systematically developed to meet the safety requirements for an offset crash and after fifteen years of groundwork and development Mercedes-Benz became the first automotive brand to offer customers a driver's airbag in the steering wheel – for which Huber became known as the 'father of the airbag'. It was followed in 1988 by the front-passenger airbag, installed first in the S-Class 126 of 1979.

In 1981, on top of his work for Mercedes-Benz, he accepted a post as a lecturer in body-shell engineering within the motor vehicle engineering department of the Technical

Bruno Sacco discussing the C III project with Peter Pfeiffer.

University of Darmstadt. He was appointed an Honorary Professor in 1987. He remained Chair of the department until July 1998 – having already retired from his post as a development engineer on 31 December 1997.

Still today, he considers the Mercedes-Benz brand's greatest service to be that it raised public awareness of the issue of vehicle safety through countless innovations and made it the norm. Indeed, many Mercedes-Benz inventions are now standard equipment in production vehicles across the globe.

BRUNO SACCO (BORN: 12 NOVEMBER 1933)

Bruno Sacco was born in the north-eastern Italian city of Udine close to the Slovenian border. In 1951, he passed his exams as the youngest surveyor in Italy. During a visit to the Turin motor show, his fascination for vehicle design was piqued after catching a glimpse of the French designer Raymound Loewy's Studebaker Starlight Coupé. 'The car took

my breath away, it was like a moving sculpture from another world,' Bruno Sacco recalled many years later. It was not until he chanced upon the same car a little later in Tarvis, where he was living with his family, that his resolve to pursue a career in design manifested itself in earnest. To what seemed like a whim to others, he moved his family 600km north-west to Turin, the spiritual home of modern designers such as Pinin-Farina, Nuccio Bertone, Gigi Michelotti and Carozzeria Ghia, to most of whom he would become a frequent visitor.

His experience in automotive design grew exponentially after managing to procure contract work with such greats as Giovanni Savonuzzi and Sergio Sartorelli at Ghia and his reputation soon came to the attention of head of testing for car bodywork and styling at Mercedes-Benz, Karl Wilfert.

Having already managed to hone his German language skills while working on the Karmann-Ghia, he agreed to a meeting and on 13 January 1958 he took up his work at Daimler-Benz in Sindelfingen as second stylist, after Paul Bracq. Looking back on his career, Bruno Sacco once said, 'All I knew was I wanted to amass as much experience of dif-

Béla Barényi in the office with the team of the Department of Advanced Engineering. People from the left: Hermann Renner, Gerhard Busch, Béla Barényi, Heinrich Haselmann, Gustav Reichstetter and Bruno Sacco, around 1970.

Bruno Sacco was inducted into the Automotive Hall of Fame (Dearborn, Michigan) on 3 October 2006.

ferent types of design as possible, France, Germany and the USA. However it turned out completely differently.' This was to be Sacco's job for the next forty-one years.

In less than ten years with Daimler-Benz, Sacco was promoted into management and placed in charge of the bodywork and ergonomics department. With no formal written rules on design, he decided that the way forward was to, first, understand the Benz culture. 'Nothing but the best',

painted on a dusty board in the factory, was where he started. 'Once I understood it, I began to evolve the form.'

As stylist and designer he was involved in various projects under the supervision of Karl Wilfert, Friedrich Geiger and Béla Barényi , including the Mercedes-Benz 600 and the 230 SL roadsters. In addition, he was made project leader for the design of the safety exhibitions of the day, as well as the so-called 'test labs on wheels', the C III-I and C III-II experimental vehicles. In 1970, Sacco became head of the body design and dimensional drawing department at Daimler-Benz. Under his aegis, this period saw the development of the ESF (experimental safety vehicle) prototypes and the 123 series.

In 1975, and now bearing the title senior engineer, Bruno Sacco took over as successor to Friedrich Geiger as head of the styling department and from then on played a vital part in shaping the overall appearance of Mercedes-Benz passenger cars. The key stages of this gradual formal evolution were the record-breaking C 111-III diesel (1978) and the W 126-series S-Class (1979). In 1978, Sacco was appointed head of the styling department.

In 1987, the board of management appointed him director of the design department, and in 1993, in his function as head of design, he became a member of the company's board of directors. In this capacity Bruno Sacco also assumed a mandated role for the design of products for the commercial vehicle division. In March 1999, after forty-one years' service with Mercedes-Benz design, Bruno Sacco handed over leadership of the department to Peter Pfeiffer.

Homogenous Affinity

From early on in his learning period, Bruno Sacco saw how designers at Mercedes-Benz had succumbed to the magical pull of a fashion trend. He noted that the Mercedes-Benz W 111 series saloons, introduced in 1959, were a prime example. Similar to virtually every other European and North American manufacturer, they sported 'tailfins' and as quickly as they arrived, they were abandoned with equal alacrity.

The tailfin models from the upper category were superseded in 1965 by the Mercedes-Benz 250 S, 250 SE, 300 SEb and long-wheelbase 300 SE models from the W 108 and W 109 series. These vehicles signalled the beginning of a new era: design without any fads of fashion, stating its point through simple elegance.

He said 'I am a designer at Mercedes-Benz not because I think "art for the sake of art" should be my motto, but because I want the cars for which I am responsible to sell successfully'. What he actually managed to do was to create a new design language. Something later referred to as 'homogenous affinity'.

The first law of this philosophy was what he referred to as the 'vertical affinity': 'A Mercedes-Benz must always look and feel like a Mercedes-Benz.' It became the central pillar

---

BRUNO SACCO AWARDS

During the years he worked at Daimler-Benz, Bruno Sacco received numerous personal awards:

1981: Honorary member of the Academia Mexicana de Diseño

1991: Received the title Grande Ufficiale dell'Ordine al Merito della Repubblica Italiana

1993: Winner of the Cover Award – *Auto & Design*, Turin

1993: Awarded the Premio Mexico 1994 – Patronato Nacional de las Asociaciones de Diseño AC, Mexico

1994: Winner of the Apulia Award for Professional Achievement

1996: Voted Best Designer by *Car* magazine

1996: Voted Designers' Designer by *Car* magazine

1997: Winner of the Lifetime Design Achievement Award, Detroit

1997: Presented with the Raymond Loewy Designer Award by the Lucky Strike brand

2002: Honorary doctorate from the Udine University, Italy

2006: Inducted into the Automotive Hall of Fame, Dearborn

2007: Inducted into the European Automotive Hall of Fame, Geneva

---

of the Mercedes-Benz design philosophy and ensured that a predecessor model did not appear outmoded following the presentation of a new model generation. The goal of this strategy was to retain the positive aura of a Mercedes-Benz on the roads by members of the public representing different cultures from all over the world, for as long as possible, and to this end, while most designers think ten years ahead, Sacco challenged his designers to think thirty years ahead.

The second main pillar of the Mercedes-Benz design philosophy was brand identity. This called for traditional design characteristics to be maintained, which would be further developed and featured in all model series simultaneously. In this context, the term Sacco used was 'horizontal affinity', recognizable by body accents, for example, in the design of the radiator grille, headlamps and tail-lights. Although there were formal differences in detail between saloons, coupés and roadsters, the family likeness remained obvious to even the most casual observer at first glance.

CHAPTER ONE

FROM 'S' TO 'SPECIAL'

'You don't simply decide to buy an S-Class: it comes to you when fate has ordained that your life should take that course. The door closes with a reassuring clunk – and you have arrived', so said the sales brochure of the first real Sonderklasse, the W 116.

Through almost sixty years of just being 'Sonder', the Mercedes-Benz 'S' now has a class of its own and has since become the ultimate reward for a lifestyle shaped by mobility, individuality, success and sophistication, and what has made the car and its predecessors unique among the world's great saloons.

The tradition of using the nomenclature 'S' for the Mercedes-Benz did not just begin with the type 220 (W 187) in 1951; its roots can be traced right back to the very origins of the Mercedes' brand itself, at the start of the twentieth century, indicating a high-end 'Saloon'.

An early, eye-catching example of this is the Mercedes-Simplex 60 PS launched in 1903. This elegant and luxurious touring saloon was once owned by Emil Jellinek, a key protagonist in the early history of the Mercedes' brand. The then top-of-the-range model is now one of the most spectacular exhibits in the Mercedes-Benz Classic collection

In the years to follow, the Mercedes and Benz sales' ranges always included several high-end, luxury 'saloons', even though open-top tourers were by far the most commonly used body form during this period. The more powerful models were also offered as luxury 'saloons' affording the ultimate in passenger comfort.

In the mid-1920s, it was a different picture. Due to ever more powerful engines and increasing volumes of traffic, which the road-building programme was unable to keep up with, safe-handling characteristics, a comfortable interior and optimum protection against wind, rain and dust, were becoming more and more important. Saloons or 'Saloons'

and Pullman saloons gradually began to replace the open-top tourers.

These high-end saloons became a welcome addition to their range of vehicles from the high-end, luxury segment, so Mercedes-Benz started to produce them as a platform to launch their latest technological or innovative advancement.

They not only meet the highest standards in terms of safety, comfort and style: due to their status as an absolutely top-of-the-range model, extremely luxurious ambience and particularly opulent and spacious interior, they are primarily tailored to meet the requirements of individuals who need to, or have to, reflect their status in the choice of their vehicle, too. This tradition follows the philosophy of a car that is always a reflection of the times. After all, with each new generation of its top-of-the-range vehicles, Mercedes-Benz has always provided convincing responses to the wishes and needs of each specific era. In a phrase that sums up the importance of the model's history right through to the present day, the S-Class and its predecessors are, and have always been, the epitome of the perfect car. Not for nothing has the S-Class been acclaimed again and again as the best car in the world.

FROM W 191 TO 'PONTON MERCEDES' (1952–59)

The first time that Mercedes really admitted to using the soubriquet 'S' to refer to 'Sonder' (special) was with the release of the type 170 S (W 136), later becoming the (W 191). Even though already essentially a bespoke high-end vehicle manufacturer, they realized that there was a market to appeal directly to successful business owners and company directors.

The upgraded Type 170 S Limousine, 1949–52 (bottom). The Standard 170 D Saloon, 1949–50 (top).

Initially developed from the W 136, and looking similar, being better appointed as well as 170mm (6¾n) longer and 104mm (4in) wider, it had more in common with the Type 230 (W 153) of 1938. This in itself marked the return of Mercedes-Benz to the bespoke luxury segment; no mean feat, considering it was only six years into the first phase of Germany's reconstruction, following the Second World War.

Following the relative success of this luxury, high-end optioned market, Mercedes decided to continue creating a 'special' line and the (W 191) developed into the (W 187). For the first time since before the war, this used a powerful 6-cylinder engine, the significance of which carried on to be the mainstay of the true 'Sonderklasse' models from the later 1970s onward.

Also, for the first time, Mercedes decided to take the model one step further and started to produce a single stand-alone luxury model to rival even the Rolls-Royce of the time, the Type 300 (W 186); it quickly found favour with business owners and statesmen alike, including that of Konrad Adenauer the Chancellor of West Germany from 1949 to 1963, who commissioned six custom versions of the Cabriolet, Saloon and Landaulet. It became so inextricably linked with his name that to this day they are referred to as the 'Adenauer'.

The 1951 300 is nicknamed 'Adenauer Mercedes' as the first German chancellor favours this model. The design is a mixture of traditional pre-war shapes and the modern 'pontoon' shape. It was the largest and fastest series-produced car made in Germany. It soon became the most popular luxury car for kings, statesmen and industrial magnates.

The Mercedes-Benz 300 D (W 189) appears at the IAA International Motor Show in the autumn of 1957 as the last of the legendary 300 series.

What had become very clear was that there was a clear market for 'special' vehicles and Mercedes continued to build the W 186, through to 1963, albeit now called the W 189 until it was replaced by the 600 (W 100)

The *Langenscheidt German–English Dictionary* defines *Pontonkarrosserie* as 'all-enveloping bodywork, straight-through side styling, slab-sided styling.

Even with its more integrated body style, the W 187 was beginning to look old-fashioned in comparison to the lower, wider look of other European and North American model designs; but, already, a new era of body design was well underway. The days of the old-style ladder chassis with separately mounted body parts was on its way out and the 'self-supporting' body was being introduced across the automotive world.

This advanced method of body mounting allowed for a much more integrated form: where hitherto large bulbous wings and running boards, for example, formed a more limited basis for shape, the 'Ponton' allowed more spacious interiors, lighter and more torsionally rigid bodies, which in turn improved agility and handling, as well as vastly improved aerodynamics. Out of this arose a harmonious and, by the standards of the day, generously proportioned, glazed passenger compartment.

This was now the point, according to many experts, at which automotive designers finally made the transition from styling to design.

FROM 'FINTAIL' TO HIGH-PERFORMANCE SALOON (1959–72)

The 'Ponton' body styling allowed designers to get more artistic and use a bit more flair and the 'Fintail' model is a case in point.

This new high-end generation represented a very special milestone in automotive history: it was the first time that the 'self-supporting' body shell, incorporating the safety cell and crumple zones devised by Béla Barényi, had been used on a series production car. Introduced in 1959 (220, 220 S and 220 SE (W 111)) they earned their nickname from the understated tailfins that adorned the rear wing. Not wanting them to be considered merely as a fashion accessory, they were officially known as 'sight lines' or 'guide fins', since they fulfilled a genuinely useful function for parking manoeuvres.

Nevertheless, these visual style elements were highly controversial. The later head of design, Bruno Sacco, even thought it necessary to make a statement in an internal memo. He wrote:

We believe that the design of the rear is not necessarily a North American feature, rather it is a product of the age, as tail wings have regularly been used by Italian body designers since the mid-1950s in connection with aerodynamic studies. If one imagines the car without the proposed tail wings, then in terms of the arrangement of design elements such as lights, bumpers. etc., the rear aspect of the 220 SE of 1959 represents the tail configuration that is the most copied and remodelled by other manufacturers of all time.

The designation 'S' continued and expanded into the SE model and, although never described as a 'Sonderklasse', the 'S' remained synonymous with any 'flagship' versions of each model and in this case the 300 SE (W 112) was presented in 1961.

It was fitted as standard with the 'Adenauer' M 189 big block 6-cylinder, fuel-injected engine, air suspension and the newly developed automatic transmission. A longer version was introduced in 1963, which again started off a new tradition in Mercedes-Benz luxury class saloons: the 'lang' (long) wheelbase offering rear passengers significantly more legroom and comfort. The 'L' designation was not used officially until 1965 with the W 109 300 SEL.

The 108 and 109 saloons replaced the 'Fintail' in 1965 with an initial line-up of the 250 S, 250 SE and the 300 SE for the W 108 and a single W 109 300 SEL.

The 108s were the generic models fitted with conventional steel springs but the 109 was offered as an air-sprung variant of the model series 109, available from the outset with a 10cm (4in) longer wheelbase. Both models introduced a V8 engine into the range, predominantly to be able to compete with the North American market.

The 108 and the 109s were the last of the ambiguous 'S'-

The W 111 300 SE flagship 'Fintail'.

Mercedes-Benz W 109 300 SEL, 1965–67.

The W 108 SE model clearly shorter than the SEL.

The forerunner to the S-Class bears the features of a competitive racing car. On test runs on the Hockenheimring racing track in preparation for three factory teams' participation in the 24-hour Spa-Francorchamps race in the summer of 1969.

The 6.3 M 100 engine 'shoe-horned' into the W 109.

The production version of the 300 SEL 6.3.

designated vehicles before the true Sonderklasse W/V116 of 1972, although there was something else that pointed the way to the future S-Class models and that was discreet power. The Americans referred to it as a 'sleeper' and the British called it a 'Q' car.

It all started with the W 109 300 SEL and a taunt from an auto journalist that Mercedes only build good 'grandpa cars and taxis'. Eric Waxenberger, head of a special development department, decided to put the German press in their place.

Working at night, in his own time and without the knowledge of his superiors, he took a rejected 300 SEL body from Sindelfingen and the 6.3 M 100 from the 600 and prepared them to race, only informing Rudolf Uhlenhaut what he was doing when it was prepared to enter the Macau Enduro in 1969. It went on to finish first in the six-hour race and then second in the Spa 24-hours.

The same journalists that taunted him earlier now had to eat their words: 'This automobile is the most the stimulating, desirable four-door saloon to appear since the Model J Duesenberg.' *Road & Track* called it simply, 'The greatest saloon car in the world'.

So successful were they, even though they were nearly three times more expensive than the entry-level 280 SEL, that they succeeded in selling 6,526; ironically using more M 100 engines than the 600.

With the addition of exceptional comfort and luxurious interior fittings, it also rivalled the performance of many sports cars of the day.

What this did for the powers that be at Mercedes Daimler was to cement the ideas that an 'Uber saloon' was necessary, and even though the 116 S-Class was already in the 'pipeline', it encouraged them that further investment in a stand-alone 'Sonderklasse' was the way to go.

UNSAFE AT ANY SPEED

For the many decades that followed the invention of the motor car, vehicle safety was usually based upon nothing more than the empirical knowledge that was gleaned from production and/or motor racing; and even then, it usually meant little more than striving for a car to be as stable and robust as possible and have good handling characteristics.

'Safety' became the 'elephant in the room' and vehicle manufacturers deigned not to even mention the word for fear of reminding potential customers that the motor car could bring with it death or injury. However, every passing year that brought an increase in vehicle numbers also brought with it a sharp statistical rise in death and serious injuries from vehicle accidents.

Ralph Nader's book, *Unsafe at Any Speed*, highlighted the serious inadequacies in vehicle safety. The opening line to his book gave not only the American automobile market (of which it was aimed) a wake-up call, but the rest of the world too:

Ralf Nader, author of *Unsafe at any Speed*, at the Senate hearing in 1966 triggered by his book.

De Haven's research provided strong evidence that the human body was less fragile than had been generally assumed, that the structural environment was the dominant cause of injury – leading to such key safety measures as the three-point seat belts and airbags.

For over half a century the automobile has brought death, injury and the most inestimable sorrow and deprivation to millions of people.

Having already set up The Aviation Safety and Research Facility at Cornell University, visionaries such as Hugh de Haven understood that the same principles that apply to aircraft safety, also apply to vehicle accidents. Against much political lobbying and opposition he managed to set up a more generic, all-encompassing crash injury and research facility. He once said:

We will get into anybody's automobile, go any desired distance at dangerous speeds, without safety belts, without shoulder harness, and with a very minimum of padding or other protection to prevent our heads and bodies from smashing against the inside of a car in an accident. The level of safety which we accept for ourselves, our wives and our children is, therefore, on a par with shipping fragile valuable objects loose inside a container... People knew more about protecting eggs in transit than they did about protecting human heads.

The world was at last beginning to understand that more could be done to save life and limb but, more importantly,

much of the responsibility was laid firmly at the feet of the 'vehicle' manufacturer.

Much was already known about 'active safety' or 'primary safety' – terms used to refer to mechanical technology such as good handling, good steering and stopping capabilities, which, in themselves, had already greatly assisted in the prevention of many accidents, but this wasn't enough.

For many years, Hugh de Haven had been viewed as a 'crackpot scientist' of little merit; however, a chance meeting between de Haven and a police investigator during a safety talk at the Indianapolis State police headquarters was the beginning of a new understanding of vehicle safety.

Sergeant Elmer Paul was investigator of RTC (Road Traffic Collision) with the Indianapolis State Police Department and he had already recognized what he referred to as the 'second impact or human collision' as being the primary cause of death and injury in vehicles. He approached de Haven after the seminar with an offer of assistance and very quickly a new term was being 'bandied' about: 'passive safety', the recognition of and components needed to protect occupants inside a vehicle. For example:

• Passenger safety cell
• Crumple zones
• Seat belts
• Interior impact resistance

FROM 'SPECIAL' TO 'SAFETY'

Mercedes, on the other hand, had visionaries such as Béla Barényi who, from the very early days of his career, decided that safety was everything, so much so that he even dared to tell Wilhelm Haspel, during his first interview, that they were 'doing it all wrong', before going on to tell him why items such as steering and steering wheel could be designed to enhance the safety of the occupants instead of 'skewering' them.

From what started as a little wood shed on the edges of the Sindelfingen plant, hand-built carriages that would propel vehicle bodies toward walls; the vehicle safety and development department became a full-blown test centre. By 1957, a test track had been built adjacent to the Untertürkheim plant, which included a skid pad featuring concentrically arranged circular tracks with different surfaces where vehicles could be tested on blue basalt, concrete, slippery asphalt and large cobblestones, with an integrated sprinkler system allowing wet-surface testing.

Bringing together the individuals previously mentioned was a master stroke in itself, not only did they bring immeasurable passion and devotion for the marque that was still trying to find its niche in the marketplace, but each individual wholeheartedly believed that innovation was not only the root to a safer product, but also a better product.

With every early innovation, came a deeper understanding and refinement of the principles of vehicle safety that would lay the foundation for many critical safety innovations for many years to come. For example, a conscious distinction was able to be made between passive and active safety, with the appropriate sub-speciality fields of study: whereas active safety, with its aspect of driving safety, conditional safety and operational safety had always played an important role for engineers since the invention of the car, the far-reaching significance of passive safety was being understood for the first time.

One of the first highlights in series production was the premiere of the safety body in the 'Fintail' (W 111) in 1959,

CLOCKWISE, FROM TOP LEFT:

Béla Barényi early experiments for the safety steering wheel and column.

Steam-powered rocket to propel test vehicles into walls and dangerous situations.

Launching vehicles into the air from ramps.

Various steam-powered rockets were used to propel vehicles, although at times they were a little uncontrollable.

developed by the mastermind of vehicle safety, Béla Barényi. His 'safety body' is based on the concept of a shape-stable passenger cell with specific deformable crumple zones at the front and rear to dissipate kinetic energy in the event of a collision and, as such, heralded the first high point of vehicle safety research at Mercedes-Benz. It soon became the international standard for passive safety in the global car design industry.

The so-called Fintail model also boasted other innovative safety features. A particularly conspicuous feature was the interior designed to reduce injury hazards: hard, sharp-edged interior fittings and controls had disappeared to be replaced by recessed door handles, a dashboard yielding on impact, padded window surrounds, window winders, armrests and sun visors, and a steering wheel with a large impact-absorbing boss. The rear-view mirror was designed to detach from its bracket under a severe impact.

Amongst his most important innovations was the door lock with securing pin, which was first presented in 1951. It not only secured the door from flying open in the event of an accident, but by remaining secure to the body form, they also gave extra strength to the safety cell.

Many of his ideas were so ahead of their time that some did not make it into series production until long after Barényi

had left active service; for example, the recessed windscreen wiper when in standby mode, which was not introduced until the 126 model series of the S-Class in 1979.

Instead of 'safety' being a word to be feared and to shy away from, Mercedes turned it into a watchword for innovation, modernization and advancement. This ultimately resulted in solutions for all series production vehicles, most often debuted in the saloons of the S-Class. These top-of-the-range vehicles from Mercedes-Benz, again and again became trendsetters for new safety topics and succeeded in establishing standards in active, passive and integrated safety for the entire automotive industry.

ACCIDENT RESEARCH AND DEVELOPMENT

While automotive corporations in other parts of the world were digging in their heels, believing that highlighting safety issues in vehicles was a constant reminder that a motorist and potential customer was at risk from injury and death, visionaries like de Haven, Swearingen, Elmer Paul and J. P. Stapp could see the other side of the coin: that they could

Colonel J. P. Stapp.

Colonel J. P. Stapp risking life and limb aboard his homemade rocket sled.

learn how to keep passengers safe through the research of accidents and consequent development to lessen the likelihood of it happening again.

Under the auspices of Barényi in 1967, Daimler-Benz started a six-month pilot project working together with police on the investigation of serious road-traffic accidents that had occurred in the district of Böblingen and on the A8 highway. So successful was this exercise that, on a cold winter's day in 1969, talks with the ministry of the interior, government and senior police officials, together with representatives of Daimler, began to discuss the possibility of a joint, long-term programme to analyse all road-traffic accidents involving Mercedes vehicles.

The Accident Research Project was officially launched on 29 April 1969, after which the interior ministry issued a directive to all the relevant police departments, ordering them to inform Daimler-Benz by telephone of any road-traffic accidents and to allow company representatives to inspect the accident report and question the duty officers on the actual sequence of events. The justification for this measure was as follows:

The interior ministry supports the research of Daimler-Benz AG because of its general import for road safety.

Buoyed by Daimler's success at gaining relevant and invaluable information, the German parliament resolved to set up its own central unit at the Federal Highway Research Institute and, in 1973, set up GIDAS (German In-Depth Accident Study). It still exists to this day, providing meticulous data for all automotive engineers to acquire the knowledge needed to develop new and even more effective safety systems.

As a result, this analysis and application of traffic accidents has continually shown that the risk of being injured when travelling in any Mercedes has been consistently declining year on year.

CHAPTER TWO

ALL THINGS TO EVERYONE

INTRODUCTION

There were fast cars, there were luxurious cars, there were big cars and small cars, there were sports cars and family cars but there was not a car that could fit into every category. The world needed a vehicle that would cope with ever-changing traffic demands, something that would cope with speed and performance like a sports car but would also be safe, smooth, reliable and comfortable.

The psychology of the car buyer had changed and the buyer had become more pernickety. They were no longer content with just owning a vehicle that would take them from A to B, they wanted to get to their destination in a timely fashion yet safely, be comfortable yet alert and be protected from wind, engine and road noise. Their bubble of glass and metal had become an extension of their needs, wants and personality. They wanted confidence in the vehicle they had chosen above all others; they wanted power on tap but not without the ability to control it; they wanted to be able to push the cars capabilities without risking losing control.

A Sonderklasse principal, if it was to have longevity, had to be all things to everyone.

UNDERSTATED ELEGANCE OF CO-ORDINATED INTEGRATION

The consumer public was waking up to more than just 'this is the best vehicle to buy'; they needed to be able to reassure themselves that the vehicle they were investing in was everything they needed'; it was no longer a simple A to B means of transport.

Even though a great deal had changed, road surface quality, improvements in road network and infrastructure had also highlighted the inadequacies of vehicles. Restrictions of use of the vehicle, poor visibility and high levels of noise, and how they continuously influence the way a driver or passenger behaves, also had to be addressed. The advancements in vehicle technology had to be weighed against the ability and ease of use; excesses in stress as well as relaxation became fundamental factors.

Co-ordinated integration is first and foremost the development of individual components and, second, of their integration into a balanced overall concept. This contrasts with less well thought-out methods of design, in which, for instance, some features become over-emphasized and exert undue influence on driving behaviour.

The performance, safety, comfort and driving characteristics of the new S-class 116 cars came together as one total entity in which all these features are matched one with another. They create the ability to cope with traffic and environmental problems and so relieve the driver of some of the stress by utilizing design features that take fully into account human psychological and physical capabilities:

- To see and to be seen – clearly and in plenty of time.
- To sit comfortably and relaxed and yet to remain alert and wide awake.
- To act quickly and to react correctly.
- To be protected from the effects of noise and vibration.
- To master the engine power, not be seduced or distracted by it.
- To exploit the car's capabilities without it overtaxing the driver's.
- To have confidence in your car and so be able to concentrate all your efforts and attention on yourself and other road-users ability to drive safely.

THE SONDERKLASSE CONCEPT

For the enthusiasts who crave definitive answers you are going to be disappointed, for although there was, more than likely' a 'board meeting' or two, perhaps to decide on the logistics of building a definitive model such as the S-Class, there was never really a eureka moment as such as it is a culmination of many factors.

The art of providing a specific item to the public is never easy, whether in a small business or large company. However, providing an item that is essentially a luxury is even more difficult. The automotive industry has a particularly difficult job and it's not a hyperbole to say that getting it wrong can very easily ruin a company or, at the very least, its reputation.

Designing a model that is immediately relevant enough to be desired over a number of years is by far the most difficult of things to do. Not only does this involve following current socio-economic trends as closely as possible, but also requires being able to predict future trends and climates for the period of availability. The answer to this is very often to adapt a current range into various model options, to include a flagship or special optioned vehicle, and this was done by every manufacturer.

A generation that had come through, and survived, the war realized that they had not only fought for their freedom from tyranny, but for a freedom to express themselves. An economic boom brought with it disposable income; for the first time the working class could set their aspirations on becoming middle class and could afford to become consumers without the feeling of guilt.

The Americans called it the 'American way'; achieving a better way of life through consumerism, became a key element of American society, influenced by mass advertising through television and the accessibly of credit made more available by the banks. Europe would follow, albeit taking a little longer: a total reconstruction of buildings, roads and companies devastated by WWII; but follow they did. The introduction of 'people's cars' such as the VW Beetle, the Austin Mini and the Citroën 2CV gave the general public a taste of vehicle ownership,

In just a couple of decades cars had gone from being a luxury afforded by only the wealthy to a necessity of the populace. The automotive market was expanding exponentially and infrastructure was adapting to cope. Large, fast parkways and freeways in North America followed the ideas of the German *Bundesautobahn* and gave people the ability to travel beyond their own towns and villages, not just for work and business but for pleasure. Weekend recreation involved families, which meant bigger and more reliable vehicles. Bigger vehicles meant more power, with more power came the need for more safety.

As people earned more money and aspired to a better lifestyle, other factors came into play too: brand loyalty was

German Bundesautobahn just before World War II. By 1950, Germany had over 2,000 autobahn routes.

A view of the
Mercedes-Benz plant
in Sindelfingen, where
the 'Stroke 8' is being
assembled alongside the
113 series SL (Pagoda).

based on reliability or simply what was available. People now had the means and ability to play with desirability, choice and fashion trends; this in itself created a trade-in market. Desirability and options brought kudos and kudos brought value: a high-priced luxury car kept a higher percentage of its value for longer compared with the lower end markets.

Most manufacturers covered the 'desirable' option with a high-optioned model in a specific range. By way of example, the Citroën DS had the Pallas, Ford had the 'Ghia' models; even high-end luxury manufacturers had special optioned vehicles in their range: Jaguar had Daimler and Rolls-Royce had Bentley. Mercedes, as already mentioned, had followed the trend with high-end cars in the range too and by introducing the 600 W 100 in the early 1960s, covered the extremely high-end part of the market, providing super-luxury for members of state, royalty, despots and dictators, film and music stars. However, the ambiguities of the 'S' models was starting to lead to much confusion in the model ranges; the W 108/109 'S' range of vehicles had been successful in their time but they were now showing their age in both style and design. If the 'S' was a flagship model, was what it offered enough to make customers feel they had bought something special? Mercedes knew that they were losing out on a 'special class' for the discerning buyer in the corporate/business market and started to work on the design of a completely new range: a stand-alone 'Sonderklasse' or 'special class'.

For the first time since the war, Mercedes had already developed a completely new line of vehicles, the W 114, they themselves referred to as the 'new generation'

The W 114 came with a completely redesigned chassis, incorporating an entirely revised suspension system, a new body style and a new range of engines ranging from 4- and 6-cylinder petrol to 4- and 5-cylinder diesels. They were built with the emphasis on safety and practicality over performance. The range covered everything from a taxi specification to a smart two-door coupé and for the first time, model numbers related to the engine size.

More than 1.8 million 'stroke 8' W 114 vehicles were built, making this upper mid-range vehicle family, the first vehicle of the brand to be produced by the million.

Much of the technology of the new 'Sonderklasse', the W 116, would be based on that 'new generation'.

THE SUPER MERCEDES

When mentioning the evolution of the S-Class, it is just not possible to ignore the 'W 100 600 Grand Saloon'. Even though the cost bracket of the W 100 was clearly for the wealthy, the 'Uber saloon' became the backbone to the principle of what was to become the 'Sonderklasse'. Its success went on to affirm the possibilities that a stand-alone high-end saloon would be well received and, just as importantly, would be fiscally successful.

'The love of inventing never ends.' With this statement, Carl Benz left a legacy to future generations of engineers that has gone on to drive developers for decades. Curiosity, creativity, the courage to embrace new ideas and a passion for the motor car – these became the traditional, core values of Mercedes-Benz.

The head of the research and development division of the time, Professor Werner Breitschwerdt, knew that it no longer sufficed to build a high-class Mercedes with just a big body, plush interior and a fast engine; neither was it sufficient simply to serve up a raft of innovations in a more modern package than the last model and hope it will appeal enough to create a stir on the day of release. On this premise, Mercedes employees at Untertürkheim and Sindelfingen were tasked with making the 'impossible, possible'.

He summed it up when he said of the Model 600:

> We wanted to build a car that could do everything that was possible, and it had to be capable of doing more than all the other cars – for the driver and the passenger.

He turned to his chief of construction and engineering, Fritz Nallinger. As chief technical director, Nallinger had already almost singlehandedly rebuilt Daimler-Benz's Grand Prix team 'Silver Arrows' into one of the most successful teams of the decade, but he had also played a leading role in the design and development of most of the large-scale engineering projects, including aircraft, marine and heavy truck development.

As an automotive visionary he had been pushing Daimler to not only build such a vehicle as the W 100, but a complete assembly system that would go on to be the backbone of Mercedes' cars of the future. He had already developed an all-round independent suspension and, as a master at engine design, had provided Daimler with huge leaps forward in reliability and efficiency. His high-speed diesel engine designs had gone on to provide a key strength in the market long after his retirement.

By the mid-1950s, he had already developed the first 'all-alloy' V8 engine for just such a vehicle and by 1959 he had a working model. Not one to rest on his laurels, he had also gone one step further and designed, alongside Adolf Wente, a 7.5-litre V12, deeming it 'a fitting partner to the V8' and was convinced that it would underline the significance of such vehicles as the W 100 and the later Sonderklasse. Although the V12 never advanced beyond the development stage at this time, his legacy was brought into fruition in the third Sonderklasse incarnation, the W 140 and, although the

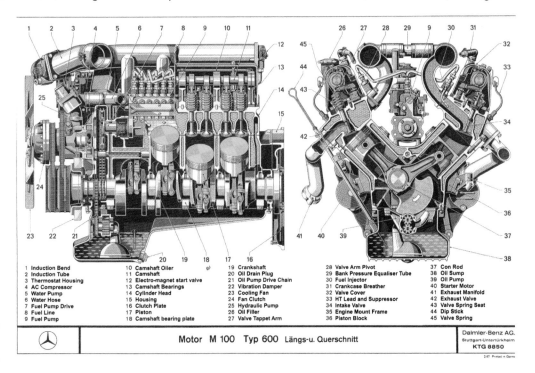

1 Induction Bend	10 Camshaft Oiler	19 Crankshaft	28 Valve Arm Pivot	37 Con Rod
2 Induction Tube	11 Camshaft	20 Oil Drain Plug	29 Bank Pressure Equaliser Tube	38 Oil Sump
3 Thermostat Housing	12 Electro-magnet start valve	21 Oil Pump Drive Chain	30 Fuel Injector	39 Oil Pump
4 AC Compressor	13 Camshaft Bearings	22 Vibration Damper	31 Crankcase Breather	40 Starter Motor
5 Water Pump	14 Cylinder Head	23 Cooling Fan	32 Valve Cover	41 Exhaust Manifold
6 Water Hose	15 Housing	24 Fan Clutch	33 HT Lead and Suppressor	42 Exhaust Valve
7 Fuel Pump Drive	16 Clutch Plate	25 Hydraulic Pump	34 Intake Valve	43 Valve Spring Seat
8 Fuel Line	17 Piston	26 Oil Filler	35 Engine Mount Frame	44 Dip Stick
9 Fuel Pump	18 Camshaft bearing plate	27 Valve Tappet Arm	36 Piston Block	45 Valve Spring

Motor M 100 Typ 600 Längs-u. Querschnitt

Daimler-Benz AG.
Stuttgart-Untertürkheim
KTG 8850

Schematic of Mercedes first petrol V8, the M 100 for the W 600.

Not just technically advanced, but aesthetically beautiful was just as important.

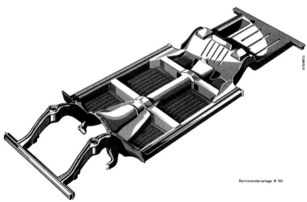

W 100 chassis design and build.

eventual engine, the M 100, that went into the 600, the 300 SEL 6.3 (W 108) then enlarged and fitted into the W 116 450 SEL in 6.9 was based on a cast iron block, the original all alloy concept eventually formed the basis of the M 116 and M 117 engines fitted in the 126.

True to the brief, the W 100 was a revelation of design. For the first time in automotive history, every engineering detail was built to act in unison with one another, none of which would compromise the other. It truly became nothing more and nothing less than the best car in the world – the true meaning of Gottlieb Daimler's motto 'Das Beste Oder Nichts'.

Head of passenger car design, Rudolf Uhlenhaut, decided on two main points of focus for an up-to-date, superior, representative vehicle: maximum passenger comfort in understated luxury and superb performance maximum safety. This culminated in concrete demands for ride comfort of the highest calibre, unrivalled to this day, and at the same time sporty driving characteristics: a large car and yet playful handling and a luxury vehicle but athletic performance.

In a changing post-war, socio-political climate, Mercedes took a radical step away from the self-promotion of the open-air landaulet design of motoring normally representative of the kind of dignitary who would be attracted to this exclusive segment of vehicle; although an open top was available, the

The M 100, although large, was by no means considered ostentatious. Its sleek yet boxy design gave it the ability to 'mingle' with other cars, with nothing more than an occasional admiring glance by the more astute passer-by.

It was astonishing that the Model 600, as sharp-edged as it appeared, had a Cd value of only 0.458. Compare this to the 230 SL with a hardtop having a Cd value of 0.515 and a Model 190 SL with a hardtop a Cd value of 0.461.

fact is that out of 2,677 vehicles built, only 59 were 'landaulet'.

The W 100 600 went on to be built for the longest period of time of any other Mercedes – an uninterrupted eighteen years from 1963 until 1981 – only matched later by the R107 SL. This showed that a single model can remain current for a very long time in automotive terms.

The biggest market by far was also one of the newest markets, even with a starting price of around $20,000 ($150,000 in today's market), close to 28 per cent of the total units were exported to the USA.

Apart from the kudos of producing nothing short of an engineering triumph to the rest of the world, what this did for Daimler-Mercedes themselves was to prove that, even against all trends, there was a 'thirst' for something special and even though a relatively meagre 2,677 units were made, the lessons learned were invaluable.

33

THE 116 SONDERKLASSE THROUGH TURMOIL

Developing a 'facelift' to a model or upgrading a style or model range is difficult enough for any automotive company, however, introducing not only a completely new class, but a flagship range, can be a leap into the unknown.

Development of the new Sonderklasse range had begun in the last quarter of 1966, only a year after the release of the 108/109 range. Daimler had already been working on a new corporate style and needed a flagship model to replace the tired-looking 108/109, which, as soon as it was released, was being referred to as the 'finless Fintail'.

The time spans in which designers are required to work, especially in a high-end market like that of Mercedes, is considerable; research and development alone can be anything from three to five years. Add to this the production period and the time a model needs to look current – it can be well over a decade. However, a major risk, separate altogether from the logistics of the vehicle itself, is the capricious nature of social, economic and political changes into which a new product will be released. The release of the first officially designated 'Sonderklasse', and the tumultuous transition that Mercedes-Benz faced in the 1970s, is a case in point.

The 116 came into being during a time when fuel prices were soaring and emission regulations were becoming stricter, especially in a relatively new market to Daimler: North America.

Long before the actual fuel embargo of 1973 triggered by the US involvement in the Yom Kippur War, fuel production was already playing a major part in controlling economies. German petroleum output had already peaked in the mid-1960s and, along with many other countries, they were becoming increasingly dependent on foreign, often unfriendly, nations' suppliers as its key resource. The first hint of the possibility that the world could be held to ransom was the 1967 oil embargo, triggered by the Middle East. Without going into the political reasoning's behind the later embargo and 'perceived' crisis of 1973, and again in 1979, what was important were the effects felt by the automotive industry via what was being felt by the consumer public.

There is no such thing as economical high performance and higher fuel prices makes driving more expensive, consequently making automobile ownership less appealing. So, Daimler had to ensure that the buyer had the confidence that the vehicle they have just spent their hard-earned money on was also economically responsible; buying true quality went hand in glove with obtaining lasting value and dependability.

Furthermore, a car built to these standards is less subject to wear and tear, and even less likely to be able to be pushed to its engineering limits, making the whole car very durable and making its normal service life appreciably longer than that of most other cars. Long service intervals and the less likely need for repairs hopefully go toward negating the worry that perhaps you are being a little less frugal with fuel.

The oil crisis kept fuel prices high for 18 months but also cut supply. Fuel stations had limited supplies.

German industrial leader Hanns Martin Schleyer
was kidnapped on 5 September 1977, by the Red
Army Faction, also known as the Baader–Meinhoff
Gang, in Cologne. It was intended to force the West
German Government to release Andreas Baader
and three other Red Army members being held at
the Stammheim Prison near the city of Stuttgartt.
However, on 18 October 1977, on learning that three of
their members had been found dead in prison, the Red
Army killed Martin Schleyer.

A counter-culture society throughout Europe was already
moving away from the post-war growth and baby-boom-
er years, and into a period of anti-authority. Readers of a
certain age may remember the likes of Baarder, Meinhoff
and the Red Army faction being involved in assassinations,
kidnaps and bombings, in the name of anti-imperialism and
anti-establishmentarianism, which became such an issue in
Germany that it became known as the 'German Autumn'.
It quickly spread in various degrees of intensity throughout much of the Western world even gaining momentum
in the USA. However, as with any other vehicle, the new
model flagship line, the 116, still had to endure these ongoing
changes in the political and economical climate, and stand
on its own merits. It had to stand for excellence, more than
just opulence

Engine performance alone is still no convincing argument in the luxury class.

Safety and comfort are just as important. It is a fact that the abilities of the Mercedes-Benz S-Class engines lie in the sports-car category. But that's to be expected and does not need to be harped on. Our goal is not to challenge drivers, but to fit automobiles to them.

The way the Mercedes-Benz S-Class reaches this goal is the blending-together of a high per-formance power plant, a safety standard which is a model for the automobile industry, and comfort that continues for hour after hour of driving. These are the construction priorities at Daimler-Benz, and they come together with a class of work-manship that is known all over the world. The advantage, of course, is not the reputation but the result: the value of the automobile lasts far beyond the norm. This is not simply a purchase; it's an invest-ment.

If you are not willing to accept compromises in your choice of an automobile, get in touch with your Mercedes-Benz dealer.

Mercedes-Benz
The way every car should be built.

An English advert for the 116 Sonderklasse.

As soon as the W 116 was released at the IAA (Interna-
tionale Automobil-Ausstellung) in the autumn of 1972, it
was declared as a vehicle of understated elegance and yet
a vanguard of modern engineering. The word 'Conservatism' became the auto-journalists' new buzz word; thank-
fully, words like: ostentatious, gas-guzzling or economically
irresponsible, were never mentioned.

THE INITIAL 116 MODEL LINE-UP

280 S

Both the 280 S and 280 SE shared the same double overhead camshaft M 110 V28 (280 S)/M 110 E28 (280 SE) engine, the only difference was that the 280 S employed a Solex 4 A 1 carburettor and the 280 SE used a Bosch D-Jetronic system. It was replaced early in 1976 with Bosch K-Jetronic.

From a technical point of view, the 280 was old news as it was a direct transplant from the previous W 114 E-Class (1967–76) of which it was also offered in carburettor and fuel-injected versions. It must be remembered, of course, that in 1970s Europe, the carburetted engine remained the 'norm'. Fuel-injection was still classed as a 'high-end' option and usually only seen on luxury vehicles.

The well-engineered engine achieved respectable performance times for a carburetted vehicle. Horsepower and torque remained the same at 160bhp and 226Nm (167lb ft), respectively. With a top speed of 190km/h (119mph) and a 0–62mph time of 11.5sec with the four-speed manual car, it was no slouch; the automatic took a couple of seconds longer but, for the time period, it was still above average.

Fuel economy, on the other hand, was poor at around 15.6mpg (18ltr/100km). This figure was acceptable in 1972, but the 1973 oil crisis was just around the corner.

At a price of DM 23,800, the 280 S was an attractive alternative to the higher end models. It came standard with a four-speed manual transmission and power steering However, as was the case with Mercedes in the 1970s and indeed the 1980s, various useful items, such as a second exterior mirror, were an extra cost option.

A five-speed manual could also be installed, as well as the characteristically smooth Mercedes four-speed automatic, with the option of floor or column shift on all models except the 450 SEL 6.9 and the 300 SD turbo-diesel. Even though column-shift transmissions had by this time faded out of fashion in Europe, they remained popular in the North American market.

Air-conditioning was offered, also at a huge extra cost.

Windows were rolled down by hand in all models (except for the 450 SEL 6.9 and 300 SD turbo-diesel; however, you could pay extra for electrically powered.

The 280 S was produced from August/September 1972 to July 1980 and it became the second most popular 116 with 122,848 being produced.

280 SE/ SEL

The E in 280 SE/ SEL stood for Einspritzung. They were a more expensive and powerful alternative to the slightly lethargic 280 S models, and consequently the SE (standard wheelbase) became the most popular 116 sold, with a total of 150,983 proving popular with private buyers who wanted a little more power and speed than the fuel-injection offered.

The fuel-injected M 110 managed 185bhp and 238Nm of torque (176lb ft), Even though top speed only increased by 10km/h to a final mark of 200km/h (125mph) a good second was knocked of the 0–62mph sprint in both the manual and auto versions. Nonetheless, minor differences like these meant a lot in this period and buyers gladly paid the DM 25,530 for a 280 SE and DM 31,698 for the 280 SEL, for the livelier and more rev-happy fuel-injected engine. Fuel-injection did little to quench the thirst of the 280 SE/SEL, with the model returning similar fuel economy as the 280 S. But for many, fuel-injection was something to brag about in 1970s Germany.

In early 1976, the 280 models received a Bosch K-Jetronic fuel-injection system. The reason behind this was partly due to the change from leaded gasoline to unleaded gasoline in Germany, but mainly because of new emission laws in Europe. The standard D-Jetronic system worked well with leaded fuel, but was nothing but trouble when having to deal with unleaded gas. Performance suffered and fuel economy worsened.

Sadly, initially the K-Jetronic reduced the power of the M 110 by around 8bhp for a final total of 177bhp. However, two years later, in 1978, Mercedes had been able to refine the K-Jetronic fuel-injection to produce the necessary 185bhp, which the M 110 so needed. While both the 280 S and the 280 SE models were produced at the same time; the 280 SEL models first appeared in October 1973, and production ended two months before the 280 S and 280 SE models were discontinued.

350 SE/350 SEL

The V8s models were for those serious about power, prestige and refinement, and it started with the 350 mod-

Side profile of the 116 SEL (top) and the 116 SE (bottom).

The SE (standard wheelbase) outsold the SEL (long wheelbase) by 3 to 1.

els. Being smoother and more refined than their smaller 6-cylinder siblings, the 350 models were aimed at a more sporty driver; its powerful engine attached to a four-speed manual transmission, worked well for the enthusiastic driver, much more so that the three-speed automatic option, which could match its sub-10sec 0–60mph time. However, Mercedes seemed at the time unable to produce a decent manual transmission. What the manual box offered in spirited acceleration, it ultimately lacked in smoothness and precision, spoiling the sensation completely. The more expensive automatic transmission actually outsold the manual 350, with more customers being interested in the more relaxed driving and cruising. The three-speed auto-

matic used a hydraulic clutch and was considered one of the best automatics available; it remained available in floor- or columnshift position.

As was the case with the 280 models, the 3.5-litre V8 engine had seen duty in the previous W 108 280 SE 3.5/280 SEL 3.5 (1970–71/1971–72). It started out at 200bhp (later detuned to 195bhp, then rejuvenated to 205bhp). The 350 consumption was officially rated at 18mpg (15.7ltr/100km), but this figure was found to be a little too optimistic and unrealistic once on the road.

The SE sold well with 51,100 units; however, consistently with the straight six models, it sold a lot less in the long wheelbase, managing only 4,266 units.

The 450 SEL outsold all other SEL 116 just under 3 to 1.

450 SE/450 SEL

For the first two years, the 450s were considered the flagship model until the mighty 6.9 came along later in 1975. It was easily one of the best sellers in the W 116 range, selling 41,604 in the standard wheelbase; however, unusually in SEL form, units built far exceeded this with 59,578.

Compared with their competitors, the 450s were well equipped and more appealing overall and actually represented value for money – a first for Mercedes. It even won the Car of the Year award in 1973 at a time when big engines and big cars were frowned upon.

The same three-speed automatic transmissions were standard for one, which did quite well managing and using the power of the engine. However, what really swung it in the direction of the 450 was the modified rear suspension, which also had the side benefit of remaining stable during high speeds or kick downs.

The 450s were by no means blisteringly fast, but the rev-happy and responsive qualities of the engine, rather than the performance factor, represented a high standard of luxury for their time. The 225bhp, 4520cc V8 engine was the same engine also serving in the R107 SL roadsters and C107 SLC coupés.

450 SEL 6.9

One thing that separated Mercedes from many other manufacturers was that they didn't just make models to fit a market already saturated with similar models. They pushed the boundaries, sometimes even scarily so, often seemingly putting themselves on a fine line between success and failure. They often did this by having complete faith in their 'teams' of engineers and designers, but they also had an innate ability to be able to learn from previous vehicles using the pros and cons to adapt to a new market.

The 450 SEL 6.9 was a case in point and something that went on to continue its theme to the present day.

To envisage the reasoning behind the '6.9', one only has to look at Erich Waxenberger's 300 SEL 6.3 as its reference point. Waxenberger ran with this concept behind the back of the Mercedes' board, taking it upon himself to build it after hours in a tucked-away garage. He only revealed the car to Uhlenhaut when he knew it was marketable and, even though they only expected to sell around fifty units of this first Q car, it went on to sell 6,526 units, actually outstripping that of their Limousine W 100 600.

Shoe-horning another large-engined 'Q-car' into a model

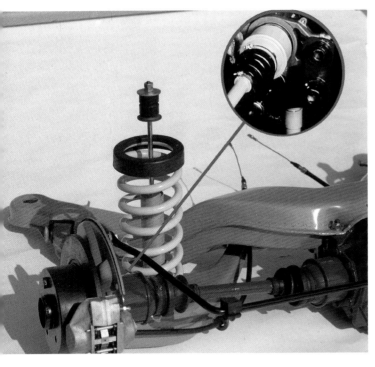

The newly developed antidive system as fitted to the rear of the 450 range.

market in the middle of a global oil crisis must have seemed reckless, but shoe-horned it was, albeit slightly delayed until May 1975.

Once again, Mercedes had applied what it had learnt from the 6.3: that an understated model would be the way to go. It became an overnight icon of engineering excellence. Even now, you only have to mention the W 116 to anyone who knows a little about Mercedes, or even just cars, and the most likely response will be '6.9' followed by a deep, knowing sigh.

Externally, apart from the 6.9 badge, wider tyres and a twin exhaust pipe, there was nothing to really distinguish it from even a basic 280 S; unless chosen as an option, it even had the steel wheels and stainless steel colour-coded wheel trims of its lower model line.

The 450 SEL 6.9 was the top-of-the-line W 116, signifying power and prestige in one package and it boasted the largest production engine ever put into a Mercedes car, keeping this record until the release of the R129 SL73 AMG in the mid-1990s.

Its cost was double that of the simpler 350 SEL but still managed to sell 7,380 units, more than both the 280 SEL and the 350 SEL.

Internally, the 6.9, had a plethora of goodies only available as extra cost option on other vehicles in the model line, such as an RPM gauge, while electric windows for both front and rear passengers, internal sun blinds and air conditioning were available as standard in some markets. Oddly enough, Mercedes even bowed to popular demand and offered leather seats for the North American market, but only in the rear for the European market.

The M 100 engine, which came originally from the previous top-of-the-line S designated W 109 300 SEL 6.3 (1965–72), had also found fame after having been used in the W 100 Mercedes 600 range. It had a cast-iron block but used aluminium cylinder heads, and used a dry sump configuration, normally only used in racing cars. It also benefitted from sodium-filled valves and hardened valve seats, something only seen in piston-driven aircraft. It was hand-built and bench-tested for 265min, 40min of which were under full load.

Despite the 6.9 badge, the engine capacity was actually closer to 6.8-litres (precisely 6834cc). Horsepower was rated at 286bhp and torque was an immense 550Nm at 3000rpm (406lb ft), This should have equated to an explosive amount of power and acceleration, but it lacked the instantaneous acceleration of its forbearer, the 300 SEL 6.3, due to its staggering weight. It still, however, managed a respectable official top speed of 140mph (224km/h), which was often pushed closer to 150mph (240km/h) and had a 0–60mph of 7.1 – quite a feat for almost 2 metric tonnes.

The engineers also devoted themselves to ride and handling: the 6.9 was furnished with a four-wheel hydro-pneumatic suspension; oil was pumped in and out of a strut at each corner, as required to meet variations in load, and this hydraulic action was combined with a stored supply of nitrogen to effect damping, and springing continually compensated ride position and firmness, depending on acceleration or braking. Stiffer front and rear stabilizing bars countered body roll of this 1,985kg (4,367lb) behemoth. A ZF limited slip differential final drive unit enhanced road-holding performance of dry road conditions, as well as improved unladen weight traction in more inclement conditions.

The US-spec 6.9s were quite a bit slower than the Euro-spec version, also due to the US crash regulations of the time. Amongst other things, the W 116s destined for North America were fitted with energy-absorbing bumpers that were long, heavy and extremely ugly.

Another issue hot on the heels of the '1973 fuel crisis', was

The 450 SEL 6.9.

The M 100 6.9 engine originally developed from the 6.3 M 100 fitted to the 300 SEL and the 600.

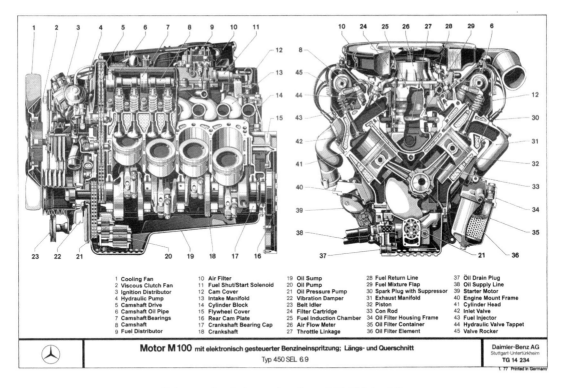

1 Cooling Fan	10 Air Filter	19 Oil Sump	28 Fuel Return Line	37 Öil Drain Plug
2 Viscous Clutch Fan	11 Fuel Shut/Start Solenoid	20 Oil Pump	29 Fuel Mixture Flap	38 Oil Supply Line
3 Ignition Distributor	12 Cam Cover	21 Oil Pressure Pump	30 Spark Plug with Suppressor	39 Starter Motor
4 Hydraulic Pump	13 Intake Manifold	22 Vibration Damper	31 Exhaust Manifold	40 Engine Mount Frame
5 Camshaft Drive	14 Cylinder Block	23 Belt Idler	32 Piston	41 Cylinder Head
6 Camshaft Oil Pipe	15 Flywheel Cover	24 Filter Cartridge	33 Con Rod	42 Inlet Valve
7 Camshaft Bearings	16 Rear Cam Plate	25 Fuel Induction Chamber	34 Oil Filter Housing Frame	43 Fuel Injector
8 Camshaft	17 Crankshaft Bearing Cap	26 Air Flow Meter	35 Oil Filter Container	44 Hydraulic Valve Tappet
9 Fuel Distributor	18 Crankshaft	27 Throttle Linkage	36 Oil Filter Element	45 Valve Rocker

Motor M 100 mit elektronisch gesteuerter Benzineinspritzung; Längs- und Querschnitt

Typ 450 SEL 6.9

Daimler-Benz AG
Stuttgart-Untertürkheim

TG 14 234

1. 77 Printed in Germany

Schematic of the redeveloped M 100 to 6.9.

At around US$40,000, the 6.9 was competing with the Rolls-Royce Silver Shadow, when even the most expensive Cadillac Fleetwood range only listed at around $18,000.

fuel consumption. Officially rated at 14.6mpg (19ltr/100km), in reality one would be lucky to achieve anything over 10mpg (28ltr/100km). And with spirited driving this would drop to around 8mpg (35ltr/100km). However, this did not deter the wealthy and famous from queuing up to own one and, even now, forty years on, it often sits proudly in the top five of polls of the world's greatest saloons.

Diesel Engines

Mercedes were no stranger to the benefits of the diesel engine. At the 1936 International Automobile and Motorcycle Show in Berlin, Mercedes-Benz introduced the world's first production diesel engine car: the OM 138 in the model 260 D (W 138 series). It consumed an average of 9.5ltr/100km of diesel fuel – the closely related model 200 guzzled 13ltr/100km of petrol. The 260 D travelled 450–500km on one tank filling – quite an asset given the rather wide-meshed gas station network at the time. What's more, a litre of diesel cost 24 pfennigs in Germany compared with 39 pfennigs that had to be paid for petrol.

With a subsidy of 5 pfennigs per litre offered to taxi drivers, the 260 D quickly gained acceptance as the tough, cheap-to-maintain vehicle of choice. This popular use also managed to convince private buyers of it virtues and diesel power as an alternative gradually found favour in all walks of life in this post-war period.

Following the end of the Second World War, economical automobiles were more than ever in demand. Mercedes-Benz again included a 4-cylinder car diesel engine in the model range in the form of the model 170 D (W 136 series). The diesel variant, launched in 1949, was powered by the 1.8-litre OM636 engine, an in-line 4-cylinder diesel developing 28kW (38bhp) at 3200rpm. As early as 1950, Mercedes-Benz introduced a modified power plant that now had an output of 29kW (40bhp). The saloon's top speed increased from 100km/h to 105km/h.

Thanks to the farsightedness of its creators, and above all the continuity of its further development, the diesel car captured a firm spot in the Mercedes-Benz model range.

The success of the 'Ponton' models 180 and 190 (W 120/121 series) in events such as the Mille Miglia and African Endurance Rally in 1959, the W 110 series (Fintail) went a long way to prove its worth to the North American market and further emancipate itself from its origins as commercial engines.

In 1968, for the first time, two new diesel models were introduced simultaneously: the 200 D and the 220 D, in the W 115 series. In 1973, the 240 D was added as the top-of-the-range version, until being replaced by the 300 D, a 5-cylinder variant called the OM617. It was the world's first 5-cylinder passenger car diesel engine. Careful engine balancing and engine suspension refinements resulted in an extremely smooth engine, easily comparable to that of a 6-cylinder.

With a volume of 3005cc, the OM617, designed as an in-line 5-cylinder, generated 59kW (80bhp) at 2400rpm and had a respectable top speed of 148km/h (92mph). With acceleration from standstill to 100km/h in 19.9sec, the new top diesel model from Stuttgart was the liveliest and fastest diesel car in the world and featured impressive smoothness and economy. Altogether, 53,690 units of the 240 D 3.0 were manufactured; in all, Mercedes-Benz sold 945,206 W 115-series diesel cars.

Going on to be used in the following W 123 range, this elegant diesel engine would be what would save Mercedes in the North American market with the introduction of CAFE (Corporate Average Fuel Economy).

CAFE describes the average fuel consumption of all models of a brand. Under a regulation issued by the US government, by 1985 the average consumption of all models of a car brand sold in North America had to be less than the equivalent of 8.55ltr/100km. The number of units of each model sold was not important. CAFE was computed simply by adding up the average consumption of all variants on offer and dividing up this figure by the number of variants. Innovative concepts like the economical OM617 diesel engine, therefore, made their mark on the consumption statistics.

The engineering target for Daimler was always to introduce a suitable diesel engine for their largest available luxury saloon and, instead of incurring huge extra costs building a powerful 6-cylinder version, it was decided to equip the OM617 with a turbo-charger. The required modifications needed to cope with higher thermal and mechanical loads were by no means small and the modification resulted in an attractive, well-balanced, economical reliable unit.

300 SD Turbo-Diesel

At the 1977 Frankfurt International Motor Show (IAA), the 300 SD 116 series was introduced. It was to be equipped with an OM617 compression-ignition engine with the addition of an exhaust-gas turbo-charger provided for performance appropri-

Even though it was exclusively produced for the North American market, the 300 SD proved to be a huge success with 28,634 models reaching American soil, despite a prohibitive price tag of $25,000.

ate to the luxury saloon. This boosted the output of the 5-cylinder diesel, familiar from the 123 series, to 85kW (115bhp).

The four-speed automatic transmission was tuned for a high-end top speed, pushing the turbo-charged diesel engine to 165km/h (103mph). Although it was never going to break speed records, it was quite a feat for a diesel back then, and such a speed could have been useful in Europe, although a moot point in the United States. This car was made for cruising, with fuel-conscious buyers in mind, and for that, the extra horsepower developed 231Nm (170lb ft) of torque at an early and very useful 2400rpm.

Obviously, the diesel's advantage was fuel economy – and, on average, the 300 SD could achieve ratings between an optimistic 8ltr/100km, and a more realistic 14ltr/100km (29.3 and 16.7mpg, respectively).

To further the course of diesel power in a luxury saloon, the experimental C111-3 made what turned out to be a multiple record-breaking run at the Nardo test track: it ran 12h non-stop at an average of 320km/h, only consuming 16ltr/100km. In doing so it proved that domestic diesel power units could mean reliability and performance.

US-spec W 116s looked very different from what the Europeans and the rest of the world were used to. The United States had a rule about bumpers withstanding impacts of up to 8mph (13km/h). Accordingly, Mercedes lengthened and strengthened the front and rear bumpers of W 116s going for export to North America. These bumpers not only made the W 116 heavier, but affected handling, and as a result, American-spec W 116s were the poorer cousins of their European counterparts. To make matters worse, there

Low-profile buttons contribute to passive safety.

Uncluttered interiors, well laid out, with everything available within reach.

was also the issue of sealed beam-lights, required on all cars in the United States.

The fact that the 300 SD was only made for the US market does not mean it was the only W 116 offered in North America. The 450 SEL 6.9 was eagerly awaited by the power-hungry Americans, and it made it over the Atlantic. The 450 SEL was also sold in the US for a while. Obviously, North America did not care about the 280s, and they were never even considered for export to North America.

However, the Americans were cutting back on their smog habits and US-spec W 116s received horrific power cutbacks. To give you some idea of the difference: a US-spec 450 SEL could be outpaced quite easily by a European-spec 350 SEL. The Europeans enforced some of their own emissions laws, of course, but not as drastically as did the Americans.

SAFETY THROUGH FORM AND FUNCTION

The 116 Sonderklasse was a big leap forward for Mercedes. Friedrich Geiger's design concept was the beginning of recognizable design accents that, later on, Bruno Sacco would take further into 'homogenous design'.

To some extent it was thought that he went too far, and a number of journalists used words like 'unadventurous' and 'unassuming', and some even saw the use of dull plastics and the lack of chrome a step backward in quality – but that was far from the truth. Apart from 'conservatism' the other watchword was 'safety'.

Safety-oriented design brought together form and function: padded dashboards and steering wheels replaced hard Bakelite and chrome; deformable plastics and flush buttons meant less damage to occupants in an accident; airy, boxy, uncluttered interiors meant better vision; and formally arranged controls meant ease of use would lead to better concentration.

The Béla Barényi taper pin door latch/lock was tested to destruction by applying tonnes of pressure.

The exterior wasn't neglected either: easily damaged parts were relocated for better protection in accidents. Previous Mercedes had a rear tail-mounted fuel tank – this was relocated to above the axle for better protection from rear-end shunts. Doors were strengthened, as were door pillars and roof frames. Rain gutters on the front windscreen were shaped in such a way as to reduce water flowing over the main surface of the screen. Even the now recognizable fluting of the rear tail-lights was purposeful as it reduced road dirt accumulating on the lights during bad weather conditions.

Béla Barényi's ingenious conical door-pin patent was once again used to almost eliminate the potential for the doors to 'pop open' during an accident, something that had taken many lives previously, as people had been thrown from the vehicle.

The double wishbone front suspension was technically advanced for its time – it limited the nose dipping and diving under heavy braking and, later on in its life, the brakes became anti-lock. The swinging rear arm of previous rear suspension units fitted to previous Mercedes was replaced by either a semi-trailing arm set-up or the super advanced self-levelling system. It gave the car a great deal of comfort, also something for which the 116 was built.

In terms of engines, the W 116 came with a somewhat small line-up of motors. Mercedes knew exactly what type of people an S-Class appealed to in those days, and planned out the range accordingly. Unlike modern S-Classes, it had a very small target market, which did not call for offering more varied engine options to widen the appeal of the car.

CRASH-TESTING DEVELOPMENT

Daimler had long been proponents of the advantage of crash testing vehicles and at the end of the 1950s, they had started practical testing for safety research purposes. Initially, individual components were tested, e.g. by means of impact tests, but entire systems were also tested, e.g. the seat belt, which became available in 1958.

In 1959, spectacular crash-testing was started using Mercedes-Benz vehicles as the basis for safety research. For the systematic crash tests, the test vehicles were first accelerated by means of a towing system, such as those used to launch gliders. With the Mercedes-Benz towing unit, saloons fresh from the assembly line could be launched into the air. This was necessary because right from the start of crash testing at Mercedes-Benz, the engineers did not just simulate collisions by running vehicles into a fixed barrier, they also simulated rollovers. To achieve this, the test vehicles were run at a speed of 75–80km/h (47–50mph) on to a so-called corkscrew ramp, which gave the automobiles the necessary twist so that they lifted off into mid-air and landed on their roofs. These tests led to the installation of stabilizing structures in the bodywork.

Hot rocket testing a 116.

The hot-water rocket sometimes didn't behave as it should. Here it didn't brake in time and 'rear-ended' the 116 test car.

The new test hall was used to test the side-impact protection abilities of the 116.

The Hot-Water Rocket

Accelerating a test vehicle with a towing unit was not an ideal method. Dr Ernst Fiala created a solution in 1962: for the crash experiments performed by Karl Wilfert's team, he designed a hot-water rocket, which propelled the vehicles without a tow rope. The device was mounted on a single-axle trailer positioned behind the test vehicle and consisted of a pressure tank, a quick-opening valve and a discharge nozzle. The tank was filled with water to roughly 75 per cent of its capacity and, in order to produce thrust, the tank was heated until the temperature of the water had reached approximately 260°C (500°F). The resulting excess pressure propelled automobile and rocket forward after the valve was opened, accelerating the unit to over 100km/h (62mph).

Crash tests without such incidents became possible from 1973 when, under the auspices of Gunter Huber, a dedicated crash hall with custom-designed facilities was built at the new test centre in Sindelfingen.

On the 65m (213ft) acceleration track, a linear motor producing a thrust force of 53,000 Newtons accurately pulled the automobiles into a 1,000-ton barrier, which rested on a very sensitive force-measuring platform; however, huge leaps forward in crash technology were made.

THE EXPERIMENTAL SAFETY VEHICLES (ESF)

In the 1960s, it became impossible to ignore a negative aspect of mass motorization: more and more people were being killed on the roads. In 1968, the US Department of Transport therefore started a programme for the development of Experimental Safety Vehicles (ESVs), and initiated the international 'Technical Conference on the Enhanced Safety of Vehicles'. In 1970, the first requirements to be met by ESVs were defined. These included an extremely demanding frontal and rear-end impact against a rigid barrier at 80km/h (50mph), and a side impact against a mast at 20km/h (12mph). The test vehicles also had to withstand minor accidents at 16km/h (10mph) without lasting deformations at the front and rear. It was also believed that American consumers would not accept having to actively put on and fasten a seat belt, therefore automatic belt systems were envisaged, which would envelop the front occupants when the doors were closed.

The American Government also issued an invitation to foreign countries to take part in this 'Enhanced Vehicle Safety Committee' (EEVC).

At Mercedes-Benz the challenge of designing vehicles with even more safety was taken up with great enthusiasm. After all, the company was already able to look back on more than twenty years of continual safety research at the time. And about ten years previously, in 1959, the fundamental basis for all future safety developments had already entered series production at Daimler-Benz: the safety body shell with impact energy-absorbing crumple zones at the front and rear, and a rigid passenger compartment between them.

From spring 1971, the ESV project went full-steam ahead in the separate safety research department founded at Mercedes-Benz in Sindelfingen in 1969. All in all, thirty-five vehicles were built and tested over the following four years. The first test took place on 12 March 1971 with a W 114 from series production, i.e. the medium-class series at the time. The car was subjected to a frontal impact on a rigid wall at 80km/h (50mph). The tests also included frontal and rear-end collisions, lateral collisions with masts and other vehicles, and also drop tests from a height of 0.5m (1½ft).

With the release of the ESF 13 at the IAA in May 1972 much work had been done to improve the vehicle structure and internal restraint system to advance occupant protection during an accident. However, Mercedes-Benz's comprehensive approach to safety as a whole founded on these experimental vehicles has become a valid legacy even 50 years later.

MERCEDES-BENZ PRESENT FOUR ESF VEHICLES TO THE PUBLIC

ESF 5

Developed on the basis of the W 114 Stroke8 ('Strich Acht') series floor pan with the now released R107 front end and presented at the 2nd International ESV Conference from 26 to 29 October 1971 in Sindelfingen.

- Designed for an impact speed of 80km/h (50mph).
- Five three-point seat belts, each with three force limiters, front seat belts self-fitting.
- Driver and front passenger airbag; also an airbag in each of the front seat backrests for rear passengers on the outer seats. This increased the weight of the front seats to 63kg/139lb each (standard: 16kg/35lb).
- Extensive structural modifications in the front end and sides.
- Kerb weight: 2,060kg/4,532lb (665kg/1,463lb more than standard).
- Overall length: 5,340mm/210in (655mm/26in more than standard).
- Wheelbase increased by 100mm/4in, so as to maintain spaciousness in the rear, despite the larger seats.
- Front-end extension including hydraulic impact absorber: 370mm/15in.
- Experimental V6 engine to gain deformation space at the front.
- Dashboard with impact-absorbing metal structure on the front passenger side.
- All relevant impact areas in the interior were padded with polyurethane foam, especially the doors, pillars and roof frame.
- Doors without quarter lights, power windows.
- Headlamp wipers, beam range control, parallel rear window wipers.
- Side marker lights, tail-lights with standstill relay and control function.
- Windscreen and rear window of laminated glass, bonded in place.
- Pedals with rounded-off lower section.
- ABS brakes.

ESF 13

Stylistically revised variant of the ESF 5, presented at the 3rd International ESV Conference from 30 May to 2 June1972 in Washington (USA).

- Restraint systems and other features adopted from the ESF 5.
- Kerb weight: 2,100kg/4,620lb (705kg/1,551lb more than standard).
- Overall length: 5,235mm/206in (550mm/22in more than standard).
- Front-end extension including hydraulic impact absorber: 420mm/17in.
- The changes to the external dimensions were primarily the result of the redesigned front and rear ends. The bumpers were now de-signed to be under run, while the deformation path remained the same. The front and rear were extended to reduce the bumper over-hang to an acceptable level.

ESF 22

Based on the W 116 series (1971 S-Class) and presented at the 4th International ESV Conference from 13 to 16 March 1973 in Kyoto (Japan).

- Designed for an impact speed of 65km/h (40mph).
- Four three-point belts, each with three force limiters and a belt tensioners.
- Driver: airbag instead of belt tensioners.
- Kerb weight: 2,025kg/4,455lb (287kg/631lb more than standard).
- Overall length: 5,240mm/206in (280mm/11in more than standard).
- Front-end extension including hydraulic impact absorber: 245mm/10in.
- ABS brakes.

ESF 24

Modified S-Class (W 116) presented at the 5th International ESV Conference from 4 to 7 June 1974 in London (UK).

- Restraint systems identical to ESF 22.
- Kerb weight: 1,930kg/4,246lb (192k/422lb more than standard).

- Overall length: 5,225mm/206in (265mm/10in more than standard).
- Front-end extension incling hydraulic impact absorber: 150mm/6in.
- ABS brakes.

ESF 13 was presented at the 3rd IESFC in Washington.

ESF 05, based on the W 114 Stroke 8, was presented at the Second International Conference on Experimental Safety Vehicles in Sindelfingen.

ESF 22 used the body of the new 116 S-Class of 1971 and was presented at the 4th Conference in Kyoto, Japan in 1973.

Once again the 116 was used for the 5th Conference, this time based in London in 1974.

This already refers to still current concepts such as driver-fitness safety through seating comfort, climate control and non-intrusive vibration/noise characteristics. Where perceptual safety is concerned, the ESF 13 featured pneumatic beam range control, a headlamp wash/wipe system, a tail-light monitoring system in the cockpit, a rear wiper and a safety paint finish with a light colour and contrasting strips. External safety features for the protection of pedestrians and two-wheeled road-users included foam-covered front and rear bumpers, rubber drainage channels and rounded door handles. Fire safety was also taken into account: the fuel tank was above the rear axle, well away from the exhaust system. The fuel pump was, if necessary, deactivated by a mechanism that depended on the engine oil pressure, a valve system prevented any spillage of fuel if the car stood at an unusual angle, the materials used in the interior were fire-retardant and a fire extinguisher was conveniently mounted on the lower front of the driver's seat.

The foundations for the current safety level of cars bearing the Mercedes star had, therefore, been laid. An extract from the summary test report (1975) stated:

> *The ESF 24 can be regarded as the completion of the project, as this vehicle represents the best possible compromise between the original ESV requirements and our current series production cars.*

SAFETY MILESTONES

1978: Premiere of the ABS as an option for the S-Class.

1981: Driver airbag and belt tensioners available in the S-Class.

1995: Belt force limiters and side airbags enter series production of the E-Class.

At Mercedes-Benz, safety was included in the development specifications for new cars as a matter of course decades before the ESV programme, and in rapid succession the ideas first realized as part of the ESF project entered series production as well.

After the ESV era, Mercedes-Benz continued to use concept and test vehicles to develop safety technology. One example of this was the Auto 2000 research car, unveiled to the public in 1981, which was used to test seats with integrated belt anchors, an integrated seat child module and pedestrian-friendly bumpers.

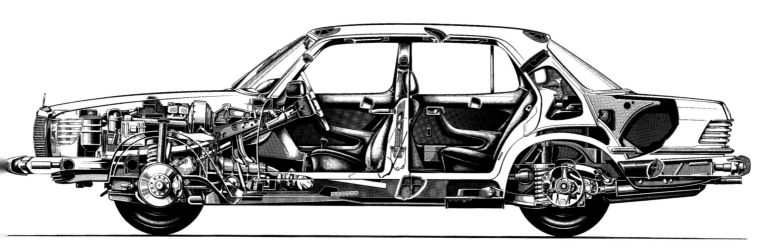

Schematic of the ESF 24 based upon the 116.

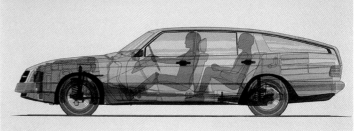

Many of these safety innovations made their debut in S-Class vehicles. ABS, for example, was presented as a world first in the W 116 model series in August 1978. However, under the direction of Guntram Huber, the 'all new' S-Class W/V 126 broke new bounds – amongst other things, it was the first passenger car in the world systematically developed to meet the safety requirements for an offset crash.

Mercedes also became the first car brand in the world to offer their customers a driver's airbag in the steering wheel, also in the W/V 126 model series as well as seat-belt tensioners.

AUTO 2000 RESEARCH VEHICLE

In the late 1970s, the Federal German Ministry for Education, Research and Technology funded, to the tune of 110 million DM, a research and development programme with the motto: 'Economical and low emissions for the future'.

The BMFT (Bundesministerium für Bildung und Forschung) stipulated that fuel consumption was not supposed to exceed 11ltr/100km (21.3mpg) for a vehicle with a curb weight of up to 2,150kg (4,730lb) – a very ambitious target in those days – and the maximum for vehicles weighing 1,250–1,700kg (2,750–3,740lb) was to be 9.5ltr/100km (24.7mpg). In addition, the car was supposed to accommodate four occupants and provide a payload capacity of more than 400kg (880lb).

Mercedes-Benz met the requirements with the 'Auto 2000', first presented to the public at the 1981 Frankfurt International Motor Show. It was very much based on the 126 platform, albeit extended. This research car had an aerodynamically optimized body with a very low Cd (drag coefficient) of 0.28.

Three different engine concepts were tested in this vehicle. Automatic cylinder cut-off premiered in a V8 petrol engine displacing 3.8 litres. When little power was required, four of the eight combustion chambers were temporarily shut down – today this is a feature of several large-displacement petrol engines from Mercedes-Benz.

The 3.3-litre diesel engine tested in 'Auto 2000' had exemplary accelerating power owing to six cylinders and two turbo-chargers and excelled with a consumption of 7.5ltr/100km (about 31.3mpg) at a speed of 120km/h (75mph).

With the third drive unit of the 'Auto 2000', the engineers realized an ambitious project: the automotive gas turbine. It had several qualities, including low-pollutant combustion,

The front nose arrangement was also modified and constructed of a new plastic material (Bayer AG), similar to that of the SL in design. Particular attention was also paid to pedestrian impact protection.

An integrated child-seat protected rear passengers, creating a mini cell.

low weight, compact dimensions, favourable torque characteristics and the elimination of water cooling. All engines were harnessed to a four-speed automatic transmission.

Subsequent model revisions improved aerodynamics compared with that of the original model with flush-mounted side windows (only the small area at the front mirror was retractable). There were further changes to the rear end to improve Cd rating, including lowering the profile and adding under-body shielding.

A seat-integrated belt system was introduced, so the belt was always in the right position to the passenger; this was later introduced as standard in the new SL type R129 in 1989.

The interior was, on first sight, very much influenced by the C126 model, which would not appear for a decade later, although much more technically advanced.

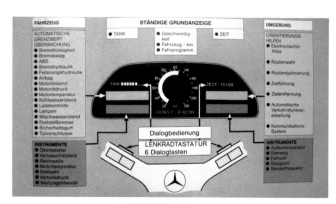

Improved side-impact protection, using struts and impact material in the interior of the doors, improved door-impact resistance. However, a clever 'locked fingers' system along the lower slam panel improved door and frame deformation properties.

Daimler also trailed a 'complete driver information system' (FIS), which included a tri computer, cruise control and an early navigation system.

The Auto 2000 was used extensively in real road traffic for experimental purposes; here, a shot from the Stuttgart urban traffic of 1982, next to a standard S-Class.

The C111 Experiment

As stunningly beautiful and elegant as the C111 looked in its bright 'weissherbst' (rose wine) orange bodywork as it sat on its platform at the 1969 IAA, it hid more than it gave away.

The car broke ground in terms of engineering and design but was only ever meant as an experimental test bed for future technologies, much to the dismay and chagrin of many hopeful customers, who all but threw blank cheques at the Daimler staff members in an effort to be the first to secure themselves one of these dream machines.

On the basis of the experience gained in testing this car, Daimler went on to produce four series of the C111 'lab on wheels' vehicle well into the nineties.

The first C111s featured Felix Wankel's rotary engine, developing 280bhp, as Mercedes, along with the rest of the world, thought this may be the future of engine technology; however, these were quickly shelved with reliability issues and emission problems.

Then, in the fall of 1973, a boycott of the oil-producing countries brought about the so-called oil crisis and crude oil, hitherto an inexpensive commodity, became a precious resource. The most obvious proposition was the low-consumption diesel engine but the compression-ignition unit was still thought to be sluggish and noisy. The Mercedes engineers installed a 3-litre, naturally-aspirated, compression-ignition engine with five cylinders in the C 111-II for the first tests and then in the car, now called C 111-IID. The

The C 111/1 being presented at the 1969 IAA, but not for sale.

Various scale clay models for the C 111 being prepared for wind-tunnel tests.

C 111 prototype in the background. In the middle is the C 111/1 presented at the IAA and on the right is the C 111/2 from 1970.

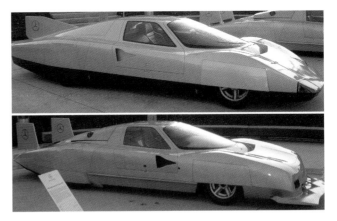

Top is the C 111/3 of 1978 and bottom is the C 111/4 of 1978/79.

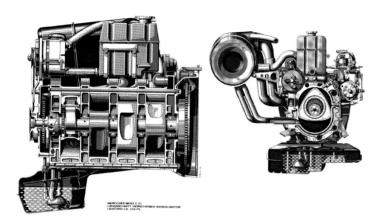

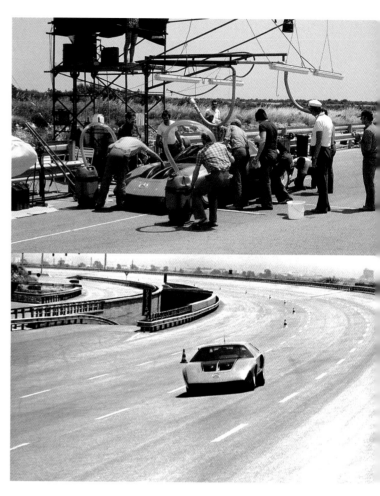

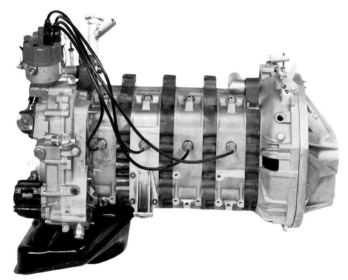

The first Felix Wankel Rotary engine.

OM617 LA engine developed as much as 190bhp, thanks to turbo-charging and intercooling, as opposed to the 80bhp output of the production engine, which powered the Mercedes-Benz 240 D 3.0 (W 115, Stroke Eight). This new TD engine went on to be used in the 123, 116 and 126.

In 1979, the C111/IV broke track records at Nardo by reaching 403.978km/h (251mph), this time with a 4.8 V8 M 117 engine, which went on to be the basis of the V8 in the second-generation Sonderklasse, the 126.

The C111 wasn't just an engine test vehicle, it went on to become a test hack for many things that we now take for granted in modern cars, from twin climate control systems to screen integrated radio antennas and drag coefficient bodywork. The brakes were vacuum assisted ABS and the

On the brand-new test circuit in Nardo, Italy, the test vehicle named **C 111-II D** establishes sixteen world records within 60h. Of these, thirteen are established for diesel vehicles and three for automobiles of all motorization types. Mercedes-Benz achieves records over 5,000 miles (8,047km) with an average speed of 252.540km/h (156.92mph), over 10,000 kilometres (6,214 miles) with an average speed of 252.249km/h (156.74mph) and over 10,000 miles (16,093km) with an average speed of 251.798km/h (156.46mph). Service stops run smoothly.

front suspension featured anti-squat and anti-dive control; once again, this was put into production in the 116. Its rear axle was a precursor to today's multi-link independent rear suspension, which started life in the W201 and C-Class range of vehicles but has continued as the basis of Mercedes rear suspension ever since.

ABOVE: **For the record-breaking run of the C III-II D, engineers use turbo-charging and charge cooling to push the 59kW (80bhp) strong 5-cylinder diesel engine of the Mercedes-Benz 240 D 3.0 to an impressive 140kW (190bhp).**

Mercedes-Benz
C-111 1970

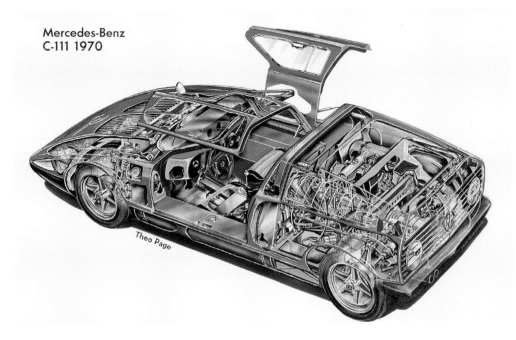

Theo Page

A skeletized drawing of the C III/2 of 1970.

INTRODUCING THE ANTI-LOCK BRAKING SYSTEM

A technical innovation of trend-setting importance became available in the autumn of 1978 exclusively in the 116 series S-Class models. This world-first anti-lock system (ALS), which had been developed together with the Robert Bosch GmbH, enabled a driver to retain steering control, even during emergency braking.

It was not, by far, just a Daimler-Benz innovation and there had been successful systems used in aircraft and railway systems since the early 1950s. However, oddly in the car, the demands on the mechanical friction wheel sensors were much higher: not only did they have to register decelerations and accelerations in wheel speeds, but they also had to react reliably on corners and on rough ground, and work perfectly even when heavily soiled and at high temperatures.

Daimler-Benz engineers had been working on a system alongside TELDIX GmbH in Heidelberg as far back as 1966. The result was in the form of contactless speed pickups, which

operated on the principle of induction. Their signals were to be evaluated by an electronic unit that controlled brake pressure via solenoid valves. Although not 100 per cent reliable, the results were promising and provided a way forward.

It took the new development partner, Bosch, five years to be able to supply the first digital control unit to Untertürkheim for test purposes. Digital instead of analogue – this meant fewer components, with the advantage of the risk of malfunction being reduced down to virtually zero.

Thanks to this digital technology, the electronic components were capable of recording, comparing, evaluating and transforming sensor data into governor pulses for the brakes' solenoid valves within milliseconds. What's more, not only the front wheels but also the rear wheels were included in the control operations.

Another eight years passed before Daimler-Benz was able to offer a reliably functioning anti-lock braking system for production cars. This time was required to give the prototype the degree of technical maturity and reliability that is indispensable for large-scale production. In development,

Key development engineers, all at one table, analysing a solenoid module for the TELDIX ABS: Dr Manfred Burckhardt (left, standing), Professor Dr Werner Breitschwerdt (seated at the table), Joachim-Hubertus Sorsche (standing) and Guido Moch (last on the right).

The (analogue) TELDIX valve system.

The first successful Bosch 'digital' ABS control system.

Mercedes-Benz early **TELDIX** anti-lock braking system. The car with the anti-lock braking system (left) keeps to its precise line, even when braking on a bend, while the non-equipped car becomes difficult to control (right).

the engineers benefited greatly from the revolution in electronics. It was not until the invention of integrated circuits that small, robust computers could be built, capable of recording wheel sensor data in next to no time and reliably actuating the valves for adjusting brake pressure.

Although Mercedes-Benz paid about half the development costs, it was agreed with TELDIX and then Bosch that, in the interest of general automotive safety, the system should also be available to any other motor manufacturers without cost.

It had taken a long time for Mercedes-Benz and Bosch to develop this system but they became the world's first motor manufacturer in August 1978 to officially launch the second-generation anti-lock braking system and to offer it as an option from December 1978 – initially in the S-Class as an extra cost option of DM 2,217.60; however, in 1984, ABS became standard equipment on all Mercedes-Benz passenger cars.

Ten years after the introduction, as many as one million Mercedes-Benz cars with ABS were being operated on the roads throughout the world.

Early successful testing on a W 114.

How the Anti-Lock Braking System Works

The principle of automatic control is simple and basically the same for all systems: as soon as a wheel begins to lock up as a result of excessive application of the brake pedal, the automatic system reduces the braking force to such an extent that the gripping capacity of the tyre is not exceeded, in spite of the full pressure on the brake pedal. The quality of the system depends on the precision of the control.

The ABS consists of the following parts:

• Sensors on all four wheels.
• Electronic control device.
• Hydraulic control valve unit with return pump.

If a wheel tends to lock up as a result of excessive pressure on the brake pedal, its rotating speed diminishes very quickly.

A signal is sent by the sensor at the wheel to the electronic control device. This compares the rate of deceleration with the highest permissible values and reacts extremely rapidly, with a warning that the wheel is about to lock up. A signal is instantly transmitted to the electromagnetic control valve to reduce the pressure of the brake fluid on the appropriate wheel far enough to stop the rapid deceleration and to eliminate the danger of it locking up. As soon as this happens, the wheel, which is now receiving less braking power, accelerates again. This fact is registered by the wheel's sensor and again the electronic unit reacts: the wheel can transmit more brake power, therefore pressure is re-applied until speed drops again and the process begins anew.

All this happens without any action on the part of the driver.

The Bosch system schematic showing working system.

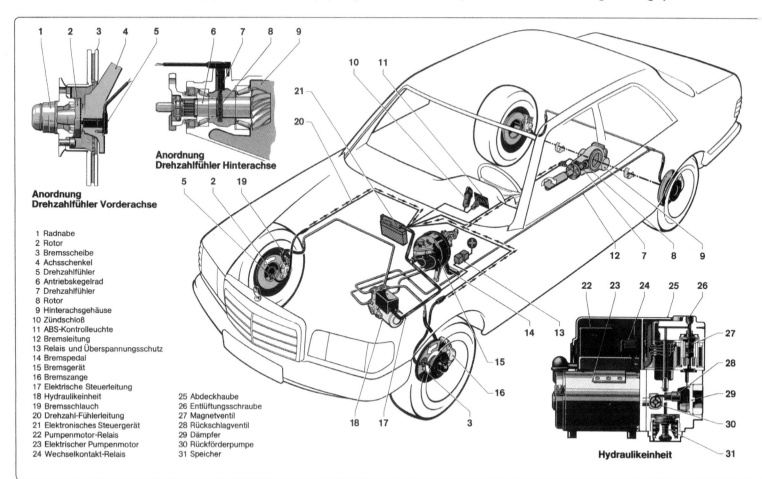

Anordnung Drehzahlfühler Hinterachse

Anordnung Drehzahlfühler Vorderachse

1 Radnabe
2 Rotor
3 Bremsscheibe
4 Achsschenkel
5 Drehzahlfühler
6 Antriebskegelrad
7 Drehzahlfühler
8 Rotor
9 Hinterachsgehäuse
10 Zündschloß
11 ABS-Kontrolleuchte
12 Bremsleitung
13 Relais und Überspannungsschutz
14 Bremspedal
15 Bremsgerät
16 Bremszange
17 Elektrische Steuerleitung
18 Hydraulikeinheit
19 Bremsschlauch
20 Drehzahl-Fühlerleitung
21 Elektronisches Steuergerät
22 Pumpenmotor-Relais
23 Elektrischer Pumpenmotor
24 Wechselkontakt-Relais

25 Abdeckhaube
26 Entlüftungsschraube
27 Magnetventil
28 Rückschlagventil
29 Dämpfer
30 Rückförderpumpe
31 Speicher

Hydraulikeinheit

Stopping Distances as Short as Physically Possible

In any emergency stop, the ABS keeps all four wheels within the wheel slip range (just before the point of locking-up), which permits optimum use of the 'grip' of the road for braking.

With conventional brakes, a car can be stopped from 60mph (100km/h) after about 160ft (50m). With ABS, the same car on the same road needs only 138ft (42m). The reduction by 24ft (8m) corresponds to a 16 per cent increase in braking efficiency. But this figure does not tell the whole story. In vehicle braking, speed does not decrease in a linear progression; retardation increases towards the end of the stopping distance.

At the point where the car equipped with ABS comes to a stop from 60mph, the normal car would still be doing 25mph (40km/h). At this speed it could still crash into an obstacle when the car with ABS would already be at a standstill.

On a wet road, the differences in stopping distances are even more dramatic. More important still is the fact that with ABS, the car remains steerable – a driver can avoid a hazard without taking their foot from the brake pedal.

A failure of the electronic brake control would have no effect whatsoever on the normal operation of the brakes.

Braking distances are considerably shortened, particularly on wet roads. Stopping distance for a fully loaded car is only very little longer than that for a car occupied only by the driver; however, braking in curves becomes possible without losing control of the car.

On a wet road, the differences in stopping distances are even more dramatic. More important still is the fact that with ABS, the car remains steerable – a driver can avoid a hazard without taking his/her foot from the brake pedal.

CHAPTER THREE

CONCEPTION TO FRUITION

INTRODUCING THE SIBLING

Neo-liberalism and *laissez-faire* economics were slowly dragging the worldwide economy, by the scruff of its neck, out of the pit of recession, but with an already stretched-to-breaking-point North American auto-industry burdened with ever-tightening CAFE fuel mileage standards, more had to be done.

A more aware world, means a more responsible world and the CAFE effect spread; 'economical' fuel-injection was becoming the 'norm', turbo was being used to increase the power of small engines, small front wheel drive vehicles became the 'responsible choice' – was there room for another large engine saloon?

Mercedes at this time took a bold step. If the 116 could be a success through the turmoil of the 1970s, so could a revised model. The way forward was to make the consecutive model not just a revision of the old one, but a consecutive model in the true Sonderklasse line. To make it responsibly meant making it lighter, more efficient, even safer, with innovation; it had to be elegant yet understated, without 'bells and whistles'. According to Professor Werner Breitschwerdt, head of development at Daimler-Benz:

> We are neither willing nor able to be prophets but we already knew at the beginning of development that our NEW S-Class would have to be an up-to-date vehicle range optimally meeting requirements prevailing at any given time, from the launch, well into the nineties.

On 13 September 1979, a new generation of the Sonderklasse was unveiled at the Frankfurt International Motor Show IAA.

THE TRANSITION PERIOD

In September 1979, model series 126 was presented at the Frankfurt International Motor Show IAA, succeeding the first S-Class type range. The production of model series 116, however, was not yet finished. Daimler continued to produce the 116 alongside the 126, ceasing only between April and September 1980, depending on the model. The last car of a total of 473,035 built units of this range that passed the final-assembly inspection at the plant in Sindelfingen was a 300 SD.

Although sad at the time, its demise made way for the growing admiration for the new Sonderklasse on the block: the 126 Sonderklasse. However, its legacy was that it laid the foundation of design that would bring excellence in engineering through understated elegance.

The Land of the Rising Sun

Approaching the end of the 1970s saw another threat on the horizon in the form of Japanese car manufacturers.

The North American market was already starting to suffer the consequences of 'resting on their laurels'. After sales peaked at a record 12.87 million units in 1978 of American-made cars, within four years this had almost halved. By 1980, Japan had become the world's leading car manufacturer – a position it has continued to hold to this day.

Japanese companies not only performed better than their American counterparts, but also operated in a fundamentally different manner. On average, the best Japanese companies manufactured cars of better quality and with superior manufacturing productivity compared with American manufacturers. They did this by introducing an approach to manufacturing and product development that is fundamentally dif-

**Last 116 off the
production line:
a 300 SD.**

ferent from the conventional mass-production system that has been the basis of US automotive manufacturing. This new manufacturing and product-development approach, was referred to as 'lean production', and was based upon a different concept of work organization and human resource utilization within and between organizations. If the US automotive industry was to remain competitive, it had to undergo structural change and adopt this new production paradigm. It wasn't until 1980 that American vehicle manufacturing decided to undertake a five-year, $80 billion programme of plant modernization and retooling. Functional aerodynamic design replaced styling in Detroit studios, as the annual cosmetic change was abandoned. Cars became smaller, more fuel-efficient, less polluting and much safer. Product and production were being increasingly rationalized in a process of integrating computer-aided design, engineering and manufacturing. Programmes of employee motivation and involvement were also given high priority.

Traditional American-built cars were always disadvantaged in major foreign markets, such as Japan and Europe, which used high gasoline taxes to accomplish energy-conservation goals and to raise tax revenues. Because they have evolved under a regime of low fuel prices, American cars have been too large and inefficient to compete, even if the official barriers to their sale in some countries were eliminated. As a result, the European subsidiaries of Ford,

General Motors and (formerly) Chrysler, developed families of automobiles that conformed to the requirements of their host countries. Even though American cars improved significantly in the 1970s and 1980s, they still carry the reputation in foreign markets of being gas guzzlers. In effect, cheap energy has been one factor that has confined American cars to the North American market.

In contrast, Japanese and European manufacturers have exported their vehicles, which were developed in markets with high fuel prices, to markets throughout the world. Their highly fuel-efficient cars were saleable in all countries, whether fuel was expensive or cheap, e.g. foreign brands account for about 35 per cent of the US market. Whereas American manufacturers have developed separate product lines for domestic and foreign customers, the Japanese and Europeans have been able to sell the same models worldwide, which gives them a significant economic advantage.

Once again, Mercedes were ahead of the game: efficiency was not just about fuel consumption, but also quality and longevity of the brand. No longer was it sufficient or necessary to just restyle a model to suit recent fashions, what they had learnt from the introduction of the new Sonderklasse 116 was that, in spite of the economy or political environment, by building recent innovation, safety and style into a new model, they could not only sell their cars, but they could sell them well.

IN DEVELOPMENT

The preliminary discussions for the development of a successor to the 116 started in 1971, essentially at the close of development of the 116. However, although only in the 'brainstorming' period at this time, the teams must have had one eye on the 116, especially considering the already discussed turbulent times that the 1970s would bring.

The brainstorming period was dominated with comments as to how to continue the Sonderklasse concept with responsibility; but much had changed over this period in the way of technical innovation, as well as legislature of safety and emissions. What was most important and was not open to compromise was that any model must remain 'typically Mercedes'. In addition, they had to make sure that new model generations built a formal link with the future without allowing their lines to neglect the starting point. This ensured that each new Mercedes-Benz was given an unmistakable identity and revealed its good breeding at first sight. It also meant that fashionable trends were out of the question for Mercedes designers, since these lacked the very ingredient that made every Mercedes-Benz different: the long-term effect.

From 1975 there were visible changes in our understanding of the car. Customers valued, above all, the practical qualities of a vehicle. Spacious bodies with large tailgates were popular, but more and more car buyers were interested in compact cars, hatchbacks and estates, which prompted Daimler to enter their first manufactured estate model: the S 123.

In the 1970s, vehicles were still painted in bright, cheerful colours. Particularly popular were yellow, orange, light green, light blue, red and beige; this also continued into the interior. However, by the early 1980s at the latest, such bright colours had served their time. Chrome decoration was also used less and less. Unpretentious dashboards were visible testimony to the introduction of electronics into automotive design.

At the same time, automotive manufacturers began using new materials, which presented designers with new challenges and opened up new opportunities. In order to save weight, bumpers were produced in plastic and aluminium. They were also mounted closer to the body, so that the two fused visually to produce a single entity and thereby improve aerodynamic values.

Indeed, the wind tunnel played an increasingly important role in automotive design – at least in Europe this was the

case. As a result, the angular designs of the late 1970s and early 1980s were increasingly replaced by slim, rounded bodies with smooth surfaces and bumpers aerodynamically integrated into the body.

Even small details pointed to the concerted effort to improve aerodynamic performance: door handles were sunk flush with the body, exterior mirrors were streamlined, gaps in bodywork were minimized and under-bodies smoothed.

Even though to some extent wind-tunnel aerodynamics had been researched on Mercedes vehicles since the 1930s, the S-Class 126 was the first Mercedes-Benz production vehicle to be systematically developed and designed with aerodynamic considerations in mind.

The wedge shape introduced in the 126 was testament to this but later more pronounced in the new small series, the 190, initially known familiarly as the 'Baby Benz'.

DESIGN

Under the guidance of Bruno Sacco the team commenced work with little more than a conceptual idea.

The author had the privilege of an interview with Bruno Sacco and, although a lot of what was discussed was very candid and personal, the result, for the author at least, was a deeper understanding of the process with which the 126 came into being.

Although at The Daimler we had a way to design, for me the 126 was the beginning of a new way, although I had taken charge as 'Chief Stylist'... I dislike the word 'stylist' if it relates to me personally but I accept it if it means what we achieved as a team was respected... I had little power or control, my job was designing, form and function alongside a team of other designers and engineers, there was no hierarchy just co-equality, co-existence. Apart from anything I never had an urge to design a car on my own. Everyone in the team sees things in their own way and led by their own strengths; it is this that creates beauty. I can draw a shape or a line, for example, but the intersection of body lines, the dissipation of light as it hits one surface and reflects to another for an example is the realm of the talented model makers. We designed as a team to create something that was good for Daimler but respected by everyone on

Interview at the Sacco office with Bruno Sacco, Marena (his daughter) and the author, Nik Greene.

A Mercedes must always look and feel like a Mercedes. However, that doesn't mean looking back at successes, or indeed failures, and repeating them; it means going forward with every aspect of design.

different levels. For the first time it was not just about the car, of course the car had to look good and fulfil the brief but it was more about how the car impacted the lives of those that drove it or rode in it. The driver would have to 'feel' the car and how it responded without fighting in its environment; without fighting to hold the wheel, without fighting to see where they were going and without fighting to concentrate on driving. The brief of safety and efficiency was as much about the feel of the car as it was the physical safety element.

With the 126 we wanted to balance style with innovation. Not design for the sake of design. That just breeds fads that look tired and outdated very quickly.

A beautiful car, well-engineered, will always be a beautiful car, well-engineered. A car that makes you sigh, in a good way, every time you get in it as a passenger or a driver is what drives us to do better.

Design Brief

The basic design brief for the 126 was simple:

- Provide higher performance, with greater practical benefits to the occupants.
- Higher standards of safety.
- More comprehensive specifications for ease of handling.
- More comfort to reduce stress and fatigue.
- Ample reserve power with improved economy.
- Better durability with retention of value over a longer period.
- Less frequent downtime in servicing and reliability.
- Considerable savings in fuel and raw materials.
- A lower consumption of energy and raw materials with less impact on the environment.
- Greater corrosion protection.
- Improved safety protection for all.
- Improved protection from damage in an accident.
- Reduction in exhaust gas emissions.
- Reduction in noise level from exterior as well as interior.
- Everything possible to aid the driver, whether in traffic in the city or out on the open road.

The result was a car for the first time that had more power yet was more economical. It was both safer and yet lighter; easier to maintain, yet more reliable than ever before.

The successful integration of hitherto essentially incompatible features with less compromise was the basis for a car that would go on to influence engineering and style on many vehicles in the future

REDESIGN, RE-FORM AND RE-FUNCTION

The focal point of all vehicles provided by Daimler was to offer a package of superior comfort and performance commensurate with thiS-Class of car and the 'all new' Sonderklasse were to be no different.

Freidrich van Winsen remarked that:

> Our S-Class limousines potentially cover about twice the mileage of the average of all cars in Germany, doing so while carrying a significantly larger number of occupants, to reduce fuel consumption without compromise we must be technically superior.

A redesign of the 116 had begun, even before its own release, but the brief was the same: to build an innovative, responsible machine with the accent on passive and active safety and reliability in an elegant form; to further improve, albeit in a sensible manner, the maximum of comfort and perfor-

Called a 'Masskonzeption', 1-1 design is an essential part of starting with the basics.

Part of the design studio.

mance based on advancements in engineering, safety and reliability, and complemented by the ultimate standards of quality expected from Daimler-Benz on all previous top-class Mercedes cars.

Up to this point in automotive manufacturing, the general rule in automotive improvements was that this inevitably meant bigger – larger dimensions, higher weights and consequently higher fuel consumption – but very early on it was decided that the opposite would apply.

Freidrich van Winsen, head of car development, made it very clear that simple 'downsizing' was out of the question. Important goals in the development of this new series were to be higher driving comfort and safety, but also the reduction of energy consumption. What was achieved would have to be through technical superiority and more sophisticated features and, consequently, become more efficient to ensure that an upper-class saloon would remain current and 'socially acceptable' without losing integrity. This was the only way that they could continue the Sonderklasse concept: engineered for the future to meet the demands of today.

The new styling emphasized clean lines free of short-lived modish embellishments, with the emphasis on ultimate functionality of design. The functionality was that of an aerodynamically perfected form that would contribute to the desired reduction of fuel consumption but not at the cost of ride, comfort or interior space; they were at last ready to discontinue production on the previous model after seven years.

The Body

First, the new 126 body style was produced with the emphasis placed on reducing weight. The use of high-quality and very expensive sheet steel, which was able to be subjected to far heavier loads, despite being lighter, successfully reduced the weight of the body shell and also contributed to an increase in stability. The overall result was an impressive reduction of weight up to 280kg (616lb) less than in previous models.

The newly updated wind tunnel and computer-aided Cd reduction technology managed to reduce wind resistance by an enormous 14 per cent. Added to a multitude of improvements on the bodywork and chassis, and development of a new four-speed transmission, there was a successful reduction in fuel consumption throughout the range by 10 per cent.

Safety

During the development of the body structure, the front end was completely redesigned. Many years of experience gleaned from real-time crash-testing and intensive accident research enabled Daimler to incorporate what came to be known as 'crumple zones'. The front and rear doors had built-in overlap framework to almost eliminate the possibility of jamming in the event of a full-frontal accident.

Comfort

Above-average comfort was always a characteristic feature of top-quality cars from Daimler-Benz; the 126 was no different.

To further suppress the pitching and rolling motion over uneven surfaces, the wheelbase of the SE models was lengthened by 70mm (2¾in) over that of the 116. The wheelbase of the SEL was also lengthened in comparison by 110mm (4in). In addition, larger metalastic bushes were employed at various link points on the front and rear axles to shield passengers from road rumble.

Notwithstanding the changes to body shape to incorporate the new advances in aerodynamics, the designers succeeded in creating a spacious, comfortable interior.

Further enhancements of the interior ensured a plush and psychologically comfortable atmosphere for both driver and passenger.

Besides the regular water temperature, oil pressure and fuel gauges, the instrument cluster also featured a new device referred to as the 'econometer'. It allowed the driver to keep an eye on how his/her driving style affected fuel

ABOVE LEFT: **The front side members and fork supports joined to the firewall were designed to absorb frontal, as well as side, impact to protect the occupants.**

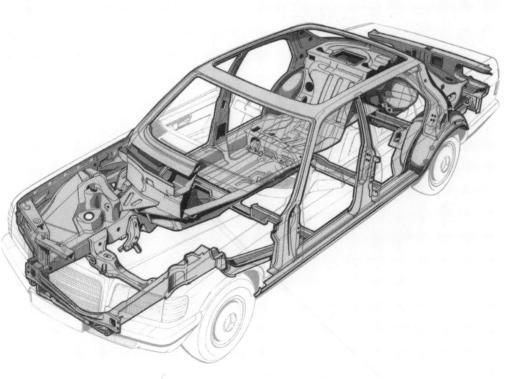

LEFT: **Maintaining strength while keeping weight as low as possible. The passenger area became a purposely designed cell with sturdier windscreen pillars to protect occupants from frontal, rearwards or sideways impact accidents.**

Larger metalastic bushes were employed at various link points of the front and rear axles to shield passengers from road rumble.

The dual 'component partition' under the bonnet also served to insulate passengers from heat and engine noise, as well as to protect certain heat-sensitive and electrical components from engine heat.

The size of the door openings changed by enlarging the head and foot areas by a few centimetres to facilitate easy access.

Even the sealing of the doors to the sill was revised so as to keep the area clean from road grime.

The dashboard and controls reflects the latest knowledge of passive safety and ergonomics.

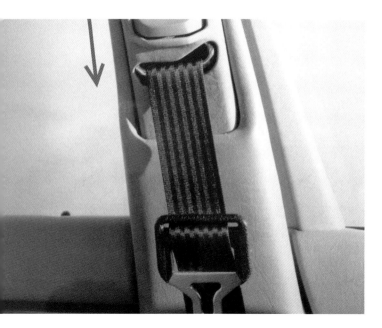

The shoulder anchor of the seatbelt is repositionable in three increments to accommodate differing heights.

consumption; even the tiniest of movement on the accelerator would be enough to take the needle from out of the red zone.

Much thought went into the design of the interior appointments, not just aesthetically but practically. The driver and passenger seat belts were laterally adjustable for the benefit of various heights of individuals,

Manual seat controls were given large, looped handles for ease of use without having to look or feel for them.

Seating size and design was to optimize comfort and reduce fatigue over long journeys. More heavily padded head-restraints provided accident protection for both front and rear passengers. The rears of the front seats were moulded to provide a comfortable leg position for rear passengers. Pull-down armrests, in both the front and rear, provided extra comfort. The SEL was given an electronically adjustable longitudinal seat position and backrest angle adjustment. All seats had an orthopaedic option of rubber bladders to provide more support, if needed.

The interior had an improved courtesy lighting system, providing puddle illumination on entrance and exit, as well as delayed action timers on main courtesy lights. The rear passenger had an optional reading light available for the C' post.

Ventilation and Heating

Daimler engineers knew that passenger well-being is not just defined by seat design and ease of use. The physical element of temperature control whilst inside the cabin was also paramount, not just for ambient conform but also for safety and concentration, regardless of all outside weather and temperatures.

The outstanding feature in the 126 was the ability to control the temperature between 16 and 32dC electronically, independent of outside temperature, this volume can also be controlled individually between front passenger and driver.

Much thought went into the ability to change stale air

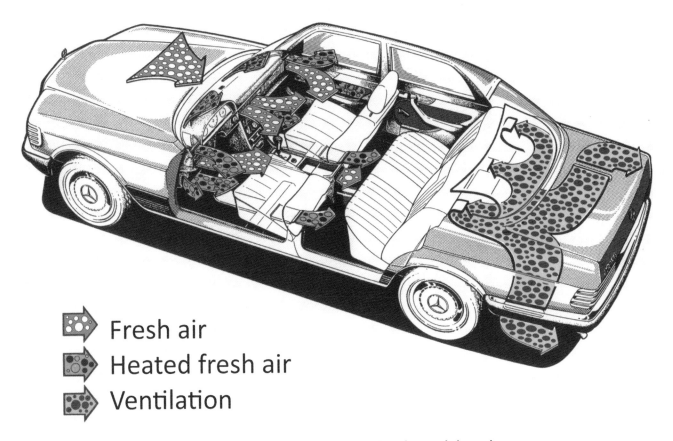

Fresh air

Heated fresh air

Ventilation

Separate ducts channelled unheated fresh air through dashboard outlets and through conduits to the rear passengers; also controllable.

for fresh air. Ducts were no longer placed in the C'Post but under the parcel shelf, which was then channelled along panels in the boot to non-return flaps behind the rear bumpers sides in a noiseless draught-free manner.

As in the past, an optional air-conditioning system was provided, but added to this was now a fully automatic climate-control system.

Engines

The range of series 126 first comprised of seven models with a choice of four engines – from the 2.8-litre 6-cylinder carburettor engine with 156bhp to the 5.0-litre all-aluminium V8-engine with petrol injection and 240bhp. Furthermore, there were two body variants: beside the normal version there was an extended variant with an enlargement of

140mm (5½in) benefitting the rear passenger leg room and the entrance width of the rear doors.

The two 8-cylinder engines of the previous series were replaced by two redesigned units with enlarged displacement and all-aluminium blocks. The 5.0-litre engine, which took the place of the 4.5-litre grey cast-iron block and the 3.8-litre all-aluminium engine, had been developed from the 3.5-litre V8 with grey cast-iron block. Due to their higher power, combined with reduced weight, the new V8-engines made for a better driving performance combined with more economical fuel-consumption.

The carburettor and injection version of the 2.8-litre 6-cylinder remained unchanged in the range and also similar to its predecessor. A 3.0-litre turbo-diesel version was produced for export to the USA 5-cylinder engine; its performance, however, was increased slightly by 10bhp to 125bhp.

The Straight Six M 110 engine and the M 116/7 V8.

Suspension

The drive layout of the vehicle basically corresponded to the previous models; however, the body had been constructed according to the newest insights into safety research. Thanks to new construction principles, the 126 series saloons were the first vehicles worldwide to fulfil the criterion of an offset crash.

The characteristic design elements of the new S-Class present themselves more in the lower zones. For the first time on a Mercedes-Benz car there were no classical-style bumpers. Instead, there were generously proportioned, plastic-coated bumpers seamlessly integrated into the front and rear apron. Broadside protection strips formed an optical link between front and rear apron, placed at the height of the bumpers between the wheel cut-outs and coloured to offer contrast between body and skirt, allowing for a more aesthetically pleasing shape.

On 17 September 1981, two years after its debut, series 126 was completed by an elegantly designed coupé version shown at the Frankfurt Motor Show IAA. The car was only

available with an 8-cylinder engine. Within the 'Mercedes-Benz energy concept' for reducing consumption and pollutants presented at the same time, the two V8-block engines had been thoroughly redesigned. Next to an increase of compression, air-circulated injection valves and an electronic idle-speed control device were on the list of improvements. An additional cam timing adjustment meant that the torque maximum could be shifted towards lower numbers of revolution.

In the case of the 3.8-litre engine, much had changed. In order to obtain a more favourable torque/bhp ratio, the bore was reduced and the stroke increased, which slightly increased displacement. In both V8 engines this resulted in a slight power reduction. However, it considerably improved economic efficiency.

In both cases, the rear axle transmission ratio was adapted to the changed characteristics of the engine. The two 6-cylinder engines were also changed in a number of details, thus also achieving some economizing effect. The power potential, however, was not affected by these measures.

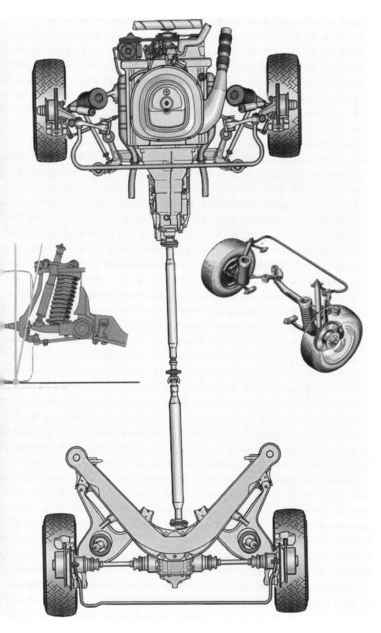

The passenger cell now was capable of handling an offset impact at a collision speed of 55km/h (34mph) without risk to passengers.

The M 116/7 engine coupled to the 722.3 transmission.

Semi-trailing arm rear axle, as well as a twin control-arm front wheel suspension with zero steering offset.

Gearboxes

The revised gearboxes deserve a mention all of their own, as they paid a huge part in the efficiency drive of the 126.

Transmissions have an effect on fuel consumption in various ways:

• Through the transmission of power efficiency. Efficiency was improved considerably by newly developed torque converters with better flow characteristics, as well as, and in spite of, being smaller in size. Mechanical losses were further reduced by two-thirds of previous models by the use of these newly designed converters, contributing to only a very insignificant higher fuel consumption compared with that of the manual transmissions.

• Through the gear change pattern. Fuel consumption was further reduced with the assistance of the gears being selected at the optimal point of fuel consumption versus desirable output.

• Through the multiplication of torque ratio. To do this, the new gearboxes have four gears as opposed to the original three gears of the predecessor model to be able to extend the torque range differences.

• The driver's influence. Through the driver's influence on the reduction of fuel consumption.

The correlation between driving at a steady pace in top gear and getting a satisfactory fuel consumption has always been known; however, there must also be a correlation between the power needed to climb or accelerate without sacrificing fuel excessively.

Economy gears, fast gears and overdrive gears almost completely vanished from the market due to lack of practical use and at times having the opposite effect as drivers failed to be bothered to use them due to the fear of being left without power when needed. So, Daimler have ensured that the new four-speed transmission has an extended torque multiplication range from 2.31 to 3.68, and when accelerating hard from standstill, the torque rise is now 6.99 instead of the original 4.62.

The control for this is that the gear will drop to its lower gear without the need to kick-down in normal use but also has the desired kick-down to two gears below when needed.

Owing to painstaking design work, and despite the addition of a forth gear, the weight of the transmission was further reduced by 5kg (11lb), as compared with that of the three-speed unit.

AERODYNAMIC DEVELOPMENT

Having survived heavy bombing during the Second World War, the FKFS (Forschungsinstitut für Kraftfahrwesen und Flugzeugmotoren Stuttgart) wind tunnel eventually passed into full Daimler-Benz AG ownership in 1970. The company then began a renovation and modernization of the complete installation project costing 8 million DM, which took nearly two years to complete.

In April 1976, the engineering department at Mercedes-Benz began operating the installation, now with four times

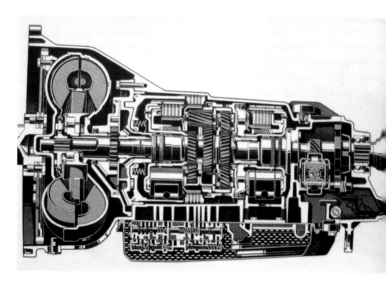

Schematic of 722.3 transmission.

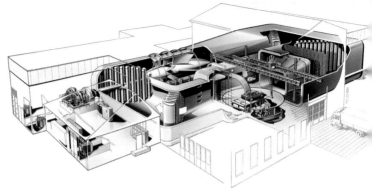

The wind-tunnel building in the 1970s with the proposed rebuild drawing.

MEASUREMENT INSTALLATIONS AND TECHNICAL DATA FOR THE WIND TUNNEL AT THE MERCEDES-BENZ PLANT IN UNTERTÜRKHEIM

- Wind tunnel weighbridge
- Multi-point pressure system
- Roller-type performance test rig
- Traversing system
- Data-acquisition system
- Length of the measurement section: 10m (32ft)
- Length of the tunnel axis: 125m (410ft)
- Air jet cross-section: 32.6m[u2] (351ft[u2])
- Maximum flow cross-section: 120m[u2] (1,291ft[u2])
- Maximum blowing speed: 250km/h (155mph)
- Maximum power input: 5,000kW
- Blower diameter: 8.5m (27ft)
- Turntable diameter: 12m (38ft)
- Swivelling range of the turntable: 180 degrees
- Maximum axle load: 10 tonnes
- Contraction ratio pre-chamber/air jet: 3.6

The new rotating base plate weighbridge can be clearly seen highlighted by the red dotted line.

The original method of using an H-shape frame and steel cables.

more capacity. As part of the capacity increase, a wind-tunnel weighbridge, a multi-point pressure system and a roller-type performance test rig were installed.

Built into a rotating base plate, the wind-tunnel weighbridge replaced the suspended balance used previously, with which the vehicle was suspended by four steel cables in an H-shaped frame, and the four steel cables were suspended by the lifting scales in the turntable. With the under-floor weighbridge now installed, the vehicle was placed on four contact plates that were fitted level in the floor of the rotating measuring plate.

The contact plates were located on four individual lift scales that were used to measure the lift forces. The rotating measuring plate made it possible to simulate and measure the effects of crosswind.

Alongside aerodynamic studies, the wind tunnel could also be used for other jobs, such as contamination measurements and measurements of the wiping precision of windscreen wipers in the high-speed range, temperature measurements at the radiator and brakes, and tests of the passenger-compartment ventilation.

The Wind Tunnel as an Engineering Tool

When the first newly developed passenger cars from Mercedes-Benz came on to the market in 1949, after the Second World War, aerodynamic drag and energy efficiency were not of primary importance. And that didn't change in 1951, when the new models 220 (W 187) and 300 (W 186) took the International Motor Show (IAA) in Frankfurt by storm. At that time, there was no official aerodynamic data for these two cars, but in the case of the model 220 at least, existing figures for pre-war vehicles with free-standing head-lamps, running boards and fenders indicate that the Cd value of the W 187 was likely to have been around 0.55.

After the war, the previous technical management team was replaced by a new generation of engineers. These included Fritz Nallinger, Rudolf Uhlenhaut, Josef Müller, Wolf-Dieter Bensinger and Hans Scherenberg, for example. In 1952, Scherenberg succeeded Max Wagner, who had held the position of head design engineer since 1926.

The presentation of the model 220 (W 180) in Geneva in March 1954 marked the theoretic shift that, for the first time, was to play a role in the design of an S-Class predecessor vehicle: the significance of aerodynamic drag.

To achieve this calculation, it was discovered that two important measured variables characterize a vehicle's aerodynamics: its frontal area A (in square metres) and the drag coefficient Cd (C = constant, d = drag, non-dimensional), which describe the airflow pattern of an object irrespective of its size.

Because the overall aerodynamics depends on both values, the most meaningful result of a vehicle measurement is obtained by multiplying Cd by A (Cd x A).

Developed in parallel, and presented seven months prior, the mid-sized model 180 (W 120), which corresponded largely to the model 220 (W 180) in terms of its body, was described by chief engineer Nallinger as embodying the 'link between the traditional Mercedes-Benz design and a new-age, aerodynamically efficient overall design'.

With a Cd value significantly below 0.50, the model 220 (W 180) meets optimal conditions for better performance with lower fuel consumption, thanks to more favourable aerodynamics, despite its larger body when compared with its predecessor.

Model	Cd	A (m^2)	Cd x
A220 (W 180)	0.473	2.07	0.9791

Yet another advancement became clear with the introduction of the W 111 model series in 1959. Compared with the 'Ponton' W 180 model series, the drag coefficient had improved by 13 per cent. Despite a 3.86 per cent larger front

surface area, the total aerodynamic resistance obtained by multiplying A by Cd dropped by 9.7 per cent. In the 'tailfin', the arched design of the roof and the high rear end of the boot lid had a favourable effect that reduced flow losses.

The following analysis was published in issue 10/1960 of the trade journal *Auto Motor und Sport*:

We were unable to work out just how 120 horse-power was enough to propel this full-sized car to a timed speed of 174km/h until we were handed the precisely measured data on the frontal surface and drag coefficient.

Model	Cd	A (m^2)	Cd x A
220, 220 S, 220 SE (W 111)	0.411	2.15	0.8837

With the appearance of the W 108/109 model series in 1965, a style icon was born. Although aerodynamic issues were not a priority at this time, it was noted that, even though the flatter roof and lower rear end of the W 108 model series resulted in a less favourable drag coefficient compared with that of the W 111 model series, the level achieved with the W 111 was essentially maintained with a 2.2 per cent higher Cd value because it was accompanied by an 1.9 per cent decrease in front surface area, resulting in a nearly identical total resistance value from the combined front surface area and Cd value.

Model series	Cd	A (m^2)	Cd x A
W 108/109	0.420	2.108	0.8854

The 116 S-Class, achieved nearly the same values as the W 111 model series due to its high rear end although it scored a somewhat better in total resistance owing to its reduced front surface area.

Model	Cd	A (m^2)	Cd x A
280 SE (W 116)	0.412	2.14	0.8817

Aerodynamics Testing of the 126

Even with the data accrued from previous models, when it came to planning the 126 S-Class, Werner Breitschwerdt,

The Pininfarina wind-tunnel in Turin.

The 126 clay model being tested in secret.

the then chief developer in Sindelfingen and later chief engineer, only focused his attention on the consumption-influencing factors of weight/power ratio. According to Bruno Sacco, initially at least, it was difficult to encourage Breitschwerdt that aerodynamic drag could play an important enough role in reducing fuel consumption to encourage him to allow extensive testing in the newly updated wind-tunnel.

We had to resort to a bit of underhand experimentation of our own using one of the 1:1 scale clay models created by the styling department. We secretly shipped the clay model to Pininfarina in Turin. At the time it was the only apparatus that would allow us to measure and analyse aerodynamic flows of a full scale vehicle in real-time and in every situation; it would even simulate the turbulence originating as ground effect under the front end of the car, which on the 126 proved incredibly important as we managed to correct a front end lift issue.

On its return to Stuttgart, Breitschwerdt had no choice but to agree with Sacco's course of action and further testing was done at the Untertürkheim wind tunnel.

As with the transition from the 'Ponton' W 180 to the 'Fintail' W 111 model series, the changeover from the 116 to the 126 model series marked not only a leap within the

The interior of the Pininfarina wind-tunnel.

Mercedes-Benz model series, but this S-Class also far out-ranked the international competition in its segment. The major optimizing factors for a favourable drag coefficient were the sharper falling slope of the roofline, the high rear end with its rearward structure slightly tucked in at the sides, the steeper inclination of the windscreen (54 degrees), the recessed windscreen wipers, drip moulding integrated into the body, a step-less transition of the front wall pillars and a seamless transition from the bumpers to the body.

The success of all these measures was impressive: the Cd value improved exponentially over that of the 116 model series by 12.9 per cent, the front surface area decreased by roughly 1 per cent and the total resistance by 13.3 per cent; greater than any other comparable vehicle of the time.

Model	Cd	A (m^2)	Cd x A
280 SE (W 126)	0.359	2.1283	0.7641

When designing the W 140 model series, which was finished in 1991, engineers likewise devoted their attention to the aerodynamics. Compared with the W 126 model series, they directed much effort towards once again significantly reducing the drag coefficient. The measures included, for instance, a rearward sloping front section, a larger radius in the transition from the radiator grille to the engine bonnet surface, a somewhat flatter slope to the windscreen, flush-fitted side windows, exterior mirrors with an integrated catch groove for dirty water, generously sized wheel trims and light-alloy wheels, less front-axle lift to minimize crosswind sensitivity and smooth-surfaced design of the under-body.

Even though it was often criticized due to its size, by introducing these measures, the engineers were able to decrease the drag coefficient by a further 16.4 per cent, thereby achieving a new record in this vehicle class. Although the frontal area increased by 12.2 per cent compared with the

Smoke trail testing for visual effects.

Combination of smoke flow profile with more detail spot tagging for close body effects.

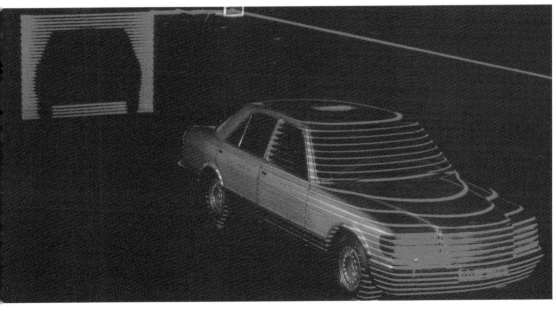

Laser profiling facility assists model makers.

Even scale models can be tested.

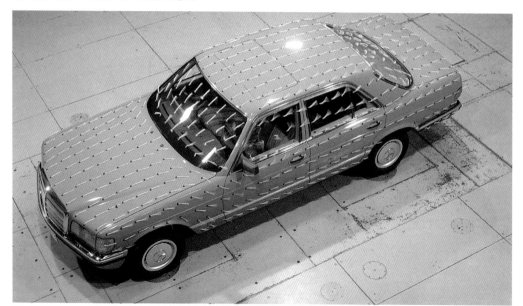

Body skin testing for fine adjustments.

predecessor (thus also earning it a new record in the comparison segment), this S-Class also had the most favourable total resistance value of all S-Class cars since the 'Pontoon' W 180 model series. This was made possible thanks to its drastically lower Cd value. The W 140 beats the W 180 in this regard by 26.8 per cent and outperforms the legendary predecessor W 126 model series by 16.4 per cent. This fact is particularly astonishing given the car's imposing overall appearance.

Model	Cd	A (m²)	Cd x A
300 SE 2.8 (W 140)	0.30	2.39	0.717

Good aerodynamics is never an end in itself, but rather has lasting effects in many directions. Still today, aerodynamics plays a major development in fuel efficiency and it all began with the 126 S-Class and a crafty journey to Turin.

WEIGHT REDUCTION

Along with aerodynamics as a path to a more efficient car, goes the reduction of weight, but along with weight reduction goes the integrity of the ride comfort and safety; the only way forward was weight reduction through innovation. Targets were set: everything that could be reduced was reduced.

An IBM computer mapping design system had already been successfully used on the 116 and this was updated to a more detailed CAD system for the 126. Using this, the technicians were able to grid map areas of the body frame that could receive a slimming treatment.

The body shell alone went through a complete revision. New thinner, high-quality, high-strength steels were used in production for the first time, enabling a reduction of around 50kg (110lb) in total.

The use of these new high-tensile steels in areas such as sill and box section, roof and door frames and sub-frame

The IBM computer aided design system used to plots body shape and styling on the 116 was used also on the 126.

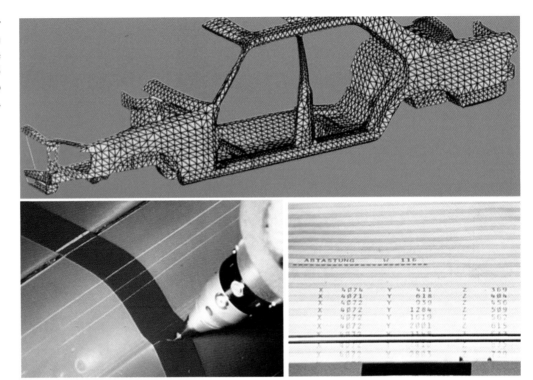

sections, enabled the reduction of weight by 7kg (15lb) alone, but without a reduction in strength.

The extended use of light alloys, such as aluminium, managed to decrease weight by 15kg (33lb), almost halving that of the 116 components. The use of post-formed plastics brought a further reduction of 5kg (11lb).

For the interior items, such as seating frames, there was a reduction of 10 per cent, saving around 4kg (9lb) in total. Even the weight of the heating system was reduced by another 5kg (11lb).

Gunter Huber, the head of body development, remarked that, 'We even removed pieces of metal, no larger than a finger nail to reduce weight'.

Much of the reduction of weight came from the engine. The V8 engines especially were now all-alloy as opposed to the 116 versions of heavy cast-iron blocks. The finished weight of the alloy block was 25kg (55lb) less than that of the cast iron.

For the first time in the Daimler-Benz history, they moved from metal bumpers to plastic composite. Apart from fulfilling advancements made in impact/crumple zone and drag resistance technologies, of which the 126 was a pioneer vehicle, they went a long way to aid the weight-loss programme.

CRASH TESTING THE 126

The many years of accident research at Mercedes-Benz have played a major role in preserving the brand's technological edge over rival automakers. That's because engineers in Stuttgart and Sindelfingen are quick to apply this knowledge in a practical manner. Over the years, the findings of such research have repeatedly provided the basis for the development of new and pioneering safety systems.

Interior Design

At the end of the 1960s, when Mercedes-Benz first began systematic accident analysis, experts initially focused on improving protection inside the passenger compartment. Although Mercedes' models were already then fitted with seat belts, very few people actually bothered to use them. For many front-seat passengers, this carefree attitude led to serious head injuries, resulting from an impact with the steering wheel, instrument panel or windshield. Accident researchers, therefore, set about identifying dangerous impact points inside the vehicle and suggested improvements to the design of various switches and handles responsible for severe injuries. Likewise, the instrument panel and interior trim materials were also reconsidered with safety in mind. Since then, design engineers have favoured energy-absorbing materials.

Test Procedures and Body Structure

Once the interior had been made safe, the attention of accident researchers and engineers turned toward improving the body structure. Once again, this followed on from initial accident analyses. Although 51 per cent of all serious passenger car accidents involve a head-on collision, experts have known, since the beginning of the 1970s, that the reality behind this term is often much more complex than it seems.

When reconstructing typical collisions with oncoming traffic, accident researchers quickly realized that vehicles usually hit one another asymmetrically, with the result that the front part of the body is more heavily impacted on one side. Experts describe this type of crash as an offset collision. In around half of all so-called head-on collisions on German roads, the impact actually affects only 30–50 per cent of the left-hand side of the vehicle front. In a further 25 per cent of such collisions, the impact occurs on the passenger side of the vehicle front.

This discovery had major consequences for automotive design. Given that a full front-end collision against a flat wall – legally required as a safety test for passenger cars – only represented a fraction of real-life accidents, Mercedes-Benz decided to go it alone. On the basis of results from the company's own accident research, engineers introduced the first offset crash tests as early as 1974 and went on to develop a design principle that provides high occupant safety, even when the vehicle front is subject to extreme partial loads. The solution came in the form of forked members – rigid longitudinal sections on both sides of the front part of the body structure, each of which forks in front of the front wall and toward the side skirts and the drive shaft hump. These cause the force of impact from a collision to spread equally between the hump, floor and side panel, with the result that the passenger compartment remains largely undamaged.

The 126 was the first of the Mercedes' models to feature forked members designed specifically to protect against off-

RIGHT: **Roll testing.**

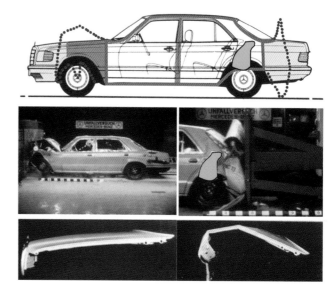

Crash testing the SEL.

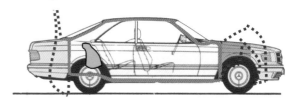

Crash testing the SEC.

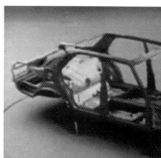

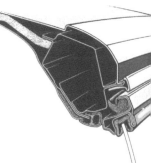

set front-end collisions. Today, a new design principle provides even more effective protection for vehicle occupants – and not only in the event of an offset crash.

Oscar: The First Crash Test Dummy at Mercedes-Benz

From the start of crash testing at the company, not only vehicles were used to assess the effects of crashes. This is because Oscar was acquired as the first crash-test dummy at the same time.

Sandbags and mannequins initially took the place of the front passenger. Nevertheless, dummies were soon also collecting crash-test data from the front passenger seat and rear bench. Individual dummy designs were used to measure specific injuries and to represent persons of different builds and ages. Increasing computer capabilities then allowed dummies to be replaced by mathematical multi-body systems. The first digital crash computations with overall vehicle models were performed for the E-Class of the 124 series.

AIRBAG AND BELT TENSIONERS

In 1981, the W 126 series Mercedes-Benz S-Class attracted a great deal of attention at the Geneva Motor Show with a new item of optional equipment: the airbag and belt ten-

sioners – two passive safety innovations – were celebrating their world premiere in the flagship Mercedes' model. The combination of a driver airbag and front passenger belt tensioners was initially only available for the 126 series from July 1981, as an optional extra costing 1,525.50 DM (equivalent of around 780 Euros) for the saloon and coupé.

During the first year, no fewer than 2,636 S-Class buyers opted for this new safety feature, ushering in the triumph of the airbag. More than 12 million Mercedes-Benz cars were equipped with airbags in the first twenty-five years of this new technology, with other brands following suit. An optional extra for the driver of 1981 has developed into a restraint system that now protects vehicle occupants with a system of airbags, belt tensioners and belt-force limiters during an accident.

A Protective Air Cushion for Car Drivers

The first ideas for an air cushion that would protect drivers from impacting on the steering wheel during a collision were already aired in the 1950s. At the time it was not possible to translate this idea into reality with the mechanical sensors and control systems available. The idea of the airbag was given a new impetus when the United States announced plans to prescribe automatic occupant protection systems for passenger cars in 1969, and in 1973 the driver airbag was even to become compulsory for new vehicles. The solutions

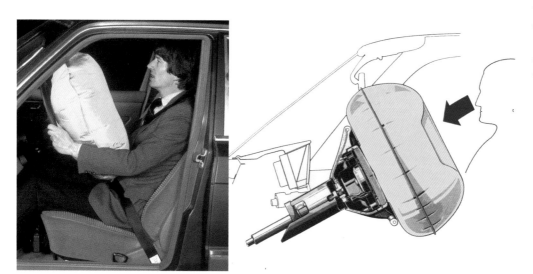

The airbag was first fitted in the 126 in 1981 as an extra cost option after ten years of testing.

presented came in for a great deal of criticism, however, and the introduction date was repeatedly postponed. Most of these projects eventually ended with no concrete result.

These developments were paralleled by continuous efforts on the part of Mercedes-Benz researchers. Work on a practical airbag had already commenced in Stuttgart in 1967. The researchers and developers had numerous hurdles to overcome in the first few years. The sensor system had to be newly developed, as did the gas generation technology and the woven material for the airbag itself. The first tests relied on compressed air and Freon to inflate the airbag. But the best technical solution proved to be a fabric bag that could be inflated within milliseconds by a pyrotechnical charge during an accident, gently cushioning the driver. The developers adopted the 'sodium azide'. This ignites a propellant charge (at the time consisting of sodium azide, potassium nitrate and sand), an explosive charge from rocket technology that deflagrates instantaneously to form mainly gaseous nitrogen and even a little water and oxygen.

In 1971, Mercedes-Benz was granted patent number DE 2152902 C2 for the airbag. Many details of this new restraint system needed to be improved and tested before it was ready for series' production. The airbag proved its reliability during more than 250 impact tests using complete vehicles, more than 2,500 sledge impact tests and thousands of tests on individual components. At the same time, 600 vehicles entered long-term trials in on-road and off-road operations, to ensure that the airbag would not be activated during normal driving.

The Evolution of the Air Cushion in the Dashpot

The airbag presented for the S-Class in Geneva in 1981 was still rather voluminous; therefore, the dashpot of the S-Class equipped with an airbag was larger than the standard steering wheel boss and, when the first front passenger

The passenger airbag was available from 1987.

airbag was presented at the International Motor Show (IAA) in Frankfurt in 1987, it was necessary to use what would normally have been the entire glove compartment space.

The Supplementary Restraint System (SRS®)

The use of belt tensioners presented in conjunction with the airbag also became a permanent passive safety feature, having been introduced in Geneva in 1981. In an accident this support system uses a pyrotechnical charge to tension the inertia-reel seat-belt worn by the front passenger within a few milliseconds. In this way, the safety technology in the W 126-series S-Class reliably fixed the front passenger in place, even if the seat belt had initially been fastened too loosely.

Airbag and Seat Belt as an Entity

The airbag is intended as a complement to the seat belt, by no means as a replacement. This was already clear to the developers at Mercedes-Benz when they began their research for the airbag in 1967. It is only the joint effect of the belt and airbag that provides the best possible protection against serious injury in an accident. Since the 1981 debut of this safety technology in the S-Class, airbags com-

From 1984, all Mercedes' vehicles were equipped with front seat-belt tensioners as standard equipment.

Even after twelve years of service, the airbag deployed as it should.

bined with seat belts have literally saved thousands of lives.

In 1992, in order to demonstrate the operational reliability of the restraint system even years after first delivery, Mercedes-Benz used the occasion of the 1-millionth airbag to be installed in one of its vehicles to conduct a crash test with a Mercedes-Benz 500 SEL produced in 1981 at the crash-testing centre in Sindelfingen. The airbag deployed exactly as it was designed to do. The service intervals recommended to ensure perfect operation are normally shorter, however.

INCIDENTAL SAFETY

Not all safety advancements make 'ground-breaking news' and the 126 S-Classes were riddled with innovations.

Steering wheels were not only padded for cushioning bodily impacts but, in conjunction with collapsible steering

columns, they would tuck themselves vertically away from chest cavities.

Windscreen wipers were tucked under the back lip of the bonnet, not just for its aerodynamic abilities but also to allow the rain to flow a safe path up the screen and away from main vision. In the 126, the all-round vision was vastly improved over the 116. Additionally, the wipers swept just over 77 per cent of the screen

Originally patented on 2 July 1958 by Daimler AG, the 'conical lock pin latch' enabled the doors to remain shut in most accidents.

The 126 latch followed very closely the design of the original.

Continuing the theme of the 116 tail-light cluster, the ribs featured in the same way – not just as a recognizable form for Mercedes, but also as a means to keep them clean and clear when soiled.

Collapsible steering column.

Screen water flow and ability to clear the screen.

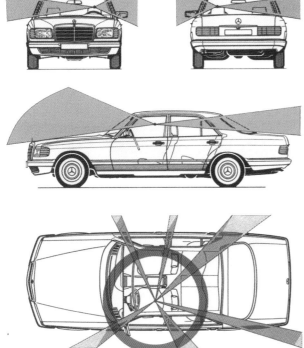

All-round vision improved.

Original conical lock-pin patent.

The ribbed tail-lights followed that of the 116.

Even on the 126 the conical safety lock pin had barely changed from its original patent design.

OPTIMIZING FUEL CONSUMPTION

Daimler-Benz always tried to reconcile the often conflicting and contradictory demands made of the car through well-balanced, forward-thinking, overall design. However, in the years following the fuel crisis, none were so important as that of fuel economy.

One such avenue was optimizing the fuel consumption of the larger V8 engines by means of a 'cylinder cut-off system', which would enable the advantages of a V8 to be maintained at optimum power requirement situations, while reducing fuel consumption by 'switching off' two or four cylinders when driving a partial load.

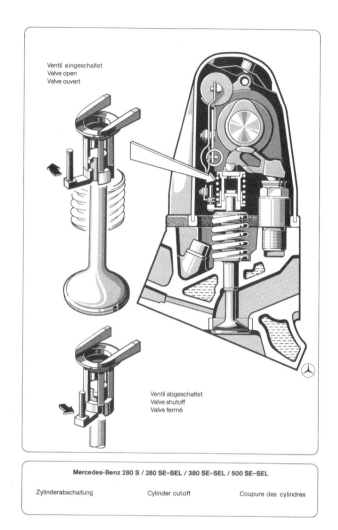

| Ventil eingeschaltet |
| Valve open |
| Valve ouvert |

| Ventil abgeschaltet |
| Valve shutoff |
| Valve fermé |

Mercedes-Benz 280 S / 280 SE–SEL / 380 SE–SEL / 500 SE–SEL

| Zylinderabschaltung | Cylinder cutoff | Coupure des cylindres |

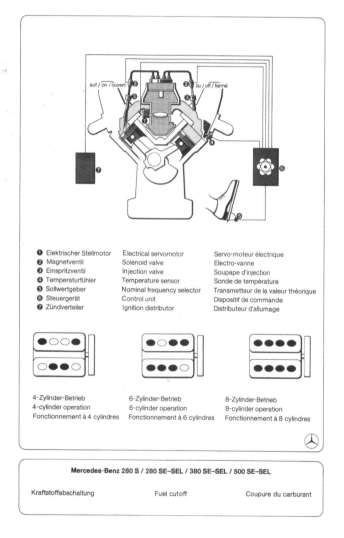

❶ Elektrischer Stellmotor	Electrical servomotor	Servo-moteur électrique
❷ Magnetventil	Solenoid valve	Electro-vanne
❸ Einspritzventil	Injection valve	Soupape d'injection
❹ Temperaturfühler	Temperature sensor	Sonde de température
❺ Sollwertgeber	Nominal frequency selector	Transmetteur de la valeur théorique
❻ Steuergerät	Control unit	Dispositif de commande
❼ Zündverteiler	Ignition distributor	Distributeur d'allumage

4-Zylinder-Betrieb	6-Zylinder-Betrieb	8-Zylinder-Betrieb
4-cylinder operation	6-cylinder operation	8-cylinder operation
Fonctionnement à 4 cylindres	Fonctionnement à 6 cylindres	Fonctionnement à 8 cylindres

Mercedes-Benz 280 S / 280 SE–SEL / 380 SE–SEL / 500 SE–SEL

| Kraftstoffabschaltung | Fuel cutoff | Coupure du carburant |

The fuel cut-off system.

A valve cut-off system.

Engineers at Untertürkheim had been working on two such methods since 1974 with the aim to use the most successful method in the 126 S-Class, as well as the SL and SLC models.

This system would render perhaps two or four cylinders inoperable solely by cutting off the fuel supply; the different operation elements would be determined by the load determined by accelerator position. This method was successfully tested and enabled a reduction of fuel consumption by about 20 per cent, especially in the lower load range of inner city driving

A particularly beneficial addition to the fuel cut-off system was the ability to cut off the valves using an electromagnetic solenoid system, which would interrupt the power flow between the camshaft and the valves, so they remained closed,

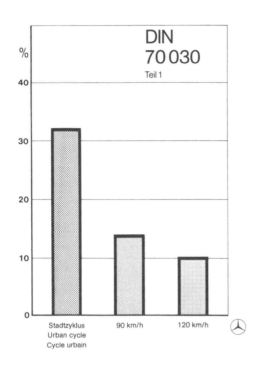

Mercedes-Benz 280 S / 280 SE–SEL / 380 SE–SEL / 500 SE–SEL

| Verbrauchsersparnis Zylinderabschaltung | Fuel saving Cylinder cutoff | Economie de consommation Coupure des cylindres |

Fuel valve cut-off benefits.

as well as simultaneously cutting fuel to those cylinders.

Despite being a more complex system, this system offered the advantage of no discernible load changes in the switched-off cylinders and would be the only way to ensure no loss of engine balance and ignition timing. This method reduced fuel consumption by over 30 per cent compared with the previous 20 per cent.

It was eventually decided that, even though the 'fuel shut-off' system was ready to go into production, it would only offer a limited short-term solution and that further develop-

RIGHT: **Adaptation of existing model; in this case using the 116 as a base can also give 1:1 definition.**

ment of the valve shut-off system would reap more beneficial results in the long term. It was not seen again until 1999 in the W 220 S-Class.

THE PROTOTYPES

Like all new vehicles, the design process took the 126 through various stages. The fluid transition between the preceding 116 model and the 126 was imperative. Even with-

Hints of Peugeot, Jaguar and even Roll Royce/Bentley can be seen in the drawings above the designer.

out following faddy styles, as can be seen from some of the images, styling cues from 'other manufacturers' was always a consideration.

Once a new vehicle has a formulated design, much more

testing takes place. However, sometimes just track testing is not good enough and it becomes necessary to take it 'on the road'.

Clay model work can give a true size definition of potential design; however, it can also facilitate aerodynamic tunnel work, even on a smaller scale than 1:1.

There are always eagle-eyed enthusiasts ready to take a snap of a partially masked vehicle, as shown in this 1977 picture snapped of the 126 with only just enough generic parts to disguise it.

Autocar **attempted to 'predict' the potential shape of the forthcoming replacement to the 116. Remarkably, it had design cues later introduced in the 140 range.**

THE FINAL RESULT

At first glance at the exterior, what was immediately apparent was how every line in the bodywork had a clearly defined function, every shape had a purpose. Classic elegance matched perfectly the logic of the new engineering style. Understated styling with simplification but not enlargement. Every panel, every curve, every shape had a job to do; everything in the bodywork had a clearly defined function that was immediately apparent.

To justify Bruno Sacco's words 'form follows function', its styling highlighted its long-term objectives not its short-lived fashionable 'bells and whistles'. He proudly announced that 'A good idea is far better than wasting money on needless metal'.

This was very true of the new S-Class 126: every contour was shaped to meet its pre-determined requirements. The flow of lines was uninterrupted, from the slightly raised boot, along its entire length and seamless downward-sloping bonnet; not just aerodynamically sound, but enabling the driver to be able to clearly see all four corners of the car with ease, making for a safer, less stressed environment.

The bumpers were large but flowed seamlessly with the shape of the car, giving the impression of continuing along its sides with the attached styled cladding. Again serving to improve aerodynamics but also being made from ABS plastic, they protect the metal bodywork from minor damage and are easily replaceable in the event of damage. The skirted bumpers at the front also minimize the tendency for the front axle to lift at speed.

Even the choice of colours available and the contrast between side cladding and body for the 126 serve a dual purpose – yes, they enhance the beauty of the styling, but enable the car to be seen clearly in many environments and weathers while on the road.

The 126 was designed and built for people who use their cars more than the average driver does; people who need to travel long distances and rarely on their own; for people who need to reserve their energy for their jobs, rather than to waste it getting to work.

It was designed with safety in mind but also with minimizing stress by giving ample space to move. Although the external dimensions of the 126 were slightly reduced over that of the 116, the space inside was actually larger. The 126 was marginally narrower; however, the front track was slightly wider with a slightly larger wheelbase measurement.

The result was better space comfort, as well as road holding. Much work had also been done on levels of noise.

Safety, power, handling, ride and operation of controls were fully integrated in the 126, coupled with additional work to refine the suspension system with focus on passive and active safety; they further simplified driver effort and kept the driver relaxed yet alert.

A big car with space for five people must have, by necessity, a relatively large 'footprint'. However, the time spent to optimize its aerodynamic qualities was well spent. Its co-efficient of drag (Cd) was around a 14 per cent improvement on that of the 116.

THE TEST TRACK

In 1967, the roads of the world converged at Mercedes-Benz in Stuttgart: following extensive expansion work, the company presented the otherwise top-secret track to the media, on 9 May 1967.

The work to extend the test track made it ideal for high-speed, endurance and rough-road testing. The possibilities for testing are as varied as the Mercedes-Benz product range – and, to this day, they continue to provide important input into vehicle development. The scenarios that can be replicated on the company's test track in Untertürkheim range from storm-swept motorways and slippery wet tracks to bumpy country roads.

Saloon and truck, Unimog or sports car, bus and racing car: by the 1950s, Mercedes-Benz had the perfect product in its portfolio to suit virtually any automotive purpose and the model range was steadily being extended, refined and further developed as demand in those early days of the 'economic miracle' continued to grow. All of which presented the development department with some major challenges. What was missing, in order for the engineers to meet these challenges as efficiently as possible, was a versatile test-track located at one of the major plants. It was an issue whose importance was stressed by Dr Fritz Nallinger, head of development of the then Daimler-Benz AG, to his colleagues on the board of management as early as November 1953.

Nallinger's suggestion: a long stretch of company-owned land directly adjacent to the Untertürkheim plant, known as the 'bottleneck', should be given over to building a test track.

The original waste-ground track at Untertürkheim, c.1908.

A planning application was submitted to the city of Stuttgart in January 1955 and, in July 1956, the board of management of Daimler-Benz AG gave a green light to the proposed investment. As 1957 dawned, the first phase of the test track was taken into operation. The layout at that time already included a skid pad featuring concentrically arranged circular tracks with different surfaces: vehicles could be tested here on blue basalt, concrete, slippery asphalt and large cobblestones. The integrated sprinkler system allowed wet-surface testing.

It soon became evident that the test track was still inadequate for the many and varied demands of the passenger car and commercial vehicle testing departments: the engineers were keen for better facilities that would allow high-speed, endurance and rough-road testing. They also wanted to be able to test commercial vehicles on steep inclines. The site was, therefore, gradually extended to accommodate all these ideas.

Major Stage for Future Potential

Activities on the test track are normally conducted in secret since, after all, this is where Mercedes-Benz also tests the prototypes for forthcoming series' models. However, once the extended and improved facilities had been completed, Mercedes-Benz seized the opportunity to present the full details of this new, major platform for vehicle development to the media, on 9 May 1967.

The two parallel tracks are connected by steep-bank curves with a diameter of 100m.

A part of the section of Incline tests.

The cumulative length of all test sections is 15,460m (50,709ft), including 3,018m (990ft) of high-speed test track.

A source of wonder back then was the seven different incline sections with gradients of between 5 and 70 per cent, along with the steep-bank curve with a transverse inclination of as much as 90 degrees. A maximum speed of 200km/h (124mph) is theoretically possible on this steep banking, but this would physically be almost unendurable for a human being.

For long-term testing purposes it is particularly important instead to be able to drive through the steep-bank curve at 150km/h (93mph) with no hands on the wheel. At this point, there are no longer any lateral forces impacting on the tyres and the vehicle remains on track through the bend without any steering input. The driver's weight nevertheless rises by a factor of 3.1, pressing him or her into the seat.

Another indispensable part of endurance testing is the 'Heide', or heathland, test section. This rough-road track in Untertürkheim was built to scale to replicate a particularly poor stretch of road in the Lüneburg Heath in the north of Germany, as it was in the early 1950s, hence its name. Here, as on other so-called washboard, boneshaker and potholed sections, is where Mercedes-Benz submits its newly developed products to lengthy endurance testing. Tests like these are so stressful that drivers have to change over every two hours. Further features of the circuit include extreme distortion tracks for commercial vehicles and off-roaders, along with ramps used to force extreme spring compression and rebound.

Handling safety in adverse weather conditions is tested with the help of a 34m-long (112ft) crosswind section. This features sixteen blowers, designed to produce gusting side winds of speeds up to 100km/h (62mph). A world first was the slalom section introduced by the head of vehicle testing at the time, Rudolf Uhlenhaut. This was a stretch of track designed to test the driving stability of suspensions at high speed and during abrupt changes of lane, using measurement loops embedded in the road surface to deliver electronic data. Such data are used in conjunction with the test driver's personal assessment to evaluate the suspension tuning. For the purposes of precise analysis, the tests have also always been recorded using radar, other measuring equipment and on film.

Since the expansion work was completed fifty years ago, the 8.4-hectare (21-acre) site, with its cumulative 15.5km (10 miles) of different test tracks, has continued to be adapted

Rumble strips and potholes to test chassis and suspension integrity.

Floodable areas to test braking under wet and deep-water conditions, as well as drivability.

91

constantly to new conditions. A section of road with a low-noise 'whisper asphalt' surface, for example, was created for the measurement of noise. This continual updating of the test track in Untertürkheim means that it remains, to this day, an important development tool for new technologies and vehicles.

Cross-wind section for testing water, fog and wind integrity.

A full view of the Untertürkheim complex, including a Google Maps overhead shot.

THE 126 UNDER TEST

The 126 Mercedes was submitted to more tests than any other Mercedes vehicle thus far to ensure longevity, as well as safety integrity.

Testing wasn't just limited to the track, real-time mechanical testing was just as important. It was not possible to run engines at full revs and full speed on a track, so much work was also done in-house.

As previously shown, track suspension testing was important but also very testing on the test-pilot, so since Daimler had invested in upgrading their IBM computer systems, much work could be done in-house.

Testing the 126 suspension.

Dry speed and turn testing.

Track turns' testing using a 280 SE and a 560 SEL.

93

Swerve and brake testing.

Much work had been completed on the IBM computer system.

Full engine and Drivetrain run-up unit made it possible to test the complete Drivetrain at full speed for long periods of time.

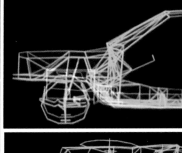

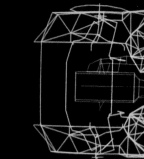

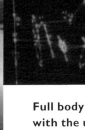

Full body stress and flex testing was now also capable with the up-graded **IBM** systems.

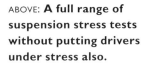

ABOVE: **A full range of suspension stress tests without putting drivers under stress also.**

RIGHT: **For the first time it was possible to use an S-Class simulator.**

CHAPTER FOUR

PRODUCTION

FACTORY REDESIGN

An important part of having a 'socially acceptable' vehicle is a socially acceptable work ethic and factory, and this meant a complete redesign of Sindelfingen.

The new S-Class would not only set new standards in engineering and design, but it would prove a market leader in production also. Even though Daimler were never really classed as a 'volume manufacturer', at least until the W 108/9 and much of the work was done to each individual vehicle by hand with individual work sheets, they were backed by the long experience gained with previous model lines.

Nothing really changed in this method for many years, much of the build route a 'vehicle in construction' took was along a standard track way: the body would arrive overhead, eventually in a position to be lowered and attached to an arriving dolly containing running gear; engines also followed a predetermined track system, although the track system became motorized to give consistency to the production time.

The human element was taken very seriously at Daimler and they continually sought to improve the build process, even offering line workers bonuses for coming up with ways to improve a particular job. It was always of the utmost importance to Daimler that their workers felt that they were a personal part of every vehicle produced and not just another machine.

Bodies arrived overhead as parts were organized on the workshop floor. Workers guided the body into place from floor level, as well as from work pits.

Although the process was refined and organized, nothing really changed for many years.

96

The 126 was the first vehicle to benefit from the revised factory and work ethic: 'Team Work'.

'Hängedrehförderer' German for hanging cradle, vastly improved the working position.

Some of the heavy, repetitive, awkward work was completed by automaton machines.

The manual part of lifting windscreens into place was now aided by machine; however, the final positioning remained a human task.

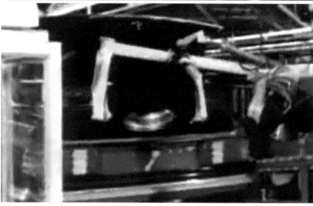

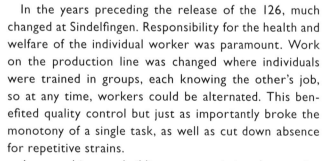

What seems like a simple job of placing a spare wheel into the wheel well can turn into a back-breaking job when done repeatedly.

Wheel fitment involved carriages that held the wheel in place before a machine automatically inserted the five wheel bolts to the correct torque.

In the years preceding the release of the 126, much changed at Sindelfingen. Responsibility for the health and welfare of the individual worker was paramount. Work on the production line was changed where individuals were trained in groups, each knowing the other's job, so at any time, workers could be alternated. This benefited quality control but just as importantly broke the monotony of a single task, as well as cut down absence for repetitive strains.

A new multi-storey building was commissioned, occupying an area totalling 65,000m² (699,400ft²), initially for the 126 but also for all future development: 19,000m² (204,440ft²) were devoted to the body shell department, 16,000m² (172,160ft²) for the paint shop revision and 30,000m² (322,800ft²) devoted to final assembly, which included the

newly created Rotisserie-style hanging cradles called 'Häungedrehförderer' to enable the technicians to carry out their work in a more comfortable position than overhead, as previously necessary.

Small, 'simple' robots were used to do what seemed to be menial jobs, such as fitting the spare tyre in the boot or fitting the battery in place, and more complicated machines were built to carry out assembly, such as fitting the fuel tank and front suspension units.

What these all had in common was not just to do with efficiency or productivity; these assembly line jobs were previously backbreaking work in awkward positions and necessitated a constant turnover of workforce; as a result, it proved productive on all sides. The machines were not only quicker and more accurate, lessening the chance of damage,

Even the vehicle battery was placed into position by a new machine.

Many women were employed by Daimler throughout the entire process from design to the production line.

but also improved the moral of the workers and improved down-time from absence and injury.

Everything that could be done to make life more comfortable for the worker on the assembly was done.

Many women were employed by Daimler throughout the entire process from design to the production line.

At Daimler-Benz, the priority was always to safeguard their reputation for exemplary standards, coupled with a continued search for higher standards. This entailed progressive perfecting of all segments of the production process.

'Automation to ensure quality' started in the new body-shell building, where computer controlled industrial robots were installed. This immediately increased mechanized welding by 50 per cent but, more importantly, it vastly improved consistent accuracy and product reliability.

For the first time, computer assistance played a large part in the complete build of a Mercedes' car, starting with the 126. Everything from computer aided design (CAD) to final testing. Banks of computers enabled the correct parts to arrive at the correct place at the correct time for each and every vehicle and then to facilitate final testing of compli-

cated parts, such as ABS and the heater-control system, to ensure perfect function right from installation.

THE PRODUCTION LINE

All 126 production was completed at Daimler AGs largest factory, Sindelfingen in the Stuttgart region of Germany. All 126s, as well as other models, were always built to order and every detail of that order was recorded in the computerized build station. Once entered, all parts, special or generic,

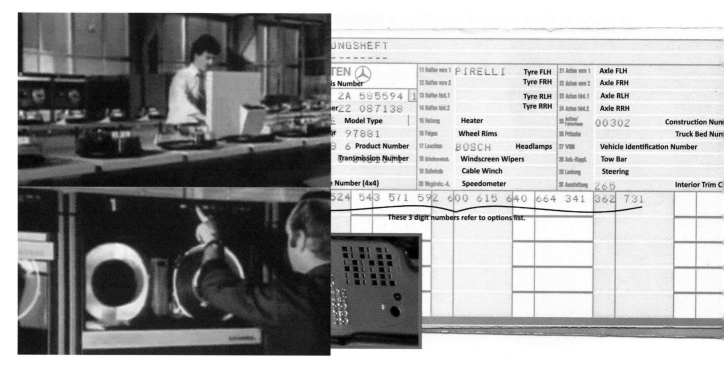

IBM played a large part in the production process, cataloguing every vehicle versus every option.

The **DATA** plate attached to the closing panel was a throwback to past times as it provided information of client options.

would be picked or manufactured at the various supply or build factories.

Every detail of the vehicle's build requirements were still contained on the data print sheet fitted in the back of every user manual and duplicated on the pressed steel data tag fitted on the bonnet shut panel, to provide concise detail in each stage of production.

A great deal of work had been completed to bring the factory up to standard and the 126 was the first vehicle to be built using their new, much of it automated, facilities, including a completely rebuilt steel press manufacturing area, built 30m (98ft) underground for stability.

Production of the 126 really started with the specially manufactured rolls of steel, lighter in weight and more refined for the special tensile strength needed for the body of the 126.

These were then transferred to the press hall containing the building-size steel presses, which would rise and fall continually as they pressed out panels and components, before being transferred to the next machine with pin-point accuracy.

As previously mentioned, Daimler increased the use of specially built banks of robotic arms to weld body sections.

Massive rolls of steel were stored on-site for easy and efficient access.

Rows of panel Weingarten and Scholer press machines, stand like waiting soldiers.

The manual construction of the 116 is evident. Workers lifted even large panels into place by hand.

The 126 was much more automated, as the body would roll around in robotic cradles as panels were fitted and welded into place.

For the 116, pressed panels arrived by belt but needed pulling and spot welding into place before moving off to a spot-welding carriage.

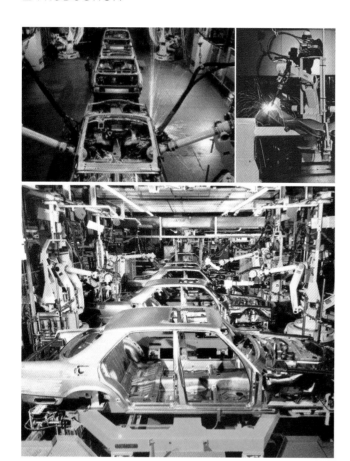

Final seam and weld finishing was always done by hand and remained so for the 126.

For the 126, rolling cradles would place the vehicle into position for completely automated seam welding.

They took over to weld the various body parts with precise movements and extreme accuracy; this improved the speed at which the bodies would traverse the build stage, but also improved weld consistency and efficacy.

It remained, however, to the human eye to ensure that every weld was clean and tidy, and lines of workers would concentrate on every join, crease and body profile.

Every panel would go through rigorous electronic and human inspection to ensure that, as each component came together to form the vehicle, it was accurate to fractions of millimetres.

Unlike many manufacturers of the time, Daimler kept a very high percentage of manufacture and production in-house. This system always ensured a high-quality end product.

Although much of the steel was pre-coated during manufacture, once the bodies were completed, they were then

Once complete, the body would move on to receive other exterior components, such as doors and bonnets.

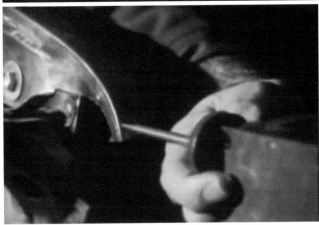

Many processes were completed in-house; here you can see the chrome plating process of the chrome grill and the veneering section.

Randomly, whole body shells would be removed for accuracy testing in the specially built measuring department. Every surface, angle and profile was thoroughly scrutinized to ensure quality and accuracy remained throughout the entire process.

subjected to an uncompromising immersion protection and priming treatment called cataphoresis or electrophoretic coating. It reached every nook, corner, boxing and panel, and substantially increased the anti-corrosion of all body parts, as well as improving subsequent paint adhesion.

The paint shop revision marked a huge step forward in quality of finish and, more notably, allowed for vast improvements in anti-corrosion protection. For the first time, a stop chip coating was applied from the waistline down before going through a primer stage.

This was then followed by a new type of PVC under-body protection. It was also applied by robot for maximum efficiency and coverage.

Once having entered the new paint unit, the body shells went through a thorough cleaning process that involved

The cataphoresis dipping process substantially increased the 126 anti-corrosion capabilities.

The new plasticized waistline stone chip coating being applied to the 126.

The 'body in white' as it's referred to, went on to be chemically washed and dried to cure the finish. It would also result in an immaculate, contaminate-free finish for the subsequent six coats of paint.

ABOVE: **Originally, the under-body corrosion and chip protector was applied by humans on the 116 – a messy and hazardous process.**

LEFT: **Six coats for flat colour and seven coats for metallic were applied throughout the process.**

The 126 system had been completely automated.

The 116 cavity wax was inserted by worker.

126 cavity wax system is measured and applied by an elaborate system of robotic probes.

In-line with continued production perfection, random vehicles were removed from the assembly line periodically to test the colour definition, depth and adhesion integrity.

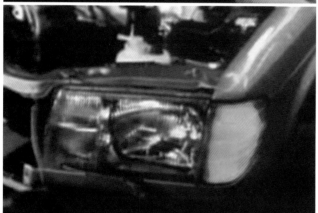

CLOCKWISE FROM TOP LEFT:

The simple installation of an indicator included connection and testing.

IBM computers kept an eye on every production process as each vehicle was signed off from its sector.

Pre-testing a complete air-conditioning unit before installation.

Pre-testing a dash cluster before installation.

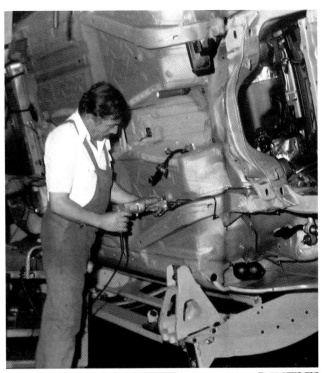

phosphatizing and dry-cleaning. The newly installed automated colour booths provided a 50 per cent more accurate and efficient finish, than was possible manually. The vehicle was then subjected to an infra-red drying process in a large tunnel to harden the coating.

The final assembly was an incredibly complicated system and relied on a central computer system to guide each and every vehicle through a parallel and intersecting production line, to ensure that each and every vehicle arrived at the correct spot at the correct time; there were thousands of permutations for a range of up to thirty differing models.

Every sector dealt with each individual component from installation and the vehicle would not move onward until the installation was tested to the correct order.

As previously mentioned, Daimler led the way with automated robotics purely to defuse many menial tasks that could ultimately lead to repetitive strain injuries to its line workers. However, for the first time, in any vehicle manufacturing process, they took it one step further by introducing 'Häungedrehförderer' – a hanging rotisserie cradle. The rotary cradle, designed by Daimler themselves and constructed by Eisenmann, enabled the line worker to easily roll the cradled vehicle into a suitable position to complete their individual tasks from a comfortable standing position, but also kept the body safe from accidental damage. Previously, workers were employed to cover finished bodywork with covers and protective paper to limit the potential for damage caused by slipping or dropping a tool or part.

Previously, much work was done bending over a vehicle on the production line or from underneath in pits and channels, where workers had to reach and look up continually.

The cradle protected the finished bodywork from accidental damage.

Eisenmann also provided completely autonomous mobile platforms to transfer vehicles in safety from one work area to another.

The 126 along the interior trim production line.

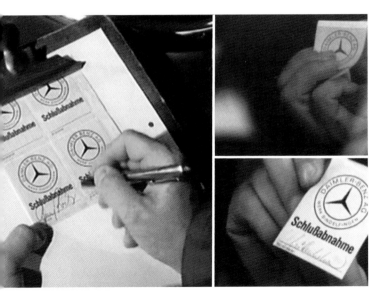

Only after passing every rigorous test did the 126 then receive the signing off label on the inside of the windscreen.

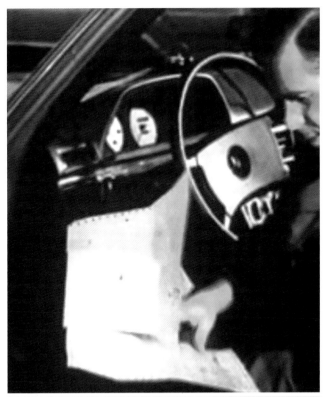

Every Daimler customer is invited to Sindelfingen to collect their new vehicle. Reminiscent of an airport lounge, the customer will sign in and retire to a waiting room where their vehicle will be delivered to them.

Even with all the robotic technologies available to Daimler, every vehicle went through a rigorous checklist. The only way to inspect the vehicle at the end of production was by human hand and eye.

For their dealer network, or for customers who cannot make it to the factory, Sindelfingen also had their own transport hub with multitudes of 'low loader' trucks and a dedicated train hub to ship each and every vehicle to over 170 countries.

PRE-PRODUCTION VEHICLES

The first time Daimler used a pilot series to pre-empt a model line was with the 123 series of 1976 and, although only minor, so successful was it that Daimler-Benz initiated what they referred to as a 'pilot series' to precede all standard production from then on. The 126 model was the second model in-line.

It worked twofold: first, so that the very first vehicle delivered to the very first customer would show uniformity of quality and production to be expected from the new S-Class, eliminating the early, potentially reputation-damaging issues that befell other manufacturers; second, it gave assembly workers enough time to familiarize themselves with the new processes involved in building the 126, without risk to customers' vehicles.

Whatever conditions that the 126 might meet in the future, under whatever circumstances, it had already experienced as a pilot model. Every part in a 126 had already been subjected to the equivalent of 3 million km, sometimes many times greater even than could be experienced natu-

rally. Countless trials and tests were made, some to destruction and dismantling to examine every part.

Separate to that of the main crash-test cars, some of the pre-production models ended up as press/photography and journalist cars. They were also used as dealer announcement and display cars. Most of the early sales' brochures had pictures of the pre-production vehicles.

Most went on to be sold to the public at a discounted price, but very few have survived. The author has only ever seen one, although recently has made contact with an owner of a second in Denmark.

There were a number of items that were different on these pre-production units; the most noticeable of course were the bumpers. The full production cars had a narrow, half-round, bead moulding around the perimeter edge just below the chrome embellisher; the pre-production cars didn't.

The plastic wheel trims were slightly different also: the centre dish was more of a raised section than the ones that actually made it into production. The reasoning behind changing them for the production vehicles was twofold according to documentation. One was that the raised area

Pre-production vehicles allowed Daimler to test vehicles in extreme conditions.

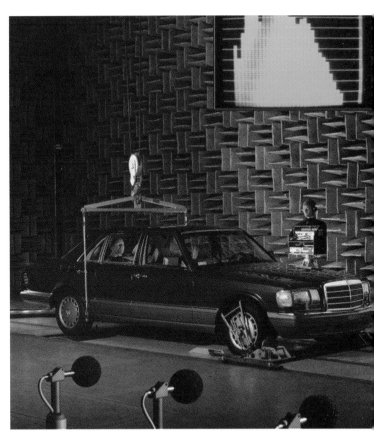

More sedate testing, such as sound testing.

There were a number of differences from the pre-production models to the production vehicles.

PRODUCTION FIGURES

Model	Dates	Output
280 S.021	April to December 1979	408 units
280 SE.022	February to December 1979	812 units
280 SEL.023	December 1979	1 unit
300SD.120	September 1979	1 unit
380 SE.032	May 1979 to January 1980	217 units
380 SEL.033	October 1979	1 unit
500 SE.036	September 1979 to January 1980	149 units
500 SEL.037	September 1979	2 units
	Totalling	**1,591 units**

VIN NUMBERS

Model	First VIN	Last VIN before change
280 S	126 021 12 000001	126 021 10 028309
280 SE/ SEL	126 022 10 000001	126 022 12 097094
380 SE/ SEL	126 032 12 000001	126 033 12 049737
500 SE/ SEL	126 036 12 000001	126 037 12 037879
380 SEC	126 043 12 000001	126 043 12 008208
500 SEC	126 044 12 000001	126 044 12 007674
300 SD	126 120 12 000001	126 120 12 052291

interfered with airflow and had a disproportionate effect on the Cd by 0.7 per cent; and, two, that the disc deflected air away from the brakes as opposed to directing it towards the disc for maximum cooling effect.

The very early pre-production models even had 116 rear-view door mirrors.

The door-lock vacuum pump was located in the engine compartment; this was relocated to the boot and housed in the recess of the spare wheel around January of 1980. The spare wheel was fitted in the boot, dish face up; once in full production, it was fitted dish face down with the additional plastic liner.

PRODUCTION IDENTIFICATION

The first two years of production, saw a model-relevant consecutive 'Vehicle Identification Number' (VIN) system, which equated to the first 281,192 cars. It may look confusing but it is actually quite simple: all VIN started with WDB126 and the model number. The last six numbers started at 000001 for each model. Once they reached the number listed as the 'last VIN before change', the numbering system changed so that the numbers increased with all 126 vehicles built and were not model-related.

Following the 'last VIN before change' list, all subsequent 126 vehicle produced followed a total production number thereafter. For example, you could have WDB126 044 1A 555555 for a 500 SEC Coupé and if the next vehicle on the build line was a 280 SE, it would be WDB126 022 1A 555556.

Sadly, this only gives you a total 126 build between numbers.

THE PRODUCTION CHANGES

As with any manufacturer, Mercedes constantly developed and evolved the 126. The list on the following three pages shows many of the important changes by date of change and, where possible, from the vehicle identification number.

Remember, as previously mentioned, that the non-model-related VIN didn't start until late 1983, so it is impossible to give you a more accurate breakdown before this.

When attempting to find the nearest build date for your own 126, remember, of course, that, even though revisions were implemented across the vehicle range from the date or VIN shown, your vehicle, even if older, may have had the revised part added at some point in its past; so for accuracy, use accumulated data, not just one item change.

The most beautiful and luxurious black anthracite velour with a number of interesting options including 'pre-heater'.

PRODUCTION CHANGES

09/1979: World premiere of the W 126 series at the 48th IAA in Frankfurt.

01/1980: Start of the main series (after pre-series) at the Sindelfingen plant. Only forty-two vehicles a day were being produced at this early stage.

02/1980: The vacuum pump was moved from the engine compartment to the spare wheel well to avoid being affected by the heat from the engine.

03/1980: The bumpers were amended by adding front and rear rub strips.

04/1980: Start of main production of the SEL models.

12/1980: SA Airbag for driver and front passenger and seat-belt tensioners were made available as a special equipment order.

07/1981: SA Air-conditioning was now activated via a switch and electronically controlled (previously manual dial), also a recirculation switch was added.

07/1981: Interior temperature sensor moved to the instrument panel in the roof frame trim; installed to improve control and performance.

08/1981: Steering gearbox upgraded for automatic play compensation.

09/1981: Introduction of the so-called 'Mercedes energy concept' for all models. This was a programme geared to reducing fuel consumption and harmful emissions. In addition to an increase in compression, the list of improvements included camshafts with modified valve timing, air-bathed injection valves and electronic idle speed control. Camshafts with modified valve timing enabled maximum torque to be achieved at a lower engine speed and, in the case of the 3.8-litre engine, torque was increased.

09/1981: Ceiling light, now with delay on exit control.

10/1981: Coupé models in 380 and 500 form were released.

11/1981: Surface heat-exchanger added below the windshield in the storage area of the windscreen to prevent snow and ice build-up.

09/1982: Fuel-level warning light illuminates immediately when the ignition is switched on.

07/1983: SA Seat-heating upgraded to feature automatic shut-off.

08/1983: New Hirschman Auto EL 6000 Automatic Antenna, which was lighter in weight and better gearing for less wear and tear on electronic motor.

09/1983: SA Burl Walnut available as option.

01/1984: Assignment of road springs and rubber seating pad bearing is calculated and constructed on a points system.

04/1984: SA Trip computer available for the V8 models all other models from 08/1984: SA trip computer available for all other models.

08/1984: SA Coupé front seats and coupé style rear sculptured singles available for the SEL.

08/1984: SA Introduction of electric seat adjustment with two memory seat positions; now also includes electric headrest adjustment from VIN A 094293.

09/1984: Seat-belt tensioners for both front seats as standard (indicated by the 'RS' on the buckle tongue) from VIN A 094293.

09/1984: SA New orthopaedic backrest adjustment by means of electrically driven vacuum pump and adjusting the seat from VIN A 094293.

09/1984: SA Headlamp wiper and washer with larger wipers and integral spray nozzle (as Gen2) from VIN A 096820.

09/1984: SA Heated outside door mirror glass available.

02/1985: Hood latches and grille slightly amended to accommodate safety hood tongue latch, similar to that of the 123 and 124 models from VIN A 134098.

09/1985: Introduction of the 2nd series from A 186069.

09/1985: New electrically adjustable steering column available for all models.

11/1985: New, lighter in weight airbag unit in steering wheel, more visually integrated to the wheel shape.

12/1985: 58D controller terminal upgraded, to improve switch illumination.

04/1986: SA New seat switches now in more modern design, similar to that of the 124 model, and new storage tray below the ashtray from VIN A 243517.

04/1986: Fanfare horn switch no longer positioned at the top of the centre console, but below ashtray similar to that of the 124 model from VIN A 243517.

06/1986: Central locking, electronic supply pump improved to respond more quickly and more quietly from VIN A 252372.

07/1986: Spare tyre mounted the other way around, now with a removable tray (as W124) from VIN A 268602.

08/1986: Introduction HPF II (*Hydropneumatische Federung*) self-levelling system with automatic lowering of the body by 24mm (1in) above about 120km/h (74mph) and operating controls for adjusting the shock absorber hardness from VIN A 281436.

08/1986: SA EDW (factory-fitted alarm system) with improved tow-away protection from VIN A 284611.

09/1986: Introduction of ASR traction control for the V8 and ASD for the 6-cylinder models from VIN A 288303.

09/1986: New surge protection relay from VIN A 288303.

11/1986: Amended stereo system with more space for larger speakers (better surround sound) from VIN A 296642.

12/1986: ABS standard on all models (previously only V8 models) from A 309743.

(*continued overleaf*)

PRODUCTION CHANGES *(continued)*

01/1987: New cruise control unit with coding for each vehicle type (unification) from VIN A 311370.

03/1987: SA EDW (factory-fitted alarm system) elimination of towing protection.

03/1987: Fault diagnosis by duty cycle now in the KE control unit.

03/1987: Revised fuel tank swirl pot with integrated separation chamber and fumes' separation, thereby avoiding splashing noises from fuel tank VIN A 327880.

05/1987: Elimination of vacuum tank for the headlamp levelling, new setting switch with incorporated shut-off valve from VIN A 338234.

05/1987: Additional security for the terminal 58D (not for trip computer) in the left instrument cluster.

06/1987: Fuel injectors made of brass with Viton seals (M 103 engine).

07/1987: Electric rear shade available as SA.

08/1987: More compact pre-tensioners with about 80mm (3in) shorter tube.

09/1987: Introduction of the up-rated V8 engine with anti-knock control.

09/1987: New instrument cluster with modified control of the tank reserve indicator to stop light flicker when cornering from VIN A 350465.

09/1987: Central vent, climate control flap receives new bar clamps from VIN A 354453.

09/1987: Icon switches for sliding-lifting roof illuminated from VIN A 357231.

09/1987: Completely new airbag system (SA) with improved electronics and triggering algorithm, recognizable by the SRS logo on the airbag; SA passenger airbag is now available from VIN A 363212.

09/1987: Heated washer nozzles now standard (SA code 875; only for LHD) and new heated windshield washer nozzles (PTC-resistor is replaced by a fixed resistor), as well as additional panels for windscreen washer jets on the inside of the hood from VIN A 363212.

09/1987: SA Air-conditioning revised, now with microprocessor control and electronic recirculation switch from VIN A 363799.

09/1987: SA Heated seats, only one controller for both front seats from VIN A 368215.

09/1987: SA New sound system available.

10/1987: The chrome rings for the door-lock pins were changed into black plastic rings from VIN A 388633.

02/1988: Comfort control relay for electric windows and seat adjustment: performance of the diode is increased from 1 to 3A.

03/1988: Amending the toolbar to the right in the instrument cluster for SA airbag, instead of RS now SRS (safety restraint system) from VIN A 407304.

03/1988: HT Lead set improved with soldered terminals improving resistance to moisture.

07/1988: Improved sound insulation – include special foam pieces around the rear speakers in the rear shelf glued into place, as well as the shelf base being covered in sound proofing material. Extra panels added to seal cable insertion slots in the rear wall and C Post. Water-drain hoses from the sunroof now sealed in the C Post with foam. Fire-proof sound-dampening fleece (20mm) loose lain over the fuel tank and into the C Post areas also between the rear seat wall and tank partition.

09/1988: New Model type 560 SE is introduced as SA only.

09/1988: Softer damping adjustment of the shock absorbers on front and rear with revised adjustment of base score in the spring selection from VIN A 428209.

09/1988: Ruffled solid pockets replaces cargo-style nets on the seat backs as standard from VIN A 428659.

09/1988: Installation of a heated exterior mirror passenger side (both mirrors now connected with a single cable set) from VIN A 430736.

09/1988: Trunk lights can be deactivated via switch from VIN A 434459.

09/1988: Wiring for anti-theft alarm system (ATA) now integrated from VIN A 434548.

09/1988: Revised wiring loom set for the exit (puddle) lights changed from VIN A 434549.

09/1988: New seat heater control unit to control power increase due to introduction of soft leather from A 439287.

09/1988: Amended resistance arrangement for the front passenger seat airbag (R32) from A 439844.

09/1988: Improved standard equipment. Four electric windows, steering wheel and gearshift lever in leather, folding armrest, head restraints in the rear and outside temperature display from VIN A 440401.

09/1988: Soft leather available.

09/1988: Introduction of twelve colours (instead of four) for the bumpers and side planking.

10/1988: New supply pump of the central locking system for increased performance and faster unlocking of the vehicle (distinguishable by white base to the motor unit) from VIN A 443217.

11/1988: Amended headlamp-control device.

12/1988: SA HPF (self-levelling system) has revised connecting piece to avoid oil flow noise during acceleration or during cornering.

01/1989: SA New relay (green) to headlamp cleaning system,

controlling shutting off the wipers from VIN A 451890.

03/1989: SA Revised electric sliding-lifting roof mechanism, eliminating the closing noise.

03/1989: New comfort control relay for electric windows and seat adjustment from VIN A 461998.

04/1989: Revised door contacts to improve glove box and exit lighting from VIN A 474336.

06/1989: Guide funnel in fuel tank filler pipe as standard (previously only KAT-vehicles and USA) from VIN A 484390.

06/1989: Brand new bumper design of the front bumper with hydraulic impact absorbers as standard from VIN A 485222.

07/1989: VIN plate change: previously known as Daimler-Benz AG is changed to Mercedes-Benz AG from VIN A 491298.

07/1989: Electronic dimmer rheostat replaces ceramic type for terminal 58D, also new warning symbol in the speedometer in SA ASD/ASR (day/night) from VIN A 491585.

09/1989: Broader transmission support with extra frame for automatic transmission from VIN A 495960.

09/1989: New ignition from A 496760.

09/1989: Steering wheel size changed to O/ = 400mm (previously 410mm) from VIN A 496760.

09/1989: New wheel covers, in addition to the already existing chrome star now with chrome ring on the edge; on special request, now painted in one of the twelve side cover colours since VIN A 496760.

09/1989: Introduction of ASR II SA (now also available for 260/300 SE) from VIN A 496760.

09/1989: Capacitor of the SA air-conditioning increased using double-fan for W and V126 only from VIN A 496760.

09/1989: Use of new soft trunk lining material only for V and C126 from VIN A 496760.

09/1989: Gear shift point increase between 2 and 3, also faster heating of the CO_2 sensor and catalytic converter – only V8 models.

09/1989: New bracket for fire extinguisher SA – taken from R129; with interior matching velour from VIN A 502270.

10/1989: Revised brake discs from VIN A 506204.

10/1989: Revised wrinkled hose to the left-hand hood air-filter intake (only M 116/117) from VIN A 513364.

12/1989: Parking lock latch (shift lock) with automatic transmission from VIN A 524864.

01/1990: Revised steering lock from VIN A 525779.

01/1990: Fuel injectors made of brass with Viton seals, in M 116/11.

07/1990: Improved check valve (noise optimization) vacuum line from the brake booster (distinguishable by black line colour).

07/1990: Introduction of Becker radios from the 2000 series SA.

SA = special equipment order only

THE PRODUCTION MARKET

There is some confusion with identification numbers as there are a few 126 with 'higher' VIN than the last. This is due to a number of factors.

First, the number only referred to the fact that the last ever 126 chosen would have to be the flagship 560 SEL and 560 SEC, so there were higher numbers in other models. Second, it is necessary to take into consideration the CKD version sent to other factories. The east London South Africa factory is a case in point. The CKD packages continued to be built after 1992, even after Sindelfingen finished making them.

Overall the different body styles of the 126 S-Class achieved a combined sales total of 892,126 units made up from a total of 818,066 saloons and 74,060 coupés. This was split between a total of 412,884 Generation One units and 479,242 Generation Two units.

Here are a few interesting facts and figures for 126:

- The highest annual production figure of any 126 model type was in 1981: the 280 SE sold in total 26,654 units. It also sold the most overall, taking just over 15 per cent of the 126 market.
- The flagship 560 SEL sold a remarkable number of 16,599 units in the year 1986.
- The best annual result for the previous flagship 500 SEL was 17,251 units in 1985.
- A total of 97,546 units were sold with a diesel engine.
- The best 126 sales' year with all models was 1983 when Daimler sold a massive 98,435 units.

Of interest is that the top three highest sellers were standard wheelbase 6-cylinder cars but the fourth highest seller was the flagship 560 SEL.

It is also interesting to note that:

- The W126 took 55 per cent of the total 126 market with 490,905 vehicles.
- The V126 took 36.6 per cent of the total 126 market with 327,161 vehicles.
- The C126 took 8.3 per cent of the total 126 market with 74,060 vehicles.

The series was extremely successful worldwide, as shown by the following sales' figures for the main export countries:

OVERALL SALES POSITION AND THE
PERCENTAGE RELATING TO ALL 126 SOLD

Model	Percentage of Sales	Sales Position Number	Model Year
280 SE	15.02	1	1979 to 1985
300 SE	12.03	2	1985 to 1991
300 SD	9.32	3	1979 to 1985
560 SEL	8.41	4	1985 to 1992
420 SEL	8.30	5	1985 to 1991
500 SEL	8.15	6	1979 to 1992
380 SE	6.53	7	1979 to 1985
280 S	4.82	8	1979 to 1985
300 SEL	4.59	9	1985 to 1991
500 SE	3.75	10	1979 to 1985
500 SEC	3.38	11	1981 to 1991
560 SEC	3.24	12	1979 to 1985
380 SEL	3.03	13	
260 SE	2.34	14	1985 to 1991
280 SEL	2.32	15	1979 to 1985
420 SE	1.57	16	1985 to 1991
300 SDL	1.55	17	1985 to 1987
380 SEC	1.26	18	1981 to 1985
420 SEC	0.41	19	1985 to 1991
350 SDL	0.33	20	1989 to 1991
350 SD	0.23	21	1990 to 1991
560 SE	0.14	22	1988 to 1991

• USA: 283,000. This doesn't include the importation of 'Grey Imports' which was estimated to be around 22,000 units a year in the 1980s.
• Middle East: 55,000.
• Japan: 45,000.
• Far East: 30,000.

These impressive figures make the cars from the 126 series Mercedes-Benz the best-produced luxury cars of all time!

THE PRODUCTION ENDS

Sindelfingen

In April 1991, the Sindelfingen plant rolled out the last saloon of the 126 series. A few chosen workers got to see and celebrate its ending.

The 560 SEL had the chassis number A605721 and the following special options (SA):

• 228 auxiliary heating.
• 291 airbag for driver and front passenger.

In late 1991, line workers gather around to celebrate the last 126 Saloon and the last 126 Coupé selected from the line back in January of the same year.

In the presence of the Mercedes-Benz CEO Professor Werner Niefer and the then Museum Director Max-Gerrit von Pein.

The last C 126 Coupé being used for a press picture.

The last saloon being driven on one of its 'regular' jaunts to keep it fresh.

All bumpers, side boards and rear view mirror backs were colour-coded to the main body.

Garland trim with #/100. The later script badging used as well as the SEC boot lid embellisher. The boot lid inner had a special trim pad. A later steering wheel was fitted from the factory.

- 300 storage box in front.
- 404 driver's seat orthopaedic left.
- 405 driver's seat orthopaedic right.
- 471 traction control (ASR).
- 540 electric roller blind for rear window.
- 620 emission-control system.
- 682 fire extinguishers.
- 872 seat heating rear seat left and right.
- 873 Seat heating driver's seat left and right.
- It was an anthracite-coloured (172) 560 SEL with black velour trim.

On 27 August 1991, the very last coupé rolled off the production line – a blue-black metallic (199) painted 560 SEC with champagne/cream leather trim. It had the chassis number A610819 and the following special options (SA):

- 228 auxiliary heating.
- 291 airbag for driver and front passenger.
- 300 storage box in front.
- 404 driver's seat orthopaedic left.
- 405 driver's seat orthopaedic right.
- 471 traction control (ASR).
- 540 electric roller blind for rear window.
- 620 emission-control system.
- 682 fire extinguishers.
- 873 Seat heating driver's seat left and right.

A total of 892,193 saloons and coupés had been produced in

almost thirteen years of production, making the 126 series, even today, the most successful upper-class series of all time!

If you take a look at the data cards of these very special vehicles, you will first notice that both were shipped on 29 August 1991. Both vehicles had the order number 291 and can, therefore, be identified as Daimler-Benz works cars.

In addition, both were ordered only in January 1991 and thus specially configured or terminated. Unfortunately, it will remain a mystery why this shipping date was listed in both data cards and who was behind the configuration of these vehicles.

In-line with Daimler tradition, the last manufactured vehicle of each series has always been stored and is now in the possession of the Mercedes Museum.

South Africa

The South Africa plant based in East London was the last factory to produce the 126. Production continued into 1992 due to the CKD kits ready to be built. When production end was imminent, it was decided to create a 'special addition': the last 100.

The author was lucky enough to be able to make contact with Philip and Les Kruger who own the beautiful 300 SE you see here; number 44 of the last 100.

There were a few differences between the European vehicles and the SA vehicles anyway due to the 40 per cent import rule established between the countries; however, the 'last 100' were a little different again.

CHAPTER FIVE

THE MODELS

THE SALOONS

In September 1979, a new generation of the S-Class was presented at the Frankfurt International Motor Show IAA. The range of series 126 first comprised seven models.

There was a choice of four engines – from the 2.8-litre 6-cylinder carburettor engine with 156bhp to the 5.0-litre all-aluminium V8-engine with petrol injection and 240bhp. Furthermore, one could decide between two body variants: beside the normal version (the SE) there was an elongated variant as had been offered for generations in the upper-class saloons (the SEL). This time the enlargement of the wheelbase by 140mm (5½in) was more remarkable than

usual; the extra length was of benefit to the passenger leg room and the entrance width of the rear doors.

Three of the important goals in the development of this new series were a higher degree of driver comfort and awareness, a higher degree of passive and active safety and the reduction of energy consumption. Using weight-reduced materials and a less air-resistant body, optimized in the wind tunnel, helped the new S-Class to reduce its fuel consumption by 10 per cent in comparison to its preceding models.

The two 8-cylinder engines of the previous series were replaced by two redesigned units with enlarged displacement and all-aluminium block. The 5.0-litre engine, which took the

September 1979 at the Frankfurt International Motor Show.

Side-by-side comparison between the 116 and the 126.

Nose-to-nose comparison between the 116 and the 126.

Tail-to-tail comparison between the 116 and the 126.

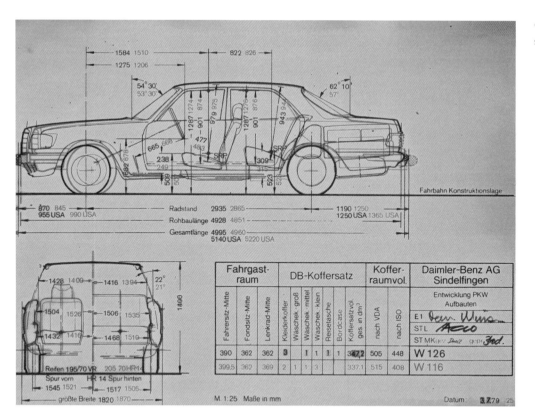

Original comparison
slide for **W 126.**

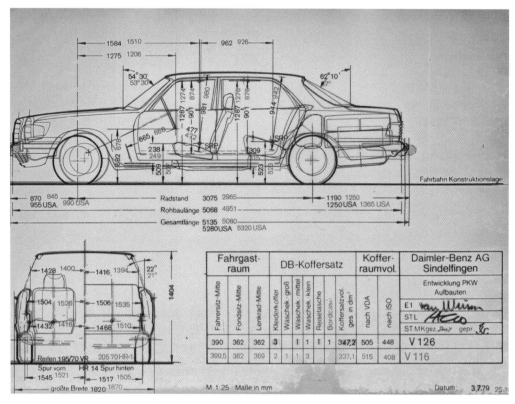

Original comparison
slide for **V 126.**

The W 126 in profile.

The V 126 in profile.

**The model line-up
in standard
wheelbase form.**

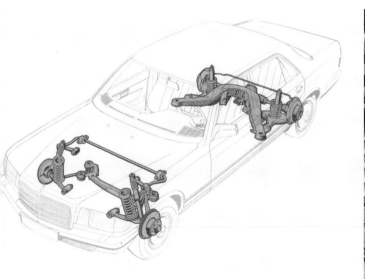

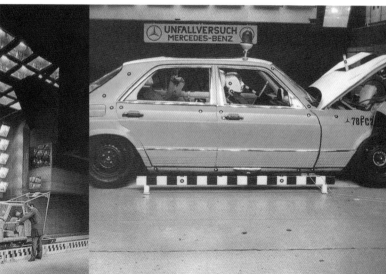

The new S-Class saloons, too, were equipped with a semi-trailing arm rear axle, as well as a twin control-arm front wheel suspension with zero steering offset.

Rigorous testing resulted in a vehicle that far exceeded the norm.

place of the 4.5-litre grey cast-iron block, was already known from the 450 SLC 5.0. The 3.8-litre all-aluminium engine had been developed after the example of the 5-litre engine from the time-tested 3.5-litre V8 with grey cast-iron block.

Due to their higher power with reduced weight, the new V8-engines made a better driving performance combined with more economic fuel consumption possible.

The carburettor and injection version of the 2.8-litre 6-cylinder aggregate remained unchanged in the programme.

Of series 126, too, a diesel version was produced for export to the USA. As its predecessor, Type 300 SD was also provided with a turbo-charged 3.0-litre 5-cylinder engine. Its performance, however, was increased by 10bhp to 125bhp. The layout of the vehicle basically corresponded to the previous models.

The body had been constructed according to the newest insights into safety research. Thanks to new construction principles, the passenger cell now also remained unharmed at an offset impact and a collision speed of 55km/h (34mph). Worldwide the 126 series saloons were the first series' vehicles fulfilling the criterion of an offset crash.

The characteristic design elements of the new S-Class present themselves more in the lower zones. For the first time a Mercedes-Benz car had no classical steel/chrome bumpers any more. Instead, there were generously dimen-

sioned plastic-coated bumpers seamlessly integrated into the front and rear apron.

Broadside protection strips formed an optical link between front and rear apron, placed at the height of the bumpers between the wheel cut-outs.

In autumn 1981, two years after its debut, to come into line with the 'Mercedes-Benz energy concept' for reducing consumption and pollutants, presented at the same time as the C126, the two V8-engines had been thoroughly redesigned, providing a considerably improved economic efficiency.

The two 6-cylinder engines were also changed in a number of details, thus also achieving some economizing effect. The power potential, however, was not affected by these measures.

Four years after the debut of the 'energy concept', the model range underwent extensive refinements, and so, in September 1985, again at the Frankfurt show, a completely revised S-Class range was introduced. In addition to a subtle facelift, which mainly altered the appearance of the bumpers, side skirts and wheels, the emphasis was on a restructured engine line-up.

Two newly designed 6-cylinder units, which had been premiered nine months earlier in the mid-range W 124 series, now replaced the trusty 2.8-litre M 110 DOHC engine. In the place of the carburettor version came a 2.6-litre direct-

Deformable **ABS** bumpers were able to resist kerb and rock stress.

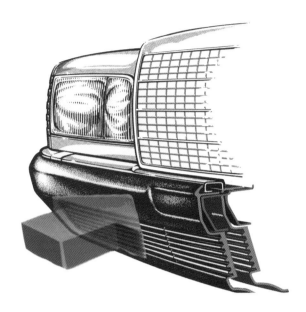

ABS bumpers were also capable of resisting a front-end impact by flexing inward; doing less damage to the vehicle but also absorbing the energy.

injection unit, while the 3.0-litre unit, which had been developed in parallel, succeeded the injection variant of the M 110. Another new addition was the 4.2-litre V8 engine, a rebored version of the old 3.8-litre unit, which it now replaced in the S-Class saloon, SEC coupé and SL. The 5.0-litre engine was also modified. Now equipped with an electronic ignition system and the electro-mechanically controlled KE Jetronic injection system from Bosch, it delivered 245bhp.

The most spectacular innovation in the engine range was a 5.6-litre 8-cylinder unit, which was developed by lengthening the stroke of the 5.0-litre V8 and which unleashed an output of 272bhp. If required, an even more highly compression version was also available that delivered a mighty 300bhp, although it was not possible to combine this unit with a closed-loop emission control system. But even without a catalytic converter, this 'ECE version' met the emissions' standards stipulated by the Economic Commission for Europe. The models fitted with this engine variant – the 560 SEL and 560 SEC – were, in their day, the most powerful Mercedes-Benz production cars ever built.

All variants in the revised model range – with the exception of the 560 SEL and 560 SEC in the ECE version – were available on request with a closed-loop emission control system with three-way catalytic converter. In each case, the series' version was the 'catalytic converter retrofit ver-

sion', for which the vehicle was delivered without catalytic converter and oxygen sensor, but with the multi-functional mixture preparation and ignition system. These retrofit versions could be fitted with the closed-loop catalytic converter without difficulty at a later date. This gave customers maximum flexibility in choosing the time to convert their vehicle – a not insignificant advantage, given that unleaded petrol was not universally available at the time. From September 1986, the closed-loop catalytic converter was standard equipment on all Mercedes-Benz passenger car models with petrol engines; the retrofit versions were available until August 1989 – with a corresponding price discount.

With the introduction of the new model range, the diesel model, which was still reserved exclusively for US export, was replaced by a modified variant. The new 300 SDL was presented with the additional space of the long version and featured an entirely new design of engine. This was based on the 3.0-litre 6-cylinder unit familiar from the mid-range 124 series, although this too was equipped with a turbocharger. The 6-cylinder turbo-diesel now delivered 150bhp – 60bhp more than the basic version without turbo-charger and almost 30bhp more than the 5-cylinder engine of the predecessor model.

As was expected, the running gear of the face-lifted models displayed no fundamental modifications. Nevertheless, a

The Generation Two W 126.

The Generation Two V 126.

few details of the rear axle design were modified in order to improve ride comfort and reduce engine noise. In addition, all models in the 126 series were now fitted with 15-inch wheels and larger brakes to match. The design of the optional alloy wheels – these were standard equipment only on the 560 SEL and 560 SEC – had been updated to match those of the compact-class and mid-range model series.

The other stylistic modifications that had been carried out on the improved models of the 126 series not only served to update the design, but had also been integrated for specific technical reasons. By lowering the aprons it was possible to further reduce front axle lift forces and improve airflow at the rear. This also had the effect of further enhancing directional stability and road adhesion when moving at speed, an aspect of considerable importance with respect to the performance of the new top-of-the-range 560 SEL.

The lateral protective strips were now smooth in design rather than grooved and, like the bumper system, they reached down lower and included additional trim on the frame side members. Because the 5.6-litre models – unlike their lower powered sister models – came with wider 215/65 VR 15 tyres as standard, the front wing and wing beading were modified in shape in order to create the necessary lateral clearance for the front wheels.

In September 1987, to counter the unusually robust challenge to the S-Class provided by the BMW 750i, higher performance variants of all V8 engines were introduced.

Compression ratios in all cases were increased to 10:1, and additional measures were taken to improve performance by between 6 and 10 per cent, depending on the model. The effect was even clearer in variants with catalytic converters. By optimizing the emission-control equipment, the designers succeeded in significantly reducing power loss due to the catalytic converter. The ECE version of the 5.6-litre V8 was discontinued without a replacement, since as a result of the treatment to increase output, the catalytic converter retrofit version was now also capable of developing 300bhp.

At the Paris Motor Show in September 1988, the 126 model range was expanded to include the 560 SE, thus making the 5.6-litre engine available in a saloon with conventional wheelbase. A very limited number were made and initially only offered to 'premier clients' as an exclusive upgrade. Very little detail was given in sales' brochures, apart from availability wording.

From June 1989, a new variant with diesel engine was produced, although this too was only available in the USA. Production of the previous 300 SDL had already come to an end in September 1987. The 350 SDL model had a new 3.5-litre 6-cylinder engine that had been developed by increasing the bore and stroke of the trusty 3.0-litre unit. The new turbo-diesel was designed more for torque than power and, with exhaust gas recirculation and oxidation catalyst, had a shortfall of 14bhp on its predecessor in spite of the larger displacement. However, the 350 SDL's 136bhp was more than adequate, especially given the speed limits that applied throughout the USA. Maximum torque was increased by almost 15 per cent and was reached at just 2,000rpm. In June 1990, the 350 SD with a conventional wheelbase was introduced to go alongside the 350 SDL.

As successors to the 126 series, eight 140 series saloons were introduced at the Geneva Motor Show in March 1991. Although the new models went into production only a month later, the plant continued, for a while, to turn out saloons of the 126 series for export.

Production of most variants came to an end between August and October 1991, although the last few armoured models did not come off the production line until April 1992. During the entire twelve-year production period, a total of 818,036 saloons left the production lines in Sindelfingen, 97,546 of them with diesel engines. That made the 126 the most successful premium-class series in the history of the company.

THE SEC

Daimler AG... The coupé is an exclusive body form. This was true even in the days of the horse-drawn carriage, when the coupé – presumably so-called because it resembled a four-seater carriage with its front end cut-off (French: 'coupé') – offered two seats in the comfort of the cab with the coachman seated up front in the open box seat. People who chose this mode of travel clearly liked to demonstrate a sense of style and individuality.

'Coupés from Mercedes-Benz have always embodied elegance on four wheels,' says Michael Bock, head of Mercedes-Benz Classic. 'Whether today, 40 years ago or a century ago – our coupés are legends of the eras in which they were built.'

The early automobiles borrowed heavily from various styles of horse-drawn carriage. The coupé retained a strong focus essentially on two people travelling in style. And since transportation in a closed two-seater was a uniquely cultivated form of travel, coupés were very often characterized by unusual lines. To this day, the coupé typifies an exclusive form of transportation.

Mercedes-Benz history offers coupés in a variety of designs. The Benz Coupéof 1895 and the Daimler Coupé of 1897 can barely conceal their relationship to the horse-drawn carriage. They established two lines of automotive coupé tradition: the Daimler Coupé of 1897, which in addition to the closed two-seater passenger cell featured the

familiar open box seat borrowed from carriage design, is considered the grandfather of so-called city coupés, which were common until the 1930s and also offered an open driver's seat. As a two-seater, the Benz Coupé of 1895 was a vehicle for the self-driving 'gentleman driver'. That made it the ideal precursor to the two or four-seater coupés with interior steering wheel, which became increasingly popular from the 1930s onwards.

But in the early days of motoring, closed vehicles, such as saloons and coupés, were the exception rather than the rule. Indeed, until well into the 1930s, manufacturers and buyers more often went for open variants, particularly where more exclusive models were concerned. Not until the modern age did the coupé establish itself as an exclusive yet iconoclastic automotive body form – for two or four occupants.

Flowing Lines for a Dynamic Appearance

The term coupé has evolved and grown over the decades. Early coupés, for example, generally only had space for two people; since the 1950s, however, they have more usually had four seats. The body, however, always incorporated a number of basic features that persist to this day.

A coupé generally has very low, flowing lines that create a stretched silhouette. It often dispenses with the B pillar altogether, and the C pillar slopes gently into the tail. The roof is generally shorter than in the case of a saloon, and curved at the rear. The side windows are usually frameless.

Nowadays, owning a coupé and enjoying utility value are no longer mutually exclusive aspirations. Although many coupé enthusiasts would contest the fact, even in a coupé, a spacious boot, folding rear seat bench and ski bag are popular equipment features. After all, the body does not reveal outwardly all the other things needing transportation in addition to the passengers.

Coupés by Mercedes-Benz and predecessor brands carry the self-image of this exceptional vehicle type in every detail. In this way the various coupés have smoothly been taking up their place in the Mercedes-Benz product range, adding a touch of sporting elegance to the brand image.

By tradition, Mercedes-Benz has always been building a special type of car which is distinguished from other models series by its high level of individuality: the Coupé.

These were the introductory words in the brand's brochure about the Coupés from the C 126 series.

> *The Mercedes Coupé embodies the rare type of a refined and sporty automobile. Its sporty character does not mean that the car has to do without comfort and safety. On the contrary, its sporty attributes combine with all those qualities which distinguish every Mercedes. The new Coupé is a car in which you can cover part of your path of life in the most sophisticated style.*

At the Frankfurt International Motor Show IAA in September 1981, models 380 SEC and 500 SEC were presented. They were coupé variants of series 126, succeeding the previous SLC models.

In concept, the new coupé generation once again was based on the S-Class saloons and not, as their direct predecessor, on an SL model. Also, unlike the SL/C models, a 6-cylinder variant was not available.

The V8-engines, already known in principal from the saloons and the SLC models, had been thoroughly redesigned within the 'Mercedes-Benz energy concept' in order to reduce consumption and pollutants.

The design of the new coupés was based on the four-door cars. From the very beginning, the elegant and harmonic Bruno Sacco penned design was seen as a great success.

The two bumpers, as well as the side protection strips, were shaped analogous to the saloons. The front apron, however, was pulled further down, with integrated fog lights to negate the lack of fog lamps in the main headlamps, as in the saloon.

September 1981 at the release of the Coupé at the Frankfurt International Motor Show.

380 SEC at the Untertürkheim test track.

The SEC range commenced with the 380 and the 500. Another concession made by Herr Sacco was the embellishing trim line, which followed the boot edge along its edge and around the corners above the tail-lights. This time purely on the grounds that it was an unnecessary addition and didn't serve any purpose.

The SEC coupé was one of the most beautiful cars Daimler had produced since the war.

A relict of the SLC range was the horizontal front grill typical for the SL.

Colloquially referred to as the 'Pantoufle' or slipper, they would keep the handles free of dirt while driving.

A remarkable construction detail was the aerodynamically optimized door handle recesses. Although disliked by the designer, he was overruled by the engineering department who insisted that their aerodynamic shape served a multitude of purposes: they directed wind, noise and turbulence away from where the door glass met the rear quarter light, particularly necessary due to the lack of a 'B-Post'.

In any case, the vehicle's aerodynamics were optimized as a whole for lower fuel consumption. This left the drag coefficient for all models of Cd = 0.34. The only exception to this was the 560 SEC model, where the value was Cd = 0.35 on account of its wider tyres.

More important were the improvements made with the V8 engines provided. Next to an increase of compression and a camshaft with an improved timing range, air-circulated injection valves and an electronic idle-speed control device stood on the list of improvements. Due to the changed cam shift adaptation, the torque maximum could be shifted towards lower numbers of revolution.

In the case of the 3.8-litre engine, it underwent a major change. In order to obtain a more favourable volume–surface ratio, the bore was reduced and the stroke increased, giving it a slightly increased displacement.

In both 8-cylinder engines, a slight power reduction had to be taken into account, compensated, however, by a considerably improved economic efficiency.

In both cases, the rear axle transmission ratio was adapted to the changed characteristics of the engine. Thanks to all these measures, the fuel consumption of the SEC coupés was drastically reduced in comparison to their preceding types.

Except for a few details, the chassis corresponded to the saloons on which the vehicle was based. Like the saloons, the coupés were also provided with a twin-control arm

Wind-tunnel testing resulted in a **Cd** of 0.34.

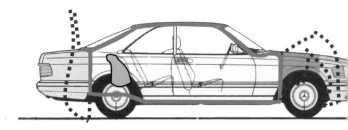

Crash testing the **SEC** was as rigorous as it was with the saloon.

Masskonzeption of the C126.

1977 prototype.

front axle, as well as a semi-trailing arm rear axle with anti-squat control.

For the first time, the front wheels of the SEC coupés were equipped with floating calliper disk brakes. Thus, larger brake disks could be used and the brake cylinder was located at the better, cooled interior, side of the wheel.

In principal, the platform, too, came from the saloon. It was, however, reduced by 85mm (3¼in). Thus the wheelbase was 30mm (1¼in) higher than in the preceding model. The passenger cabin was also much broader as in the SLC models.

The body had been constructed according to the newest insights of safety research and the construction principles, already applied at the saloons, were reinforced by further measures.

In order to compensate for the missing centre pillar 'B-Post', the roof frame constructions had been improved and the A-pillars provided with welded-in high-strength pipes, enabling the coupés to correspond to the high safety standards of the S-Class saloons.

Electrically operated belt hand-over's (commonly referred to as 'seat-belt butlers') were an interesting detail of equipment. They had the task of bringing the seat belt at all four seats into the field of vision and to be easily obtainable for driver and passengers alike. On demand, an airbag for the driver and a seat-belt pretensioning device for the front passenger were also made available.

Generation Two C126

Four years after the debut of the SEC coupé, the model range underwent an extensive package of refinements, and so, in September 1985, again at the Frankfurt show, a completely revised range of S-Class saloons and coupés was introduced.

In addition to a subtle face-lift, which mainly altered the appearance of the bumpers, side skirts and wheels, the emphasis was on a restructured engine line-up.

Another new addition was the 4.2-litre V8 engine, a rebored version of the old 3.8-litre unit, which it now replaced in the SEC coupé, S-Class saloon and SL. The 5.0-litre engine was also modified. Now equipped with an electronic ignition system and the electro-mechanically controlled KE Jetronic injection system from Bosch, it delivered 245bhp.

Although the Generation One engines were powerful and efficient for their time thanks to new electronics that controlled starting and fuel injection, more restrictions in pollution regulations were around the corner.

The West German Government at Bonn were looking to fight pollution with a number of measures with the focus mainly on protecting German Forests.

Both the US and Japanese markets had already strengthened anti-pollution legislation and the EU was looking to take similar steps.

Increasing the original 5ltr engine to 5.6ltr negated to some extent the power loss of the new catalytic convertor system but also gave the engine a boost of around 60+HP, giving Mercedes a top of the range engine that would compete with the highest end of the luxury market at the time.

Increasing the cylinder stroke to 94.8mm from 85mm increased the cylinder capacity. However, the advances went

The stunning lines of the SEC are indisputable, even surrounded by the best architecture.

The SEC showing the 'pillarless coupé' with the windows down.

deeper; the new engine had 8 rather than 6 counter weights, a different position height, a twin four into two exhaust manifold, and larger air filter. The cylinder head and block was a high tech light alloy reducing the engine weight by 20%.

The improved design of the new engine helped to reduce both emissions and fuel consumption. The EZL electronic system used a micro-processor to find the most favourable ignition point depending on load. The KEIII fuel injection system adjusted fuel injection with load and engine speed and temperature to further assist efficiency.

All the V8 engines in the S class were offered with or without the catalytic converter so they were able to use both leaded and un-leaded fuel the 5.6 was no different, in the early stages of the Generation two a 300HP ECE engine was available.

As the use of the catalytic convertor advanced amongst other manufacturers and un-leaded fuel became the norm, Daimler faced challenges from other high end vehicles, namely the BMW 7 series and the new Toyota luxury brand, the Lexus.

To negate this challenge it became necessary to improve performance across the range, compression ratios were increased to 10:1 on all engines and alongside other performance enhancing adjustments and optimisation of emission control systems an increase in performance of between 6 and 10% was achieved.

The 300HP ECE engine was discontinued in September of 1989 as a result as all 5.6 engines with the new high compression engines were capable of 300HP. They were referenced as the RUF engines.

As was expected, the running gear of the face-lifted models displayed no fundamental modifications. Nevertheless, a few details of the rear axle design were modified in order to improve ride comfort and reduce engine noise. In addition, all models in the 126 series were now fitted with 15-inch wheels and larger brakes to match. The design of the optional alloy wheels – these were standard equipment only on the 560 SEL and 560 SEC – had been updated to match those of the compact-class and mid-range model series.

The other stylistic modifications that had been carried out on the improved models of the 126 series not only served to update the design, but had also been integrated for specific technical reasons. By lowering the aprons it was possible to further reduce front axle lift forces and improve airflow at the rear. This also had the effect of further enhancing directional stability and road adhesion when moving at speed, an aspect of considerable importance with respect to the performance of the new top-of-the-range 560 SEL.

A marked difference to that of the saloon was the interior; Recaro-style sculptured seats in the front gave a sportier feel.

THE C 126 SERIES IN THE PRESS

Auto, Motor und Sport, Germany, issue no. 26/1981, on the C 126 series:

> *The feeling of space and the clear layout in the new Coupé are quite outstanding, especially in a comparison with the direct predecessor, the SLC. No less impressive is the handling of the car which weighs as much as 1,634 kilograms and is almost five metres long. The SEC handles like a dynamic mid-sized car and can be controlled most easily thanks to its precise power steering.*

Road & Track, USA, April 1982, on the Mercedes-Benz 380 SEC:

> *The new Mercedes coupé is a stylish personal car that does so many things so very well. It has much of the performance and road manner of a lusty GT car, the elegance and plushness of a limousine, and the prestige of the 3-pointed star (missing from the hood as an upright ornament, but found there as an emblem). Critics by question the price, but the excellence is indisputable.*

Road & Track, USA, September 1985, after a speed test with the 500 SEC:

> *You've got to be fairly strong to keep this throttle glued to the floor all the time; it's pretty heavy. The car is incredibly quiet at maximum speed. It's very comfortable and the steering is dead positive, only needing a bit of correction coming into the quartering wind along the straight. The seats are firm but comfortable in the Germanic fashion. It feels like a large car, which it is, but nevertheless goes fairly quickly, and, again, the lack of noise is remarkable.*

The lateral protective cladding (commonly referred to as 'Sacco boards') were now smooth in design rather than grooved and, like the bumper system, they reached down lower to cover the sill and included additional trim on the frame side members.

Because the 5.6-litre models – unlike their lower powered sister models – came with wider 215/65 VR 15 tyres as standard, the front wing and wing beading were modified in shape in order to create the necessary lateral clearance for the front wheels.

In September/October 1991, almost ten years to the day since the launch of the SEC coupé, production was halted. The total volume of 74,060 units built gives an impression of the huge popularity of this model family. The production volume exceeded that of its SLC predecessors to the tune of more than 11,000 vehicles, and this despite Mercedes-Benz no longer offering a cheaper entry-level model analogous to the 280 SLC.

By far the rarest version was the 420 SEC, of which just 3,680 units were made.

THE NORTH AMERICAN MARKET HISTORY

For an export-oriented brand like Mercedes-Benz, the US car market was of considerable significance. What made the market so alluring was the sheer size of the country and the fascination its people had for the automobile. Sales of Mercedes' vehicles only really began to take off after the Second World War; up until that point relatively few vehicles had been shipped across the Atlantic. However, corporate history records that Mercedes-Benz models were occasionally built specifically for American buyers and never even saw the German domestic market.

American Mercedes, 1905

In the early years of the twentieth century, cars from the Old World were highly desirable objects in America, but shipping and import duties of 45 per cent made them expensive. The solution that Daimler-Motoren-Gesellschaft came up with was a car manufactured in New York – the *American Mercedes* – which was essentially a duplicate of the 45bhp Mercedes. This car celebrated its premiere in January 1905 at the National Automobile Show in New York City. The first vehicle was delivered the following year with a price tag of 7,500 US dollars. For some reason, red was the standard colour. A contemporary newspaper advertisement awakened considerable interest: 'The American Mercedes is the car for speed, power and noiseless running. It is the pinnacle of reliability.'

The *American Mercedes* was built by the Daimler Manufacturing Company at its plant on Long Island. Derived from the 45bhp Mercedes, it had a 4-cylinder engine with 6.8-litre displacement, four-speed transmission and boasted a top speed of around 80km/h (50mph). An early American promotional article ran: 'If you want the best, of course you want a foreign car. If you import, of course you import the Mercedes – the finest car in the world. The *American Mercedes* is an exact duplicate of the 1905 Mercedes of 40–45 H.P. No detail is omitted.'

It is not known exactly how many *American Mercedes* were built. In mid-February of the year 1907, a blaze devastated the factory destroying eight road-ready vehicles, as well as forty still under construction. Production was never resumed.

Mercedes-Benz 300 SL Coupé, 1954

The story of the 300 SL coupé (W 198) is a rather extraordinary one; not just because it is an icon on wheels that has lost none of its fascination even today, but also because no other German manufacturer has ever produced a sports car more or less specifically for a foreign market. After all, the 300 SL came about at the insistence of the American importer Maximilian Hoffman. Had it not been for him and his sure instinct for the market, the automotive world would have been one dream car the poorer.

Once the Mercedes-Benz board of management had taken the decision to put the 300 SL coupé into series production in 1953, events progressed rapidly. Within a few months, two prototypes were produced and presented at the International Motor Sports Show in New York in February 1954 – a logical venue for the premiere, since the car had been conceived largely for the American market. Maximilian Hoffman sent a telegram describing the warmth of the response generated by the 300 SL Gullwing and the 190 SL roadsters: 'Motor Show tremendous success – Mercedes stand best at show and new sports cars the talk of the town = Hoffcar'. The board of management gave the green light for series production. A total of 1,400 units of the Gullwing had been built by 1957, almost all of them destined for America. After that, the model was superseded by the open-topped 300 SL roadster, which also met with enormous popularity in the USA.

It is also necessary to see the 300 SL in its chronological context.

This was the era of new departures following the hardship of war, and the 300 SL was a messenger carrying the gospel of hope that things at last were on the up. Of course, anyone who claimed ownership of a Gullwing had already made it in life – in financial terms, at least. The sports car was able to list industrialists, nobility, politicians, celebrities and artists among its clientele. The celebrities added sparkle to the 300 SL's image, and vice versa. The car was quite simply the ideal blend of all ingredients – perhaps the most perfect sports car ever built.

Mercedes-Benz 190 SL, 1955

The Mercedes-Benz 190 SL (W 121) is often referred to as the little brother of the 300 SL – and with good reason. It was designed at the same time and clearly shows a remarkable family resemblance. The 190 SL, however, was conceived from the start as a sporty touring vehicle, well-equipped and with excellent handling qualities, whereas the 300 SL coupé was a thoroughbred sports car.

The origins of the 190 SL can also be traced back to the initiative of the American general distributor, Maximilian Hoffman. The highly appealing two-seater was built on the shortened floor assembly of the successful 180 sedan, though it was given a new engine. Production started up in May 1955.

At the start of production, the 190 SL came in three variants: as a roadster with a soft-top; as a coupé with a removable roof but no fitted roadster soft-top; and as a coupé with a hardtop, as well as a roadster soft-top. A few of the roadsters were also available to customers as racing versions with lightweight doors and a small Plexiglas 'fly-screen'.

One can safely say that the 190 SL was a dream car for the 1950s. It sold well and of the 25,881 units built, the majority found their way to the United States.

Mercedes-Benz 300 CD, 1977

Diesel vehicles had been enriching Mercedes-Benz's US portfolio for some time. Ever since the oil crisis of the early 1970s they had cemented their place in the product range. When the 220 D was first shipped to America in 1971, it rapidly became a legend – and no less legendary was the advertising slogan that accompanied it: 'An economy car so economical it doesn't even use gasoline.'

The 300 CD, launched on the American market in September 1977, also belonged to this tradition. It combined elegance with homeliness and a highly economical drive system. For anyone who regularly drove long distances on American highways, the 300 CD was an attractive option. The car offered a high degree of ride comfort, as well as minimal fuel consumption. The engine generated 78bhp (58kW) from its 3.0-litre displacement, and automatic transmission came as standard. In total, 7,502 units of the 300 CD had come off the production line by August 1981. Then in seamless succession came the 300 CD with a new 3.0-litre turbo-diesel engine offering 121bhp (89kW). By the time production of this special coupé ceased in August 1985, a total of 8,007 had been built.

When the new turbo-diesel engine was introduced for model year 1982, the brochure announced: 'The 300 CD pioneered the idea of practical diesel power in an exotic limited-production touring coupé. For 1982, the 300 CD pioneers the idea of high-performance turbo-diesel power in this sporting body style – making an exotic automobile immeasurably more so by making it one of the fleetest diesel automobiles the world has ever seen.'

Mercedes-Benz 300 SD, 1978

Mercedes-Benz began to establish a tradition in America with its extraordinary diesel passenger cars – relaxed and comfortable motoring on America's highways, combined with minimal fuel consumption. This tradition also included the elegant 300 SD, destined only for the American market.

The first 300 SD, which still belonged to the 116 model series, was built from May 1978 onwards. It had a 5-cylinder diesel engine, which developed initially 111bhp (82kW) and later 121bhp (89kW) from its 3.0-litre displacement. Power was delivered to the rear wheels via a four-speed automatic transmission. A total of 18,634 units were built.

The North American 126

For the first 18 months, the W 116 held potential S-Class buyers at bay while the 126 was being readied to suit the market. This time though the model range was initially limited to only two models: the standard wheelbase 3-litre diesel (300 SD) and the long wheelbase 3.8 V8 (380 SEL)

Much work had been done by the Sacco team to negate the perceived 'ugliness' of the DOT additions, such as bumpers and lights. Without a second look, the US versions looked similar to their European counterpart.

Some US style items were added, such as under-dash coin trays, matching carpet on the door map pockets and swage line pin-stripes on the exterior to give a more home market feel.

The 116 for the North American market was dressed in large rubber bumpers to come up to DOT regulations.

The North American market 300 SD Generation One with the individual DOT headlights.

The new 300 SD turbo-diesel launched in October 1980 – power output remained initially unchanged from that of the 116; however, from October 1982 onwards, the engine delivered 125bhp (92kW). Unit numbers were impressive: 78,725 units had been built by August 1985.

A 1982 brochure proclaimed: 'One year after its introduction as the most advanced diesel-powered automobile ever placed in regular production, the 300 SD Turbo-Diesel Sedan remains alone and apart, its uniqueness unchallenged. This reflects no laxity on the part of other car makers. The 300 SD's technological sophistication seems simply too formidable to be emulated in so short a span of time.'

In February that same year, the 300 SDL turbo-diesels were launched featuring a new engine capable of 150bhp (110kW) thanks to its exhaust gas turbo-charger. A total of 13,830 units had come off the production line by September 1987. After a brief interlude, diesel power returned to the S-Class in June 1990 in the form of the 350 SD turbo-diesel and the 350 SDL turbo-diesel long-wheelbase versions.

Although the 3.5-litre engine developed only a comparatively modest 136bhp (100kW), it boasted a ferocious torque rating of 310Nm at 2,000/min.

In total, however, only 4,991 units were produced.

In the western states of the US the 3.0-litre engine was fitted with a 'trap oxidizer' from 1985 onwards as an emission-control system. The four models with this engine became the first production vehicles ever to feature this advanced technology.

A newly developed 3.8-litre engine for the 380 SE/SEL was developed from the original long-stroke, cast-iron block 3.5-litre of the 116; however, Daimler found it difficult to bring this design into line with the ever-changing US federation emission changes. It was decided to radically redesign the combustion chambers; not an easy decision at this point in a new model release.

The displacement volume of the original was 3818cc; however, to meet the new emissions regulations, it was necessary to increase the bore and stroke dimension to 3839cc. Coupled with the catalytic convertor and emission-control equipment, the engine suffered a decrease in bhp from 218 to a miserly 155.

All European models kept the original 3818cc engine.

The lack of performance was not a great issue in the US as the national speed limit was 55mph and by far, it was down to the 300 SD anyway to continue the enthusiasm building

Much work had been done by the Sacco team to negate the perceived 'ugliness' of the DOT additions, such as bumpers and lights.

for the diesel-powered Mercedes, as oil prices rose once again in response to the Iranian Revolution.

Dr Kurt Oblander (head of vehicle engine testing since 1971) was tasked with correcting this issue and developing improvements across the range. In 1975, Kaiserslautern University recognized his 'achievements and contributions to the development of low-pollutant vehicle engines' with an honorary doctorate – at a time when the Federal German Government had already appointed him to the steering committee of the 'automotive emissions' research and development programme, as well as to the expert committee for 'gasoline fuels and automotive emissions'. He had made a name for himself around the world. The subject of his action has always been the improvement of engine combustion in both gasoline and diesel engines, with the primary objective of reducing pollutant components, without, however, causing a deterioration in efficiency.

Commencing with the 3.8 M 116, he managed to reduce fuel consumption by just over 10 per cent with some very minor changes to piston shape and valve operation. However, further reductions were made with lighter pistons and alloy connecting rods, an improved cooling system to allow

for faster warm up of the engine, higher compression ratios and re-profiled camshafts.

The new engine management system indirectly yielded the highest of benefits. Over run fuel shut down with a reduction in engine idle speeds reduced fuel wastage but also increased the torque curve to give more power over a wider rev-band, which allowed the use of a taller final drive differential to give a further decrease in fuel economy.

Although the North American market didn't receive the 500 SEL 5.0-litre V8 until the autumn of 1983, it also received Oblander treatment of a similar concept to the Michael May 'squish and swirl' (fireball) cylinder head. This new high-efficiency cylinder head delivered 89 per cent of the available torque from as low as 1,000rpm all the way to 4,400rpm but sacrificed a little of the top end; also not a problem in the US with their low national speed limits.

Automatic gearbox improvements allowed a longer hold on to the higher gears with a second gear start and easier kick-down system to give acceleration when needed the most.

In 1983 the NA market also received the driver airbag options alongside the seat-belt tensioners, with ABS coming available as standard a year later.

CHAPTER SIX

THE POWER UNITS

THE PETROL ENGINES

The V8 M 116 Detailed Analysis

A number of factors influenced the choice of developing a V8 configuration in the early 1960s. The primary requirement was to provide a larger capacity power unit for the important US market. However, although West German and European fiscal laws heavily penalized any size bigger than 2.7 litres, there were whispers that the German tax laws would be changing in the very near future to allow for bigger engines. It was also noted that imported cars, like the 3.4- and 3.8-litre Jaguars, remained good sellers amongst marque enthusiasts.

A secondary consideration was that Daimler-Benz was becoming more and more safety-conscious and realized the need to build in a crush area ahead of the engine, which was either empty or full of 'soft' components. It was felt that a 3.5-litre 6-cylinder engine with modern over-square cylinder dimensions would be unacceptably long and would have entailed a longer bonnet or encroach on to the driver-passenger area of the interior.

Having got around to considering cylinder arrangements, the success of the M 100 engine gave the engineers a great starting point to make improvements and a V8 engine was the obvious choice. Its shape is easier to fit between front suspensions than a flat engine and does not compromise steering lock. Furthermore, there is room between the cylinders and under them for exhaust systems and ancillaries.

Daimler initially looked into using a flat-plane crank arrangement due to their simplicity and lighter weight; they also benefitted from a much freer rev-range, giving better performance and efficiency.

The main consideration of the time was that the engine should run for at least 50,000 miles (80,000km) without major attention, as well as maintaining its emission characteristics for this mileage. At the same time, the unit had to be economical to produce, had to develop 200bhp and should be capable of running at full power indefinitely.

The cross-plane crank would be more likely to fulfil these criteria due to the flat-plane crank's propensity to create a great deal of mechanical resonance vibration, especially on higher displacement engines.

The price of this balance and smoothness is weight and size. A cross-plane crank is inherently larger, since it's got crankpins on two axes, and it's much more heavily counter-weighted and balanced, all of which require a larger, heavier crankcase to hold it all, which makes a less favourable overall weight and centre of gravity.

Following on from the M 100, it was decided to use cast iron for the cylinder block. At the time this caused a little consternation, as a cast-iron block seemed an old-fashioned material for the cylinder block of an advanced engine from one of the most respected companies in Europe. However, it should be borne in mind that the engine was designed at the period of maximum disillusionment with light alloy in the USA, where the Mercedes was intended to be sold. Mercedes also had their good reasons for the choice. Cast iron is economical to buy, predictable and has good wearing and sound-damping properties.

The weight penalty was 30kg (66lb) compared with aluminium but it was reckoned that at least that weight of sound-damping material would have been needed to subdue the increased noise transmission from a light alloy block. Also, West German noise regulations called for a noise measurement from the side of the car and it was deemed uneconomical to sound-damp the sides of the engine bay just for this purpose.

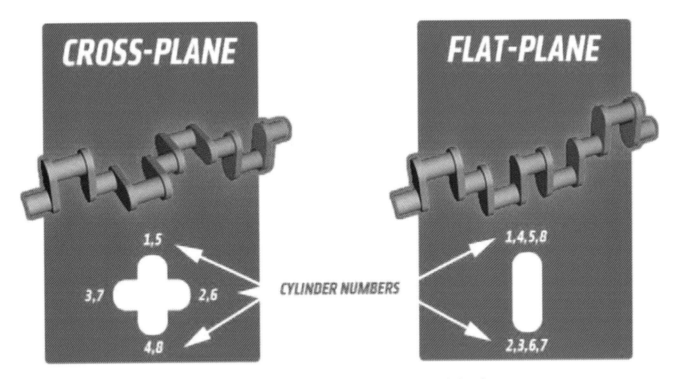

CROSS-PLANE 1,5 3,7 2,6 4,8

FLAT-PLANE 1,4,5,8 2,3,6,7

CYLINDER NUMBERS

A cross-plane crank engine achieves higher torque with fewer revolutions and thus less wear. The unevenly-spaced firings in each cylinder bank keep the engine balanced but also gives cross-plane V8s that distinctive burble sound.

Another desirable attribute in an engine is rigidity. Cast iron is better in this respect than aluminium. The short stroke also makes for a compact and, therefore, stiff cylinder block and crankcase unit. Every effort was made to keep size down and, therefore, weight. The result is a casting that measures only 10½in (26.7cm) high and 16in (40.6cm) wide in its machined state. These dimensions included the crankcase walls, which extended 2½in (6.4cm) (below the crankshaft centreline almost to the bottom of the crank swing. The object was to increase the beam stiffness of the unit with the gearbox.

To further increase stiffness, the five malleable-iron main-bearing caps were each retained by four bolts in-line. They do double duty as ties between the crankcase walls. The bearing caps fit into mortise recesses in the crankcase partitions for accurate side location.

Ample water jackets are provided right round the bores and the full depth of the cylinders. These are essential to get as much heat as possible away from the engine when it is working at full power inside a hot engine compartment on a hot day.

Five 64mm (2½in) main bearings support the forged and nitrided two-plane, four-throw crankshaft. With the 90-degree cylinder angle, this arrangement is free from primary and secondary out-of-balance forces and gives equal firing intervals. However, irrespective of firing order, the exhaust pulses on each bank are irregular and cross-over exhaust pipes are required, as Daimler wanted the V8 burble to be almost eliminated.

Large balance weights formed on the end webs are drilled for final balance. Thrust is taken at the centre main bearing and the high-speed garter spring lip seal, working on the flywheel boss, retains oil at the flywheel end.

An ingenious point is that the boss is ground with a spiral pattern that acts as a micro-groove Archimedean pump to push stray oil back into the sump. In order that the main-bearing cap faces and recesses can be machined at one pass of a milling cutter, the seal is carried in a separate, bolt-on diaphragm.

The compact dimensions of the engine have not been achieved at the expense of an unfavourable connecting-rod to stroke ratio. The 135mm (95¼in) rods (between centres) give a ratio of better than 2 to 1. Apart from reducing piston side thrust, there is room to use a longer stroke crank in conjunction with a taller block, using the same rods. The rods themselves are steel forgings, carefully proportioned to avoid stress raisers, with balancing pads at both ends. The cap dowel-bolts have knurled heads, which are an interference fit in circular recesses in the shoulders of the rods. This avoids the stress-raising notch that is usually milled across the shoulder to go with a D-head bolt.

Big and small end sizes are 52mm and 26mm (2 and 1in), respectively. Lubrication to the fully floating gudgeon pins is via a drilling through the connecting rods and from oil traps in the faces of the pistons. These are light alloy forgings with cast-in steel anti-expansion rings. Bearing in mind that customers are likely to drive the engine flat-out from the word go, all the rings have molybdenum sulphide inserts. Two compression and one scraper ring per piston are fitted. The second compression ring, interestingly, has a recessed 'nose' ground in the lower face and a backing spring.

Going against the trend towards bowl-in-head pistons, the M 116 was given cross-flow wedge heads with large squish areas. Mercedes found that the large quench areas so formed remain hotter than small ones and reduce hydrocarbon emissions.

The size of the vestigial combustion chamber is virtually defined by the 44mm (1¾in) inlet valves, which are inclined at 20 degrees from the vertical and work on cast-iron inserts in the light alloy heads. Inlet throat diameter is 40mm (1½in) with 38mm (1½in) tracts. This diameter suggests a mean gas speed of 280ft/sec (85m/sec) at full speed, which is relatively slow and is the probable reason for the high speed, 4,000rpm, at which maximum torque is produced. However, the torque curve is flat, with 170lb ft developed at as low as 1,000rpm and 211lb ft at 4,000rpm. Exhaust valves are sodium cooled and special attention is paid to getting water flow round the guides.

Even though hydraulic valve lifters were used on the M 100, Mercedes preferred to operate the valves of their overhead camshaft engines by means of rockers, as they have always done on previous engines, rather than following the trend for bucket tappets. Their reasoning behind this was that they are dealing with a known quantity and that the valve clearances can be adjusted quickly by most engine mechanics. While they agree that shimmed bucket tappets will usually go the Federal-required 50,000 miles without attention, there was a distinct possibility that they might need it before that and, most assuredly, will shortly afterwards. With good reason at the time, they pointed out that not every workshop in the USA would be able to take on the job.

Rocker layout was set up so that they pivoted on spherical-headed, adjustable posts. This ensured that line contact with the cams is maintained and leaves the door open to make a simple conversion to hydraulic adjustment at a later date by substituting hydraulic adjusters for screwed posts. Each rocker weighed 80g (22oz) of which 28g (1oz) are reciprocating weight.

It is interesting that Mercedes, like Jaguar, have chosen chain drive instead of belts for their camshafts. The main reasons for the choice were the known long life of chains and the fact that belts would have to be replaced at approximately 25,000-mile (40,000km) intervals. The layout is also the same as that of the Jaguar V12. A single run, duplex chain is driven by an 18-tooth sprocket on the crankshaft and passes round 36-tooth sprockets on the camshafts and under a 36-tooth distributor drive sprocket located in the V of the engine. Long, rubber-covered, spring-steel guides check lash on the drive side of the run and hydraulically backed spring tensioners controls the slack side. The whole assembly is contained by a simple die-cast alloy cover in which are formed the water pump and distributor drive housings.

Lubrication is provided by a gear pump slung beneath the front main-bearing cap and driven by a chain reduction gear from the front of the crank. Mercedes prefer chain for this application because of the high loadings that go with skew gears. They only tolerate them for the distributor because of the very light loadings. Oil is picked up from the wall of the stepped sump by a collector fitted with a specially shaped diaphragm-pickup. It maintains suction even when the oil is surging under 1G cornering forces. The rather shallow sump well is dictated by the need to keep the engine overall height to a minimum (27¼in/69cm) to help their stylists achieve a low bonnet line.

Oil is pumped to an oil radiator, usually in front of the main radiator, before being filtered and passed to the crankshaft. Separate drillings from the main gallery, located in the angle of the V, are taken to copper pipes running the length of the cam boxes and feeding the camshaft bearings. The camshaft chain is lubricated by oil mist.

Cooling is straightforward by means of an involute pump cast into the front face of the timing cover. It is driven, along with the steering pump, by twin-belts from a multi-groove pulley on the crankshaft nose. The fan, with a thermal clutch, is mounted on the outer end of the water pump pulley. Water is pumped first into the jackets with the aim of getting a good scouring action in this area before it passes into the inlet.

Fuel-Injection and Ignition

With Bosch only just around the corner, it was only natural that Mercedes should go to them for all their electrical and petrol-injection equipment. The Bosch transistorized ignition and electric fuel-injection is triggered by the ignition distributor driven by the camshaft chain.

Induction air is ingested through a pancake air-cleaner into a vertical trunk, where the throttle butterfly is located. The trunk in turn feeds a horizontal manifold located in the V, from which four swan-neck pipes each feed a pair of inlet ports. Fuel is injected through vertically disposed solenoid-

controlled injectors immediately upstream of the valves. In common with the Bosch mechanical system, the injection pulses are not exactly timed to valve opening. There are four pulses to two turns of the crankshaft and each pulse injects fuel into two tracts paired in the order 1 and 5, 4 and 8, 6 and 3, 7 and 2; which is in phase with the firing order. For example, group one injection takes place after the inlet valve of number one cylinder has been open for 30 degrees of crank rotation and the inlet valve of number five is due to open when the crank has rotated a further 60 degrees.

The injections' 'computer' takes into account inlet ambient temperature, barometric pressure and cooling water temperature. The last-named sensor is constantly variable and actuates a slow-running bleed behind the butterfly valve.

The virtue of this injection system is that it does the work of an eight-choice carburettor system that should be viewed in this light when considering cost. Although the power output is no better than if carburettors were used, hydrocarbon emissions are lower and more easily controlled.

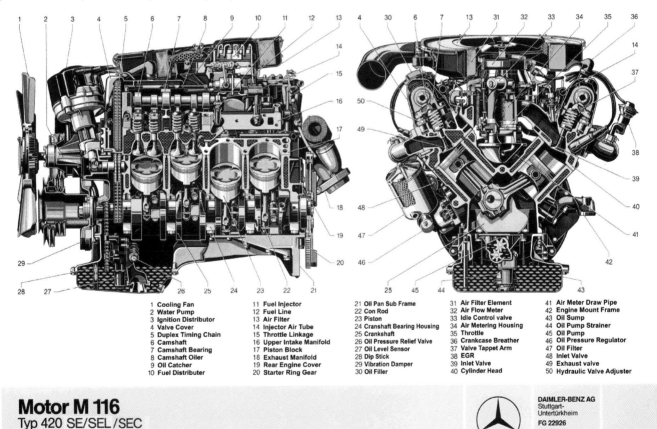

1 Cooling Fan	11 Fuel Injector	21 Oil Pan Sub Frame	31 Air Filter Element	41 Air Meter Draw Pipe
2 Water Pump	12 Fuel Line	22 Con Rod	32 Air Flow Meter	42 Engine Mount Frame
3 Ignition Distributor	13 Air Filter	23 Piston	33 Idle Control valve	43 Oil Sump
4 Valve Cover	14 Injector Air Tube	24 Cranshaft Bearing Housing	34 Air Metering Housing	44 Oil Pump Strainer
5 Duplex Timing Chain	15 Throttle Linkage	25 Crankshaft	35 Throttle	45 Oil Pump
6 Camshaft	16 Upper Intake Manifold	26 Oil Pressure Relief Valve	36 Crankcase Breather	46 Oil Pressure Regulator
7 Camshaft Bearing	17 Piston Block	27 Oil Level Sensor	37 Valve Tappet Arm	47 Oil Filter
8 Camshaft Oiler	18 Exhaust Manifold	28 Dip Stick	38 EGR	48 Inlet Valve
9 Oil Catcher	19 Rear Engine Cover	29 Vibration Damper	39 Inlet Valve	49 Exhaust valve
10 Fuel Distributer	20 Starter Ring Gear	30 Oil Filler	40 Cylinder Head	50 Hydraulic Valve Adjuster

Motor M 116
Typ 420 SE/SEL/SEC
Typ 380 SE/SEL/SEC

DAIMLER-BENZ AG
Stuttgart-Untertürkheim
FG 22926
Printed in Germany
1.86

M 116 schematic 380 and 420 engines.

M 116.

BELOW: **The revised M 117 500 and 560.**

COMPARISON SPECIFICATION

Block height
M 116: 215.85–216.0mm (minimum after decking: 215.65mm)
M 117: 244.85–245.0mm (minimum after decking: 244.65mm)
Rod length
M 116: 137.95–138.05mm
M 117: 154.45–154.55mm
Rod journal and wrist pin
Aluminium block
M 116(Europe): 52/26mm
M 116(USA, AUS, Japan): 48/23in
M 117(Europe): 52/26in
M 117(USA, etc.): 48/23in
Iron blocks
M 116/117: 52/26in
Combustion chamber
Aluminium block
M 116: 44.5–45.5cc
M 117: 55.5–56.5cc

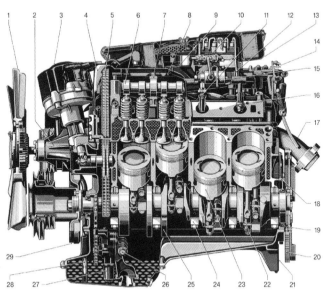

1 Cooling Fan	11 Fuel Injector	21 Oil Pan Sub Frame
2 Water Pump	12 Fuel Line	22 Con Rod
3 Ignition Distributor	13 Air Filter	23 Piston
4 Valve Cover	14 Injector Air Tube	24 Crankshaft Bearing Housing
5 Duplex Timing Chain	15 Throttle Linkage	25 Crankshaft
6 Camshaft	16 Upper Intake Manifold	26 Oil Pressure Relief Valve
7 Camshaft Bearing	17 Piston Block	27 Oil Level Sensor
8 Camshaft Oiler	18 Exhaust Manifold	28 Dip Stick
9 Oil Catcher	19 Rear Engine Cover	29 Vibration Damper
10 Fuel Distributer	20 Starter Ring Gear	30 Oil Filler

31 Air Filter Element	41 Air Meter Draw Pipe
32 Air Flow Meter	42 Engine Mount Frame
33 Idle Control valve	43 Oil Sump
34 Air Metering Housing	44 Oil Pump Strainer
35 Throttle	45 Oil Pump
36 Crankcase Breather	46 Oil Pressure Regulator
37 Valve Tappet Arm	47 Oil Filter
38 EGR	48 Inlet Valve
39 Inlet Valve	49 Exhaust valve
40 Cylinder Head	50 Hydraulic Valve Adjuster

Motor M 117
Typ 500 SE/SEL/SEC
Typ 560 SE/SEL/SEC

DAIMLER-BENZ AG
Stuttgart-
Untertürkheim
FG 22927
Printed in Germany
1.86

The M 110 schematic.

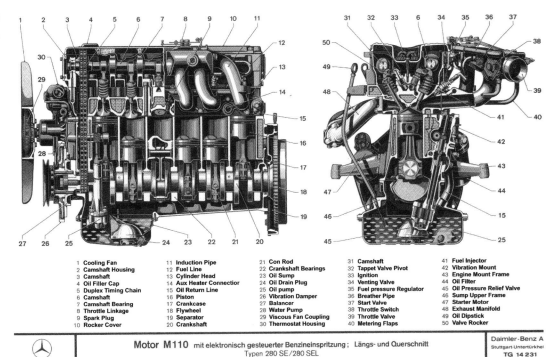

1 Cooling Fan	11 Induction Pipe	21 Con Rod	31 Camshaft	41 Fuel Injector
2 Camshaft Housing	12 Fuel Line	22 Crankshaft Bearings	32 Tappet Valve Pivot	42 Vibration Mount
3 Camshaft	13 Cylinder Head	23 Oil Sump	33 Ignition	43 Engine Mount Frame
4 Oil Filler Cap	14 Aux Heater Connection	24 Oil Drain Plug	34 Venting Valve	44 Oil Filter
5 Duplex Timing Chain	15 Oil Return Line	25 Oil pump	35 Fuel pressure Regulator	45 Oil Pressure Relief Valve
6 Camshaft	16 Piston	26 Vibration Damper	36 Breather Pipe	46 Sump Upper Frame
7 Camshaft Bearing	17 Crankcase	27 Balancer	37 Start Valve	47 Starter Motor
8 Throttle Linkage	18 Flywheel	28 Water Pump	38 Throttle Switch	48 Exhaust Manifold
9 Spark Plug	19 Separator	29 Viscous Fan Coupling	39 Throttle Valve	49 Oil Dipstick
10 Rocker Cover	20 Crankshaft	30 Thermostat Housing	40 Metering Flaps	50 Valve Rocker

Motor M110 mit elektronisch gesteuerter Benzineinspritzung; Längs- und Querschnitt
Typen 280 SE/280 SEL

Daimler-Benz A
Stuttgart-Untertürkhel
TG 14 231
3.74 Printed in Ger

Onwards to the M 117

As with the M 100 and onwards, technology, not just of the engine itself but that of the engineering processes to build with better tolerances, moved on. Daimler introduced the larger M 117 in 1971 in the 280 SE/SEL W 108 in 4.5-litre form. It retained the cast-iron block, while the M 116 kept its cast-iron block until 1978.

The M 110 6-Cylinder

The M 110 6-cylinder petrol engine was a finely engineered unit that first saw use in late 1971 in the 280 W 114. From the beginning, Daimler realized they needed a future-proof stock engine that be safety, reliability and ecologically sound.

Daimler-Benz AG technicians were justifiably proud of their new 'baby' – a completely new 6-cylinder, in-line twin overhead camshaft engine of 2.8-litres capacity. It was initially available with either carburettors or electronic fuel-injection. It also embodied the latest in newly conceived vibration damping techniques.

To meet the demands of today's traffic, the new engine had to fulfil two basic requirements. First, because of the

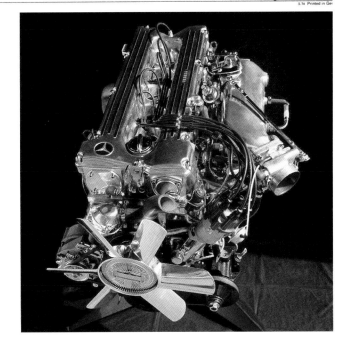

The M 110.

need for increased active safety, it should be as powerful as possible. Yet because of the ever-growing awareness of the need to protect our environment, it had also to be as 'clean' as possible.

The new M 110 engine ran quietly and smoothly, it burnt its fuel so cleanly that it earned the label 'friend of nature' from its engineering parents.

From the beginning, the engine developed 160DIN/hp (118kW) in carburettor form and 185DIN/hp (136kW) with fuel-injection (180 and 215 gross SAE/hp, respectively).

Optimal mixture combustion was ensured by semi-spherical combustion chambers. The valves, which are arranged in a V-shape, are directly operated by rocker arms from the two overhead camshafts. This was an expensive engineering method, usually only found on engines built for sports cars, but it produces a free-revving engine capable of up to 6,500rpm. This was made possible since there was only the minimum amount of weight moving back and forth in the valve gear. The two camshafts were driven by a duplex roller chain. An intermediate gear drives the distributor and oil pump. Viewed from the direction of travel, the inlet valves lie on the left side and the exhaust valves on the right. Both had a hardened valve seat to accommodate the future development of lead-free fuels; the exhaust valves were sodium-filled for cooling and thus less were through heat.

The two overhead camshafts each had their own housing, which gave the motor a distinctive appearance. They could be easily removed for repairs without having to dismantle the cylinder head, enabling cooling water to remain in the engine and cutting down repair times.

At the 'bottom end', the crankshaft rests on seven main bearings and there were no fewer than twelve counterweights on the crank webs. A new type of double-weight vibration damper was introduced to further damp down engine oscillations. Despite the high-revving ability of the engine, this resulted in an unusually smooth flow of power.

A special oil injector was incorporated in the connecting rod to assist with the cooling of the piston crown. Extensive research was undertaken before the optimum shape of the combustion chamber was devised to ensure that the best combustion properties (and, therefore, the most favourable utilization of the fuel's power) were obtained. It also made certain that the exhaust emission and fuel consumption figures would be as favourable as possible.

The Daimler-Benz engineers used a series of very effective measures in order to be able to comply with the future fuel regulations: the valves have been arranged slightly asymmetrically. The fuel/air mixture is forced into a swirling movement by the raised piston head; together with the relatively low compression, this means that the engine can

be kept safely clear of the knocking limit. The engine, therefore, would run successfully without pinking and damage-free, even on a low-lead content petrol.

Initially, the 280 and 280 C models were equipped with a completely new type of carburettor called the dual compound carburettor. This was a two-stage carburettor with each stage working on a different principle. The first stage works on the fixed-jet principle, like those fitted to the 230, 250, 250 C and 280 S 6-cylinder carburettor-engined models. The second stage, however, worked more according to the constant vacuum principle, similar to the type installed in the 200 and 220 4-cylinder models.

This combination gave good consumption and exhaust emission characteristics. For cold starts, an automatic starter device was fitted, which was heated up electrically according to the temperature of the cooling water.

In the 280 E saloon and 280 CE Coupé models, an electronically controlled fuel-injection system was used. Electromagnetically controlled injection valves situated just in front of the inlet valve, fed with impulses from an ECU, triggered them exactly when to open and admit a fine spray of fuel into the combustion chamber.

Fuel supply to the injection valves was by means of a constant high-pressure electric pump. The amount of fuel injected was determined by the time the valve is open. This in turn, calculated by the timing device, after taking into account the number of revolutions of the engine, the position of the accelerator, the prevailing air pressure and the temperature of the engine, ensured that the amount of fuel injected was matched extremely precisely to the operating conditions and wishes of the driver.

A transistorized ignition system was also fitted to the fuel-injection engine. This placed only a relatively low loading on the contact breakers, reducing burning of points and ensuring that, once set, the timing remained correctly adjusted for long periods. This was particularly important in achieving good power output, fuel consumption and 'clean exhaust values.

Finally, timing adjustment was made extremely easy and extremely precise by a new setting device on the engine designed to be used in conjunction with an electronic workshop instrument.

The M 103 6-Cylinder

Daimler knew that the M 110 was beginning to come to the end of its useful production life, especially for the upcoming

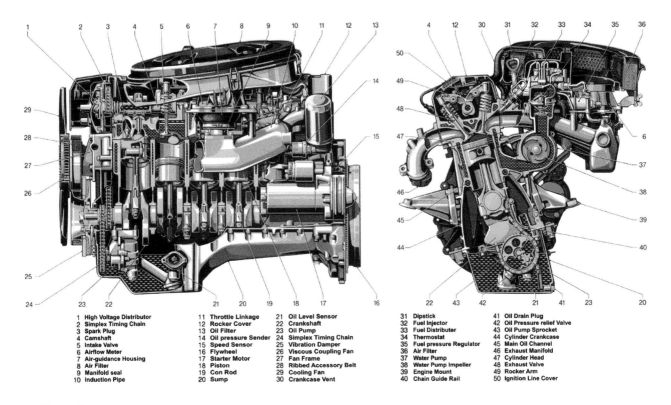

1 High Voltage Distributor	11 Throttle Linkage	21 Oil Level Sensor
2 Simplex Timing Chain	12 Rocker Cover	22 Crankshaft
3 Spark Plug	13 Oil Filter	23 Oil Pump
4 Camshaft	14 Oil pressure Sender	24 Simplex Timing Chain
5 Intake Valve	15 Speed Sensor	25 Vibration Damper
6 Airflow Meter	16 Flywheel	26 Viscous Coupling Fan
7 Air-guidance Housing	17 Starter Motor	27 Fan Frame
8 Air Filter	18 Piston	28 Ribbed Accessory Belt
9 Manifold seal	19 Con Rod	29 Cooling Fan
10 Induction Pipe	20 Sump	30 Crankcase Vent

31 Dipstick	41 Oil Drain Plug
32 Fuel Injector	42 Oil Pressure relief Valve
33 Fuel Distributer	43 Oil Pump Sprocket
34 Thermostat	44 Cylinder Crankcase
35 Fuel pressure Regulator	45 Main Oil Channel
36 Air Filter	46 Exhaust Manifold
37 Water Pump	47 Cylinder Head
38 Water Pump Impeller	48 Exhaust Valve
39 Engine Mount	49 Rocker Arm
40 Chain Guide Rail	50 Ignition Line Cover

ABOVE: **Mercedes started production of the M 103 3.0-litre in-line 6-cylinder engine in 1985. It also included the 2.6-litre version (the M 103 E26).**

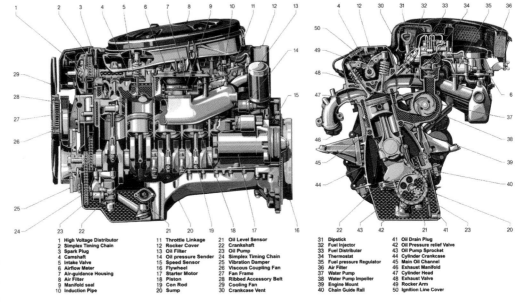

RIGHT: **The slightly larger M 103 in 3 litres.**

1 High Voltage Distributor	11 Throttle Linkage	21 Oil Level Sensor
2 Simplex Timing Chain	12 Rocker Cover	22 Crankshaft
3 Spark Plug	13 Oil Filter	23 Oil Pump
4 Camshaft	14 Oil pressure Sender	24 Simplex Timing Chain
5 Intake Valve	15 Speed Sensor	25 Vibration Damper
6 Airflow Meter	16 Flywheel	26 Viscous Coupling Fan
7 Air-guidance Housing	17 Starter Motor	27 Fan Frame
8 Air Filter	18 Piston	28 Ribbed Accessory Belt
9 Manifold seal	19 Con Rod	29 Cooling Fan
10 Induction Pipe	20 Sump	30 Crankcase Vent

31 Dipstick	41 Oil Drain Plug
32 Fuel Injector	42 Oil Pressure relief Valve
33 Fuel Distributer	43 Oil Pump Sprocket
34 Thermostat	44 Cylinder Crankcase
35 Fuel pressure Regulator	45 Main Oil Channel
36 Air Filter	46 Exhaust Manifold
37 Water Pump	47 Cylinder Head
38 Water Pump Impeller	48 Exhaust Valve
39 Engine Mount	49 Rocker Arm
40 Chain Guide Rail	50 Ignition Line Cover

126 Generation two, it continued to be used in the 123 until 1986 and the G-Wagen 460 models until 1989.

A new engine, the 4-cylinder M 102 had been produced from scratch for the early 124 range. It had a new cast-iron cylinder block and an aluminium 8-valve cylinder head with one camshaft. Late engines (until 1984) didn't have hydraulic tappets/lifters. The diameter of intake valves was 43mm (1¾in) and the exhaust valve 39mm (1½in).

The 2.0l M 102 from the beginning had a single-strand chain, which was very unreliable, but from 1987 this chain was replaced by a double-row chain.

In 1984, the engine got new light connecting rods and crankshaft, as well as hydraulic tappets/lifters and a new oil-filter. Together with the in-line 4-cylinder engine, Daimler produced the unified, as much as possible, in-line 6-cylinder engine – the M 103 3.0 litre.

The main features of these engines were a thin cast-iron crankcase and an aluminium cylinder head with a single

TYP	ENGINE	PRODUC- TION YEAR	DISPLACE- MENT cm³	STROKE mm	BORE mm	MAX.OUTPUT AT SPEED (DIN)		TORQUE AT SPEED		NUMBER OF CYLINDERS	DRY ENGINE WEIGHT KG
						kW	V/min	Nm	V/min		
260D	OM138	1936	2545	100	90	33	3300			4	
170D	OM636	1949	1697	100	73,5	28	3200	96	2000	4	
180D	OM636	1953	1767	100	75	31	3500	101	2000	4	
190D	OM621	1958	1897	83,6	85	37	4000	108	2200	4	
2000	OM621	1965	1988	83,6	87	40	4200	113	2400	4	
2000	OM615	1967	1988	83,6	87	40	4200	113	2400	4	
2200	OM615	1967	2197	92,4	87	44	4200	126	2400	4	
2400	OM616	1973	2404	92,4	91	48	4200	137	2400	4	
3000	OM617	1974	3005	92,4	91	59	4000	172	2400	5	
2000	OM615	1976									195
2200	OM615	1976									197
2400	OM616	1976			AS ABOVE						197
3000	OM617	1976									229
300CD	OM617	1977									229
300SD	OM 617 A	1978	2998	92,4	90,9	85	4200	235	2400	5 TURBO-CHARGED	244

This image details the historical rate of progress in engine performance.

camshaft for reduction of the engine weight and production cost. It had two valves per cylinder.

Valves were the same as the 2.0-litre M 102 (intake valve diameter – 43mm/1¾in; exhaust valve diameter – 39mm/1½in).V-shaped valves operated via rocker arms with hydraulic lash adjuster, KE-Jetronic gasoline injection and unit drive via maintenance-free belt drive.

The main reason for this step was the legislative measures required to reduce the environmental impact; in particular, reducing exhaust emissions and noise levels. Another important aspect was the reduction in fuel consumption, which could be achieved through consistent lightweight construction. In the M 103, for example, the internal friction was reduced by about 22 per cent (based on the 3.0-litre) – a great leap forward.

The new in-line 6-cylinder engine is 43mm (1¾in) shorter, 57mm (2¼in) lower and a whopping 42kg (92lb) lighter than its predecessor engine (3.0 litre compared with the M 110 2.8 litre). The inclination of the motor by 15° degrees to the right resulted in optimum space utilization.

THE DIESEL ENGINES

The OM617

In 1936, Daimler-Benz introduced the first diesel passenger engine with a 4-cylinder 2.6-litre engine in car model 260 D.

Today's success with diesel cars had its roots in 1948, when the 170 D was put into production as a fuel-efficient alternative to the petrol-powered vehicle. However, it was the overhead camshaft OM621 in the 190 D in 1958 that laid the foundation for today's modern diesel-powered engines and became the predecessor to the 4-cylinder OM616 with its 2.4-litre displacement and 91mm (3½in) bore.

The engineering target was a suitable diesel engine for the largest available saloon at the time and after much consideration of various alternatives, including a completely new 6-cylinder engine, it was decided to add an extra cylinder to the OM616. It was at the time, the best compromise in terms of cost, weight, bulk and engineering downtime.

Adding a fifth cylinder to become the OM617 was to become a further milestone for Daimler, passenger car development. The 1974 300 D became the first passenger vehicle ever to be installed with a 5-cylinder engine. With the addition of careful engine balancing and engine suspension refinements, the result was an incredibly smooth engine as close to a 6-cylinder engine as it could possibly have got.

So successful was it, in terms of refinement, that it was soon decided that it would be added to the first Sonderklasse 116. However, as a larger saloon, it would need more power: a turbo-charger.

Much work had already been done to aid with cooling between and around the cylinder bores but a few more modifications were necessary for it to be able to cope with the higher thermal and mechanical loads that a turbo would put on it, not to mention what was involved in the physical installation of the turbo-charger and waste-gate control. The resulting engine became the OM617A and was immediately fitted to the top of the line 300 SD W 116 and was the final step in complying with the new Energy Act of 1977.

Development Review

In the beginning of 1976, in spite of all the uncertainties that existed regarding the future of diesel engines in terms of NOx standards, the decision was taken to develop a diesel

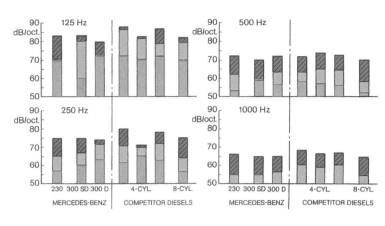

Comparison of emissions and fuel economy of Normally Aspirated OM617 versus the Turbo-Charged OM617A

Interior noise level using an 'Octave Band Spectra' system of various Diesel passenger cars

30MPH   55MPH   80MPH

Exhaust emissions OM617TD.

engine for the flagship 116 S-Class. The object was to offer an extremely fuel-efficient vehicle in the largest saloon possible.

Preliminary tests, including experiences obtained on even the largest of diesel engines, established the suitability of the Mercedes' pre-chamber combustion system of the OM617 for turbo-charging. The mechanical behaviour of the prototypes was equally good, so the decision for mass production could be taken with faith.

In 1977, sixteen class and three world records were obtained with a pre-prototype engine having an output of 140kW (190bhp) installed in the experimental CIII, e.g. 10,000 miles (16,909km) at an average of speed of 251.798km/h (156mph).

On the basis of these preliminary tests, it was possible to list and describe the necessary changes to be performed to the naturally aspirated engine right at the outset of the development of the turbo-charged version, which, interestingly, allowed for an expedited process of development. The resulting comparison test proved that there was a 43 per cent increase in performance with only a 7 per cent weight addition. Series production for the North American version 116 began in the early months of 1978.

The Combustion System

Daimler believed that the selection of a suitable combustion system for high-speed diesel engines in passenger vehicles must be based upon the following criteria.

While other manufacturers of diesel engines have selected other combustion systems, Daimler has always considered the 'pre-chamber' system as the best compromise because it displays better results in most of the criteria set out below.

It's only recently that Daimler's criteria have proved

The octave band spectrum ranges from 125 to 1000Hz at three frequently used vehicle speeds.

correct and been chosen as the best system for modern diesels.

Exhaust Emissions and Fuel Consumption

A comparison of exhaust emissions (illustrated) shows that both hydrocarbon and carbon dioxide of the turbo-charged version are considerably lower than that of the normally aspirated (NA) version of the same engine. At the same time, although the NOx levels were slightly higher than the NA version, it still managed to come below the 1978 NOx certification standards of just below 2.0gpm, which proved, as mentioned earlier, that looking to hydrocarbon and carbon dioxide emissions was a much better way forward. Combined fuel economy also improved by around 6 per cent.

Noise-Limiting Abilities

For a critical examination of the interior noise level of an automobile, a lot of factors have to be considered and it is by no means satisfactory to simply measure the overall noise level in dB. One of the most important criteria is the overall pattern of frequency bands.

It is interesting to see, especially at high vehicle speeds, that there is no significant difference between Mercedes' diesels and 4-cylinder petrol engines with similar power. At all speeds, octave band levels decrease uniformly and moderately with higher frequencies.

One of the reasons for this excellent noise behaviour is the extremely low radiation of the Mercedes' engine design. The combustion system, many refinements and the amount of experience gained over many years, also contributed.

Engine power comparative betweem OM617 NA Engine and OM617A TC engine

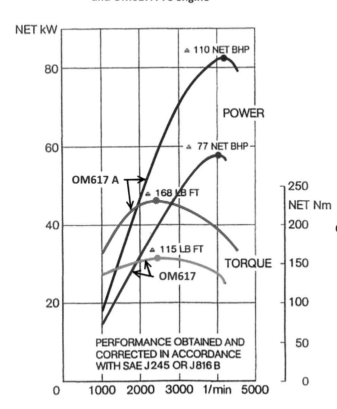

Engine power comparative for **OM617 naturally aspirated and the OM617A Turbo.**

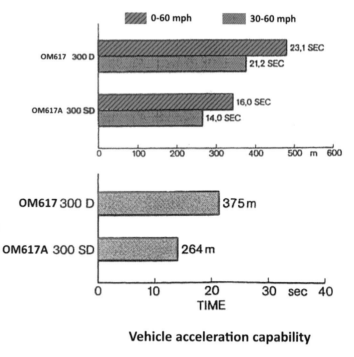

Vehicle acceleration capability

Although a good increase in 0–60 times was achieved, the passing/overtaking capabilities also increased, without a gear change.

Smoothness of Operation

Daimler's idea of going with the 'pre-chamber' engine was by far the best contributor to its ability to operate smoothly. The system allows the engine to stabilize very quickly its heat, combustion and pressure ratio at all engine speeds, including at low-idle, it's most vulnerable.

Cold-Start Capability

The 'pre-chamber' system, with its divided combustion chambers, enables the use of cold-start glow-plugs. The only difference to that of the NA engine was a warning system that informed the pilot of a failed glow-plug by means of a flashing light on the dash.

Specific, Comparative Performance

The argument for turbo-charging an engine must be on various levels, not just power and torque but also efficiency and durability. The OM617A not only returned a 46 per cent increase in torque, but also a 43 per cent performance increase.

Low exhaust opacity was achieved by means of tuning the boost pressure to a thermodynamically favourable air excess ration. Considerable progress was achieved in terms of 'time and distance' requirements in both 0–60mph and 30–60mph.

Durability

The OM617A 5-cylinder became the most powerful diesel engine of the entire Mercedes' range, as well as becoming the world's first turbo-charged diesel engine to be installed in a passenger car. Much work had been done to give the engine refinement and durability, but only time would prove reliability.

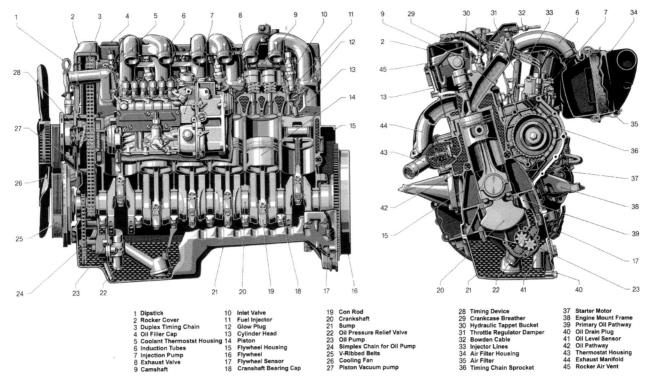

1 Dipstick	10 Inlet Valve	19 Con Rod	28 Timing Device	37 Starter Motor
2 Rocker Cover	11 Fuel Injector	20 Crankshaft	29 Crankcase Breather	38 Engine Mount Frame
3 Duplex Timing Chain	12 Glow Plug	21 Sump	30 Hydraulic Tappet Bucket	39 Primary Oil Pathway
4 Oil Filler Cap	13 Cylinder Head	22 Oil Pressure Relief Valve	31 Throttle Regulator Damper	40 Oil Drain Plug
5 Coolant Thermostat Housing	14 Piston	23 Oil Pump	32 Bowden Cable	41 Oil Level Sensor
6 Induction Tubes	15 Flywheel Housing	24 Simplex Chain for Oil Pump	33 Injector Lines	42 Oil Pathway
7 Injection Pump	16 Flywheel	25 V-Ribbed Belts	34 Air Filter Housing	43 Thermostat Housing
8 Exhaust Valve	17 Flywheel Sensor	26 Cooling Fan	35 Air Filter	44 Exhaust Manifold
9 Camshaft	18 Cranshaft Bearing Cap	27 Piston Vacuum pump	36 Timing Chain Sprocket	45 Rocker Air Vent

OM603.

It has become known as the 'million miler' for obvious reasons. A fitting engine to enter the flagship 'Sonderklasse' line.

The OM603

The OM603 engine was a straight-6 diesel used from 1984 to 1999. The 603 engine has a capacity of 2996cc and was an engineering marvel in pre-chamber design and a technological leap forward from the earlier 5-cylinder OM617. It produced 143bhp at 4,600rpm (euro market without catalytic converter produced 148hp) and 195ft lb at 2,400rpm with a compression ratio of 22.0:1. Versions 603.96x and 603.97x are turbo-charged.

Only turbo-charged models of the 603 series were available to the US market in the 126 350 SDL. The single camshaft and injection pump are driven by duplex chain from the crankshaft. A separate single-row chain drives the oil pump. The camshaft operated the valves via hydraulic bucket tappets; valve clearance adjustment is automatic.

A Bosch PES in-line injection pump with a 'piggyback lift pump' was attached to an indirect fuel system that inject-

ed measured fuel into a pre-combustion chamber with a mechanical governor and vacuum-operated stop control. It was lubricated by a connection to the engine oil circulation system. Preheating was by glow plugs with automatic control of preheating time.

The 603 engine was notable for several reasons: the emission controls imposed in the US market led to the creation of a diesel particulate filter, otherwise known as a trap oxidizer. As these were mounted at the cylinder head (modern traps are mounted further away), heat from these trap oxidizers caused failure of the aluminium cylinder heads on the first generation of 603-engined vehicles; debris from the traps could also damage the turbo-charger. This first version was sold in the US from 1986 to 1987. Daimler-Benz removed these traps for free, and if the turbo-charger had been damaged, it was also replaced. Even without the heat from the trap oxidizers, the original #14 mould cylinder heads were weak and if overheated could crack, as with any overheated engine. In general, the later model #18 or #22 mould cylinder heads are considered to be the definitive cure for cracked heads.

In 1990, the 350 SD/SDL debuted, using a larger-displacement 3496cc OM603.97 engine that had more torque and

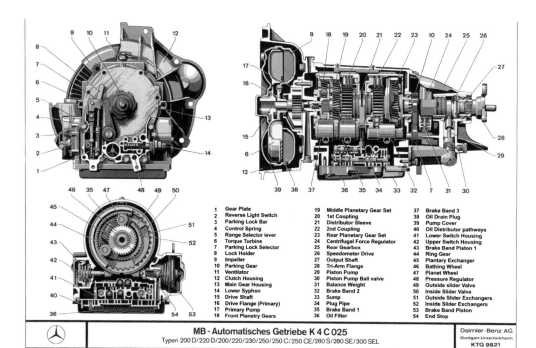

LEFT: **722.0/1/2.**

1	Gear Plate	19	Middle Planetary Gear Set	37	Brake Band 3
2	Reverse Light Switch	20	1st Coupling	38	Oil Drain Plug
3	Parking Lock Bar	21	Distributor Sleeve	39	Pump Cover
4	Control Spring	22	2nd Coupling	40	Oil Distributor pathways
5	Range Selector lever	23	Rear Planetary Gear Set	41	Lower Switch Housing
6	Torque Turbine	24	Centrifugal Force Regulator	42	Upper Switch Housing
7	Parking Lock Selector	25	Rear Gearbox	43	Brake Band Piston 1
8	Lock Holder	26	Speedometer Drive	44	Ring Gear
9	Impeller	27	Output Shaft	45	Plantary Exchanger
10	Parking Gear	28	Tri-Arm Flange	46	Bathing Wheel
11	Ventilator	29	Piston Pump	47	Planet Wheel
12	Clutch Housing	30	Piston Pump Ball valve	48	Pressure Regulator
13	Main Gear Housing	31	Balance Weight	49	Outside Slider Valve
14	Lower Syphon	32	Brake Band 2	50	Inside Slider Valve
15	Drive Shaft	33	Sump	51	Outside Slider Exchangers
16	Drive Flange (Primary)	34	Plug Pipe	52	Inside Slider Exchangers
17	Primary Pump	35	Brake Band 1	53	Brake Band Piston
18	Front Planetry Gears	36	Oil Filter	54	End Stop

MB - Automatisches Getriebe K 4 C 025
Typen 200 D/220 D/200/220/230/250/250 C/250 CE/280 S/280 SE/300 SEL

Daimler-Benz AG
Stuttgart-Untertürkheim
KTG 9821

BELOW: **722.3.**

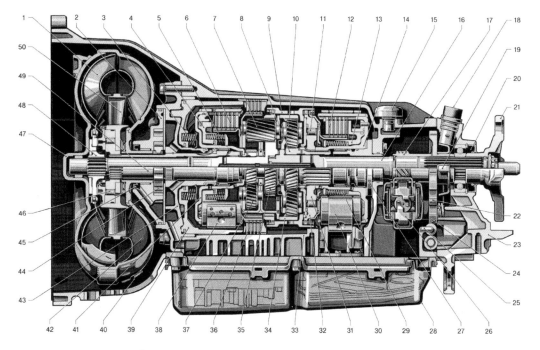

18	Inductor (Tacho)
19	Pulse Wheel
20	Rear Oil Seal
21	Drive Flange
22	Parking Gear
23	Rear Housing
24	Parking Lock Pin
25	Parking Lock Actuator
26	Centrifugal Force Regulator
27	Support Flange
28	Sump
29	K2 Compression Spring
30	Brake band 2
31	Inner Flywheel Ring
32	Freewheel Ring
33	Gearbox Housing
34	Rear Hollow Wheel
35	Drive Shaft Sun Gear
36	B3 Package
37	Front Small Planetary Wheel
38	Brake band 1
39	Reverse Piston
40	Fluid Drain Screw
41	Carrier K1
42	Impellor
43	Front Housing
44	Oil Pump drive (Primary)
45	Front Oil Seal
46	Freewheel Convertor
47	Pump Wheel
48	Turbine Wheel Flange
49	Main Drive Shaft
50	Secondary Drive Shaft

1	Torque Convertor	4	Piston K1	7	Planetary Front Gear	10	Rear Planet Wheel	13	Piston K2	16	Output Shaft
2	Primary Pump Housing	5	Compression Spring K1	8	Rear Sun Gear	11	Freewheel Gear	14	Disc carrier K2	17	Helical Gear
3	Compression Return Spring	6	Disc pack K1	9	Power Connector	12	Disc package K2	15	Vent		

4-Gang-Automatic-Getriebe W 4 A 040
Typ 500 SE – SEL

Mercedes-Benz AG
Stuttgart-
Untertürkheim
FG 25 409
Printed in Germany

a lower top rpm. The engine lived on in the W 140 chassis after the W 126 production ended, as the 300S D or S 350, with a larger yet turbo-charger, and thus more power and torque. By the time of the 3.5-litre engine, the cylinder head issues of the early 3.0-litre engine (US 1986–87) had been corrected. However, in the 3.5-litre there exists a different situation that appeared on some engines: eventual head-gasket erosion, and thus passage of oil into the #1 cylinder. As the 3.0-litre engine uses the same head oil passage design, yet does not appear to exhibit the problem, it might be that the larger bore in the 3.5-litre engine, the higher pressures and the resulting smaller head-gasket surface area, could conspire to cause a gasket-erosion issue. Elevated oil consumption is an early warning of imminent problems. Some anecdotal sources suggest that the connecting rods are weak. With a bent rod comes ovaling of the bore as the 3.5-litre block does not have sufficient bore material to allow for sleeving. If one catches the problem before it has progressed too far (after elevated oil consumption starts, but before the bent rod occurs), the issue can be alleviated with a head-gasket replacement. Generally, these problems seemed to appear more in engines before they reached 75,000 miles (120,000km) of service, than they did in engines after 75,000 miles of service.

A secondary problem with either the 3.5-litre (though true for any of the OM60x family diesels) is lack of maintenance of the motor mounts, which results in hard engine vibration from the engine resting on the frame members. Especially in the OM603, the vibration helps loosen one of the myriad of small screws in the crankcase, which primarily hold on the filter tray. If these small bolts and screws find their way into the oil pump or passages, the resulting oil starvation can cause bearing failure, and subsequent broken or thrown rods – often cracking the block. Proper motor mount maintenance eliminates these issues.

The result of both these issues was that some 603.97x engined cars had engine problems. While never formally recalled, Daimler-Benz replaced some engines under warranty, even somewhat after the original warranty term expired.

The Transmission

A big part of the efficiency drive for the 126 was the redevelopment of the Mercedes in-house built 722 transmissions.

MERCEDES 126 TRANSMISSION CODES

Model	Years	Code
280 S	1980–82	722.301
280 SE/SEL	1980–82	722.300
260 SE	1985–90	722.412
300 SE/SEL	1986–91	722.351/319
380 SE/SEL	1981–82	722.304
380 SE/SEL/SEC	1982–85	722.310
500 SE/SEL	1980–84	722.302
500 SEC	1980–85	722.311
500 SE/SEL	1984–86	722.311
500 SE/SEL/SEC	1986–91	722.356
420 SE/SEL/SEC	1986–90	722.355/324
420 SE/SEL/SEC	1990–92	722.355
560 SE/SEL/SEC	1986–89	722.323
560 SE/SEL/SEC	1989–92	722.350

Similar to that of its three and four-speed predecessors, the 722.0/1/2 was a hydraulically operated non-lock up transmission, which was much improved over its original vacuum operated shift system.

The 722.3 four-speed torque convertor transmission now benefitted from a number of electronic advantages:
• Improved acceleration.
• Improved fuel-consumption at idle.
• Smoother gear change.
• Increased responsiveness on manual operation.

From 1979 there were a couple of model-related changes. With the 280- and 380-engined models, the transmission would idle in second gear. It wasn't until the accelerator was pushed, even slightly, that it would drop into first gear. This system minimized creep, synonymous with first gear, but also improved idle fuel-efficiency and acceleration response.

The 500 models behaved slightly differently due to the high torque of the 5-litre engine. The transmission would start off and idle in second gear; however, it would only drop to first if the accelerator was snapped into kick down.

CHAPTER SEVEN

SPECIAL AND BESPOKE

THE SPECIAL PROTECTION VEHICLES

The special protection vehicles are popularly referred to simply as armoured or bullet-proof cars.

Daimler had always considered a very special clientele with special vehicles; be it the 'Big Mercedes' (770K, W 150) before World War II or the Mercedes 300 (W 186), which today is nicknamed 'Adenauer' – named after its most famous driver, the first Federal Chancellor of the Federal Republic of Germany, Konrad Adenauer.

Then in September 1963, Mercedes-Benz presented a new, exclusive prestige vehicle to meet the requirements of the most demanding customers – the 600 model, which became an instant legend. It was outstanding in every respect – generous dimensions, majestic design and exceptional technical characteristics. Its V8-injection engine developed 250bhp from a displacement of 6.3 litres and allowed the almost two-and-a-half-tonne vehicle to attain a top speed of more than 205km/h (127mph) with a 0–100km/h acceleration time of 10sec. The standard-fit air suspension, whose shock absorbers could be adjusted from the steering column while the vehicle was moving, ensured excellent ride comfort. The Type 600 was available as a five to six-seat limousine with a 3,200mm (126in) wheelbase and also in several Pullman variants with a wheelbase of 3,900mm (153½in).

It was only a short time after the launch of the top-of-the-range model that the German Government asked Daimler-

The armoured Pullman limousine had a raised roof element so that Her Majesty did not have to remove her hat.

On special request, Type 600 limousines and Pullman limousines were also built with special protection for private customers. One included for the Vatican and Pope Paul VI.

Benz AG to build an armoured version for state visitors. Although Mercedes-Benz had a remarkable track record in building special-protection vehicles, this on its own was not enough as the technical fundamentals had changed dramatically, not least because of the adoption of the self-supporting body. As a result, the engineers and materials' experts at Mercedes-Benz embarked on nothing less than the reinvention of the concept of special protection.

Thus it was that a small team set out to develop a new approach. In May 1964, at the Sindelfingen plant, they conducted the first armour tests with new steel grades and prepared the first design drawings. They eventually decided on high-alloyed steel grades, using double layers in certain situations and weight-saving ceramics for some flat-surfaced components. At the same time, working with a glass manufacturer experienced in equipping banks, they came up with a solution for the windows, the vehicle requiring not only a curved windscreen, but a curved rear window, too.

In June 1965, a bullet-resistant Pullman limousine was produced – the first special-protection vehicle built by Daimler-Benz since the war. Working under the pressure of an extremely tight schedule, the company managed to com-

plete it just in time for the state visit of Queen Elizabeth II. The generous headroom subsequently benefited other state visitors, many of whom wore hats in those days.

To make it easier to open the doors, whose weight had increased dramatically because of the protective elements, the engineers installed a hydraulic system for the rear compartment. It was activated at the touch of a small button housed in the door handle recess – security staff and hotel doormen were instructed accordingly.

Along with a number of 'normal' Pullman limousines, this vehicle remained in the company's fleet, ready to be hired to the government or other users, when required. A second version of this special variant was built in 1980. This, too, spent its working life in the company's fleet before joining the Mercedes-Benz Classic vehicle collection.

Between May 1971 and November 1980, several special-protection 600 models were built. However, unlike the two vehicles in the company fleet, these models had a standard-height roof.

After the model 600, which was built as a one-off, Daimler-Benz initially gave no further consideration to the production of special-protection models. This changed in 1970

155

A rare SPV 116. Not the wider trim around the windows and the lack of quarter light in the rear doors.

when several diplomats in Latin America were attacked, kidnapped and, in some cases, murdered. The German foreign office felt it necessary to provide a number of its heads of mission with specially protected vehicles. Several German federal authorities suggested that Daimler-Benz should build armoured vehicles as the comfortable, reliable and powerful limousines from Stuttgart were highly regarded by many governments; a reputation that had been established by the Type 300 'Adenauer' in the 1950s. It quickly became clear that this was a lucrative market and, considering Daimler already made standard vehicles in this range, it was not difficult to extend the market.

Before the W 116, specially armoured vehicles were either built on a 'one-off' manner or shipped to other coachbuilders to 'remanufacture', which entailed buying a ready-built vehicle and dismantling it fully to upgrade its security. However, for the first time the 116 was offered with an in-house armoured option.

The attacks by the Red Army Faction terrorist group in the 1970s led to a sharp increase in demand for protected vehicles. Daimler-Benz, therefore, decided that the all-new luxury-class generation – with the internal model-series designation W 116 – which was launched in September 1972, should also be offered in the form of a special-protection variant. The company's experts built on the experience they had acquired developing the special-protection 280 SEL 3.5 and improved the protection technology continuously. The special-protection variants of the 8-cylinder 350 SE, 350 SEL, 450 SE and 450 SEL models were supplied to a select group of customers, including many government bodies in Europe and overseas.

In order to provide even greater protection from projectiles and explosives, the authorities and Daimler-Benz resolved to work together closely during the subsequent years – indeed, this relationship continues to this day – as no other German car manufacturer was able to offer special-protection vehicles at the time. Together, they developed appropriate and feasible technical standards.

The Mercedes-Benz engineers began by testing individual components for their suitability. In the next phase, complete vehicles were tested by firing different types of ammunition at them in various conditions. Finally, the vehicles were also subjected to testing with explosives. Daimler-Benz established its own firing range in 1983.

The results of these tests were used to prepare requirement profiles for different situations – examples being opportunistic crimes such as attacks while cars are waiting at traffic lights, robberies committed using small arms and terrorist attacks with military weapons. This phase was conducted by the official ballistics' authorities and Mercedes-Benz specialists who were responsible for many technical innovations. These first technical descriptions formed the basis for today's test regulations for the different resistance levels.

126 Series S-Class Saloons

Enhanced special-protection technology resulting from an intensive development programme was continued with the 126. Particular mention should be made of two 500 SEL models that were built with a 200mm (7¾in) longer wheel-

base and a 30mm (1in) higher roof element. The first one, which was completed in January 1983, joined the company's own fleet of prestige vehicles. The second limousine was built at the request of the Vatican for the Holy Father and was presented to Pope John Paul II in August 1985.

For the first time with a 126 a special protection vehicle (SPV) was developed from the ground up in parallel with the production model, albeit in a separate area at Sindelfingen. The first production SPVs were delivered in late 1980/early 1981.

The short SE models were mostly used by special police units, e.g. GSG9. It was less about the opulent comfort of the SEL models than the protection of the occupants – the car was a means to an end.

To the uninitiated at first glance the armoured models of the 126 appeared little different to their original standard form.

There were no other major external changes compared

to the normal series; however, although the wheels used were either the Baroque alloys made by Fuchs or the later 15-hole dish wheels, they were of a different part number. They were made to endure so much higher axle loads than the non-armoured vehicles and be able to defend against a side blast or rifle fire.

The most vulnerable part of the wheel is the tyre; under attack, the wheels are also one of the most important means of escape. Many types of tyre were used over the early development of the 126 SPV but around the mid-1980s, Continental AG came up with a solution: the CTS-1 system.

The tyre and rim are integral and do not fit via a rim system as with normal tyres. The wall of the tyre is reinforced with a higher grade thicker vulcanized rubber and the alloy wheel rim is moulded into the side wall so, should it suffer a direct attack, the tyre keeps its shape enough to escape and retain control.

The **GSG9** special services vehicle.

The vehicles were used for many reasons, including support vehicles for transporting cash, as can be seen here during the euro currency transformation.

A closer look will reveal externally thicker rubber screen seals and wider window embellishers on the doors and around the windscreen.

The downside is that the tyres cannot be replaced; it is necessary to replace the whole unit, alloy and tyre together, at a cost of around 1,200 euros each.

Many of the innovations and methods of construction are kept 'in-house' for obvious reasons, and every vehicle was hand-built to the owner's specification. There was no 'standard' pricelist but some items were standard.

These vehicles had very thick special glass, which on the one hand had to cause no optical interference (distortions, etc.) but also had to be resistant to bombardment. A windscreen, for example, costs almost 30,000 euros in exchange.

As standard, there were no opening windows apart from the driver's window, which used a similar system of hydraulics used in the 600 W 100. However, as with most things, an option to have all four windows operable was provided using the same electro-hydraulic system of operation. They could also be closed in the event of a defect or attack with a special crank from the inside.

Everything was possible from the intercom (to be able to contact the outside world when the windows were closed) to the danger alarm and the fire extinguishing system in the engine compartment. Some vehicles contained special areas in the doors where it was possible to be able to fire a

ABOVE RIGHT: **On the front windscreen, a metal cover plate finished the lower section to hide the increase in thickness.**

RIGHT: **The Continental CTS-1 package.**

ABOVE: **From an interior perspective, the door panels were deepened to allow for the extra-thick glass. This image clearly shows the interior trim, as well as the glass.**

LEFT: **As can be seen in this GSGP vehicle, provision could also be made to store a weapon for quick release and use.**

weapon from inside to outside without opening any windows.

Although the engines were standard V8 units, some were uprated for improved acceleration abilities, the surrounding bodywork was reinforced to protect from bullet penetration and heavy duty under-engine skid trays were used to protect from an IED blast from the road surface. Automatic transmissions were considerably uprated to compensate for the extra weight involved, as well as having reinforced casings. There were also versions that had different reverse gear ratios to enable the driver/chauffeur to reverse out of trouble very quickly. The limited slip differentials were also strengthened and shield protected. The maximum allowable weight of the 126 SPV was 3.4 tonnes.

There was usually a second alternator to be able to provide addition power to a secondary battery; this would power a closed off, filtered air supply in the case of chemical attack.

Most armoured cars were ordered from the factory with velour equipment – it was, at the time of the 126,

simply the most luxurious feature, from the perspective of customers.

Unfortunately, there can never be 100 per cent protection. The attack on the Deutsche Bank board spokesman Alfred Herrhausen on 30 November 1989 is a case in point.

Herrhausen was in an armoured, government-supplied 126, the middle car of a three-vehicle convoy, with bodyguards ahead and behind. The Red Army Faction planned their attack well, planting their bomb in a satchel on a bicycle parked beside the route. The bomb was linked to an infra-red beam that terrorists, posing as workmen, had set up across the road. The terrorists allowed the lead car through and then activated the beam. When Herrhausen's car broke the beam, the bomb went off. It consisted of 10kg of explosive and a 2kg copper plate, aimed so that it would strike the rear passenger door.

Even though the 126 appeared decimated, the fact it held together as well as it did was down to the SPV engineering. The rear passenger door suffered a direct hit and the plate pierced the armoured limo, wounding Herrhausen in the legs. It is believed that had the emergency services reached him sooner, he may have survived. The chauffeur was severely injured but survived.

Most 126 SPVs are still used today in government circles, embassies and large public limited companies in Germany, although perhaps playing 'second fiddle' behind one of the successor models. In crisis areas, such as Afghanistan and Iraq, many are still being used.

Daimler continued the 126 SPV production between January 1981 until April 1992 producing 1,465 units.

Although there are a few 126 special purpose vehicles still being used, many cars, at the end of their useful service, were returned to Mercedes to be deliberately and systematically dismantled, and all parts destroyed, to protect their construction integrity.

Most SPV were delivered with a dual communication system.

Deutsche Bank board spokesman Alfred Herrhausen attacked by terrorists.

On 7 September 1986, after months of planning, the FPMR attacked President Augusto Pinochet's car in an assassination attempt. Five of Pinochet's bodyguards were killed and eleven wounded. Pinochet, however, only suffered minor injuries. He was riding the car with his then 10-year-old grandson, who survived unharmed.

This image was on the occasion of the 1,000 produced special protection car – a 500 SEL in 1988.

QUANTITIES OF 126 SPV BY TYPE

380 SE (1981–85)	86 units
380 SEL (1981–85)	88 units
500 SE (1981–85)	3 units
500 SEL (1981–85)	376 units
420 SE (1985–91)	229 units
420 SEL (1985–91)	63 units
500 SE (1987–90)	7 units
500 SEL (1985–92)	262 units
560 SEL (1986–92)	49 units

FRED OEHMKE 500 SEL STATION WAGON

This 'station wagon, break, or estate' started life as a normal 1982 500 SEL from Japan until purchased by a stone sculptor by the name of Yayoi Kusama (born 22 March 1929).

In 1984, the artist decided to change the vehicle into a new design. The car was completely disassembled (including axles plus engine disassembly) and rebuilt again.

The design was completely original and all sheet metal body was made by hand. The bodywork was extended from above the rear window line, extending the 'C-Post' to form the station wagon; the tailgate was constructed

Yayoi Kusama-designed station wagon. The rear of the vehicle, along with the tail-lights, bumper and closing section of the boot, was kept as the original. The interior grey leather/238A has been completely replaced in its entirety by original equipment in the mid-red/477 leather. In addition, a variety of burl walnut additions were installed to complement the design.

to make use of the original rear screen. An additional rear quarter light was fitted into the C-post.

The rear of the vehicle, along with the tail-lights, bumper and closing section of the boot was kept as the original. Non-Mercedes chrome roof rails were fitted to complete the aesthetics.

All design documents and sketches commissioned by the eccentric artist were destroyed to ensure the uniqueness of the design. However, there were rumours of another, but no evidence of this has been confirmed.

The original exterior colour of 904 dark blue was completely removed when the body was stripped and 934 China

blue was chosen in its place; nothing remains of the original colour. The plastic side cladding and bumpers were colour-coded to the body.

Re-Commissioning 2017/2018

The vehicle was bought from the current owner in October 2017 by the renowned classic dealer, Rosier of Oldenburg. The headlights were changed for LHD European units and the air-conditioning was converted to R134a. Due to its very long service life, much work was done to bring it up to standard. All axle elements, such as bearings and suspension parts were renewed. All lubricants were flushed and changed in a full service.

Having now received an historical recognition certificate, the vehicle will be used for shows, private presentations and classic car rallies.

NELSON MANDELA

In the late 1980s, Mercedes-Benz South Africa was the first of the local automotive companies to formally recognize a black labour organization. The union later became the now formidable National Union of Metalworkers of South Africa (NUMSA).

When Nelson Mandela's release was announced, the story goes that the NUMSA heads sat down and tried to find a way to honour him. They decided to build a top-of-the-range Mercedes-Benz, built in their spare time for no pay. The union bosses approached the company who donated the parts, and the workers put in extra hours to put the car together quickly, over just four days. In recognition of their great Madiba the 126 was hand-built from start to finish. Workers would lift the body, from work platform to work platform. Every part placed on the car was hand-selected and labelled with 'Dr Mandela's car'.

The model was to be the 126 500 SE. The chassis was inscribed with the South African flag and Nelson Mandela's name. According to those there at the time, the attention given to this particular car was unparalleled.

Mercedes-Benz employee to this day, Philip Groom, recalls how he was asked to hand over the key to Mr Mandela. He says he was so nervous, he asked his father to help with the speech. He was, of course, to meet the newly free, struggle leader, and hand over the car in front of 30 000 people. The car sparked a friendship between Nelson Mandela and Mercedes-Benz South Africa.

In 1998, when then Daimler-Chrysler AG chairman Professor Jurgen Shrempp announced a billion-rand investment in the plant, Nelson Mandela was standing next to him. At that ceremony, a brand new S-Class was given to Mandela, and the red 126 500 SE was retired to take up a proud spot in the Mercedes-Benz collection in East London.

The car left the factory 'blemish free' – many agree that this was the best Mercedes-Benz S-Class ever built by the plant.

The Madiba car was presented to then Dr Nelson Mandela on 22 July 1990 at the Sisa Dukasha Stadium in Mdantsane, near East London. Employee Philip Groom had the honour of presenting Nelson Mandela with the keys.

After the death of Mandela on the 5 December 2013, the car was put on display at the Apartheid Museum in Johannesburg, as part of a larger exhibition on the life of Nelson Mandela. The car has been registered with a personalized number plate: 999 NRM GP – standing for Nelson Rolihlahla Mandela.

RALF WEBERS ZENDER 560 STATION WAGON

At the start of the seventies, Zender had become a reference point in the sector of automotive design. In 1974, Ford Werke AG and Volkswagen AG became Zender clients, thanks to new development technologies that permitted the production of aerodynamic parts for car bodies, made of the highest quality PUR-RIM and ABS materials.

Zender grew over the years and refined its production of accessories for automobiles, gaining a large distribution network, which, in 1977, covered more than forty countries

Front view remains unchanged.

BELOW: **Side profile showing the very tasteful lines and Zender wheels.**

worldwide and became a brand synonymous with quality and ingenuity, expressed in prototype cars, futuristic design and innovative technology.

During the 1980s, tuning and modifications became very popular with Mercedes' owners and the sky was the limit as far as cost went. Overall, they tended to be a little more subtle than some of the other known tuners.

ABOVE: **Rear/side showing how tastefully the design kept the integrity of the original 126 lines.**

From left to right: Ralf Weber, Bruno Sacco and the author, Nik Greene.

THE 1000 SEL

During the 1980s, there were many companies offering various, for the want of a better term, tuning 126 cars and it would be impossible to deal with them all. However, some may have seen a badge with 1000 SEL on a 126. These were never built by Mercedes-Benz or, more accurately, even 'rebuilt' by them, and you could not purchase one from any main dealership. They were essentially aftermarket conversions of mainly the Mercedes 500 SEL and 560 SEL S-Class of the W 126-type (1979–91).

Generally, the cars started out as factory-fresh S-Classes and were modified (mostly in Germany and the UK) by tuning and coach-building companies like Chameleon, Kugok, Robert Jankel Design, Styling-Garage/SGS, Trasco and Vantagefield. Variations on the 1000 SEL-theme were even given names like 1001 SEL (Gemballa), 1000 SGS (Styling-Garage), 5000 GFG (GFG), 5000 SEL (Gemballa) and 10000 SEL (ABC Exclusive). Modified Mercedes-Benz SEC coupés

were also given similar names but instead of 1000 SEL it was a 1000 SEC. It was even possible to purchase a badge separately from any coach-building company.

The exterior of the 1000 SEL could include many extras and options: more chrome, gold instead of chrome, paint instead of gold, new rims, bumpers, spoilers, skirts and a boomerang-antenna on the boot lid for the TV.

A 'real' 1000 SEL Mercedes has a new interior. This interior should at least have new upholstery, most likely in leather and preferably in white, cream or red. A centre console that runs through the whole car is also very important. This console was, in most cases, finished in the finest wood veneers and fitted with all kinds of compartments to store personal belongings.

A champagne cooler and a TV for the passengers must be included. High-end over-the-top HiFi-stereo by Clarion or Pioneer was no exception.

All were options. In fact the badge '1000 SEL' meant that anything was possible, as long as you paid the bill.

Exterior SGS could include gold embellishments.

An unusual four single seats.

Interiors were whatever you wanted them to be.

Styling-Garage

After Styling-Garage got into trouble with Mercedes-Benz they were officially not allowed to use the 1000 SEL name. Since it was too similar to official Mercedes-Benz nomenclature, they had to change the name from 1000 SEL to 1000 SGS. This did not change anything about the contents of the Styling-Garage 1000 SEL/1000 SGS formula. Basically anything was possible when ordering a 1000 SGS in Pinneberg/Schenefeld.

Most of the time a 500 SEL was used, but there are examples of Styling-Garage converted 1000 SGS that use a 280 SEL as base. The options were endless, as seen in the illustrations. From the official pricelist, Styling-Garage could offer you the following options:

Styling-Garage 1000 SGS exterior options (03/1985):

600-style (W 100) bonnet.
SEC-style front end (bonnet, grille and bumper).
SGS front bumper with four foglights.
SGS rear bumper.
SGS side skirts.
Chrome wheel arch covers.
Sports suspension.
Centra, BBS, Remotec or SGS rims with Pirelli P7 tires (SGS and Centra wheels were optionally painted in exterior colour if the car).
Special rear lights that fill up the space of license plate.
All original exterior chrome work painted in the car's exterior colour.

Styling-Garage 1000 SGS interior options (03/1985):

Dashboard covered in leather matching colour of interior.
Curtains for rear windows.
Burr walnut interior trim.
Burr walnut picnic tables with lighting, integrated in rear doors.
Burr walnut picnic tables, integrated in the rear of the front seats.
Small console placed in-between the front seats cooled by the air-conditioning.

During the early 1980s, Daimler still built the W 100; this may have been a homage to one.

Special burr walnut console between rear seats with minibar and small cooling compartment.
Larger burr walnut console between rear seats that contains minibar, small cooling compartment, TV and video-equipment.
Burr walnut shift knob.
Wooden sports steering wheel.
S-Class separate rear seats, electrically adjustable.
Conversion of the rear bench into separate seats.
Fridge in the trunk.
Cooling compartment for the middle console.

Alarm system.
Stereo options, Nakamichi, Clarion or Pioneer.
TV between front seats in a burr walnut console.
Make-up mirrors with lights, integrated in the front head-rests.

Usually a full-option Mercedes-Benz 500 SEL (W 126) was used as a starting point and then all the options could be added. The customer could basically order whatever he or she wanted, even options that weren't on the list, as long as bills were paid. Styling-Garage made most of the 1000 SGS conversions prior to their first bankruptcy in 1986. How many were made is unknown.

Trasco

Trasco was founded in a time that was the turning point for a lot of companies – some went bankrupt, others found new customers in Japan and left the Middle-East for what it was.

The first cars introduced by Trasco were, however, still of very Middle-Eastern taste, with bright colour schemes and flashy interiors.

According to the Trasco pricelist dated June 1986, Trasco offered two different types of conversions on the regular-length Mercedes-Benz 500 SEL: the Trasco 600 SEL 5.0 and the Trasco 1000 SEL. The Trasco 600 SEL 5.0 had similar specs as the Trasco 1000 SEL; however, it did not have TV/video, no SEC-seats in the back and lacked various other options. The difference in price was about 40,000 DM (148,000 DM for the 600 SEL 5.0, 185,000 DM for the 1000 SEL).

As elegant as the coupé is, it didn't escape from a number of 'tuners' who thought they could do better. Chris Hahn of SGS created a 'Gullwing' version. Styling-Garage strengthened the roof and also added steel beams in the door sills so the car wouldn't bend as a result of cutting away parts of the original SEC roof.

As you can imagine, this was a very costly operation and so Styling-Garage would demand 83,000 DM in 1985 for converting a standard Mercedes SEC into a Gullwing, all extras not included. Just to put into perspective: 83,000 DM was about the same as the price of a new Mercedes-Benz 500 SEC at the time. Styling-Garage is rumoured to have made fifty-seven of these cars over the years, some of them used by other tuners and coach-builders for further modification.

CLOCKWISE FROM TOP LEFT:

The blue car has been equipped with the full Trasco body kit. The wheels are Rial 16. The candy apple red car has a full body kits and Remotec wheels. It also has the 1980s-style boomerang aerial on the boot.

The interior completely in sync with the exterior: beige leather, centre console with TV and storage compartments. The dashboard is interesting in that it has a full gold-plated Clarion G80 system installed. The white leather has the same centre console with TV as the above beige with a custom Raid steering wheel. Note the interesting way the upholstery on the seats has been done.

The **SGS** Gullwing.

The Sbarro Shahin

About two years after Styling-Garage unveiled their 500 SGS Gullwing, Swiss car creator Franco Sbarro displayed a very similar car at the 1983 Geneva Car Salon. The car was named Sbarro Mercedes 500 Portes Papillon 'Gullwing' with a pricetag of 200,000 DM.

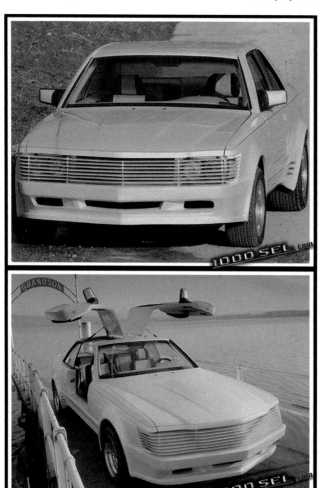

The **Sbarro Shahin Gullwing**; most ended up in the Far East due to their prohibitive price.

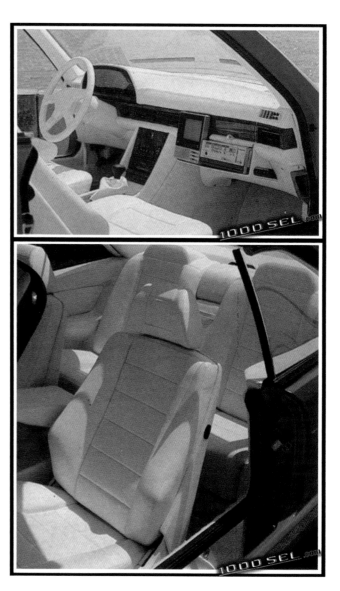

The **Sbarro Gullwing** interior.

AMG

Tuning cannot be mentioned as far as any 126 is concerned without mentioning AMG. Not only did AMG make the W 126 S-Class seriously quick with engine, exhaust and suspension modifications, but the looks of the SE and SEL were also enhanced by the German tuner.

AMG developed several body kits for the W 126, starting with the first-generation model 280 SE/500 SEL that was made until 1985.

The body kits that were made for the first generation W 126 S-Class differed quite strongly from those for the post-1985 S-Classes.

Also, there were US-versions of both first- and second-generation models and the second-generation model also had a version meant for the Japanese market only.

Generation One **AMG** body kits.

Generation two body kits, including the top one with a C 126 front bumper and bonnet.

The **AMG M 117 6.0-litre engine. The top image is complete; however, the bottom image shows more clearly the twin cam per bank covers.**

The **6.0-litre AMG engine for the Japanese market towards the end of the 126 production was known as the M 117/9, similar to that of the M 119 from the 140 S-Class.**

Carat by Duchatelet

Duchatelet was a Belgian company and they also offered some very classy modifications for the Mercedes-Benz S-Class in different stages. Each stage was given a classy name:

Carat Clarity
Carat Cullinan
Carat D'Arrow
Carat Diamond
Carat Executive

The 'Carat Clarity' was what you could call the mid-range spec upgrade for the 500 SEL/560 SEL (all other W 126 SE and SEL models could be fitted as well, but I doubt many

were done on a model other than the top-spec 500 SEL and later on the 560 SEL). It was positioned between the 'Carat Clarity' and the top-spec 'Carat Diamond'. The specifications for the 'Carat Cullinan' were as follows: first and foremost, all exterior parts of the Carat Cullinan, including bumpers, side skirts and wing mirrors, were sprayed using the 'Japan technique', which was a very exclusive finish and involved forty-eight layers of paint, thirty of which were clear varnish. The exact method of application was kept secret – even journalists visiting the Duchatelet factory weren't allowed to have a look in the spray booth.

The Carat Cullinan could be fitted with new Duchatelet-designed bumpers and side skirts. It could also be fitted with new rims, which usually were the Centra-type 31 wheels, and an electrically operated sun roof above the front seats with a special air rim in the roof that reduced wind noise.

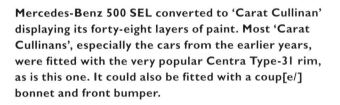

Mercedes-Benz 500 SEL converted to 'Carat Cullinan' displaying its forty-eight layers of paint. Most 'Carat Cullinans', especially the cars from the earlier years, were fitted with the very popular Centra Type-31 rim, as is this one. It could also be fitted with a coup[e/] bonnet and front bumper.

Most interesting is the configuration of the Clarion stereo. The basic components are positioned in the centre console, but an extra component, which comes from the Clarion G80 series, is placed on the right-hand side of the steering wheel. This was a common setup used for 'Carat Cullinan' and 'Diamond' interiors.

The most important modifications on most Carat by Duchatelet cars are, however, to be found on the inside and there were plenty. The finest leather was used everywhere: fifteen hides were used to cover the complete interior, including the roof liner, steering wheel, seats, all pillars, dashboard and centre console. The seats were completely redesigned for better back support. Easy to spot are the new headrests, which are much larger than the standard Mercedes-Benz items, and make it easy for anyone to recognize a Carat by Duchatelet car. As well as leather, Duchatelet also added a lot of very high-quality walnut-veneer wood. Lamb's wool carpets were placed to cover the floor of the car. A small centre console was added to function as an armrest with storage space and the dashboard was modified by Duchatelet to accommodate a small storage compartment for a car phone or other personal items. An optional TV could be placed filling the glove compartment. The obvious high-end stereo system could, of course, also be ordered from Duchatelet.

Needless to say, the Carat by Duchatelet 'Carat Cullinan' conversion was rather pricey. A 1985 pricelist shows there was a 'Standard Carat Cullinan' and a 'Luxury Carat Cullinan': the standard 70,000 DM (German pricelist) and the luxury version 100,000 DM. But prices could rise considerably when you went to the options-list: 9,000 DM for the in-dash colour TV, a video-system placed underneath the rear seats 10,500 DM and a Cartier-clock for 1,300 DM. The list of option was rather endless, so it would be no problem to convert your 500 SEL for another 200,000 DM. Remember, the prices are all without the base vehicle.

Monteverdi

Peter Monteverdi started his company near Basel in Switzerland and worked on a number of vehicles to create an exclusive market. Only three 126 versions were built.

The front end of the Tiara featured an angular design instead of the more streamlined design on the S-Class. Monteverdi installed a vertical, heavily chrome-plated front grille with four round headlights. The grille was made of chrome-plated struts. The front fenders were also modified and the hood was redesigned to be smoother and smaller than the Mercedes-Benz.

The shape of the headlights and their surrounds cited classic design elements of the Aston Martin DBS; however, some observers felt they were more reminiscent of the Alfa Romeo Alfetta of the third series. At the rear end, the line of the boot was also designed more angular. The tail-lights were the same ones used on the Peugeot 505; likely, in an attempt to create a similar appearance with those of the recently presented Rolls-Royce Silver Spirit. The bumpers were also new. Instead of the large plastic units of the base vehicle, Monteverdi used very narrow bumpers, which were bordered in chrome and reached into the car flanks.

The Monteverdi Tiara was offered in 1982 at a price of 172,000 Swiss francs. A year later, the base price was 187,000 Swiss francs, making the Tiara nearly three times as expensive as a Sierra and twice as expensive as a corresponding Mercedes-Benz S-Class.

Lotec

In 1984, a small German company, Lotec, was asked by the manager of the Tokyo bank, who wished to remain anonymous, to build the most exclusive Mercedes possible. The result was a car Lotec Ambassadeur, so far from the original that Lotterschmidt gave it his own name. In fact, from the Mercedes 560 SEL W 126 there was only a base – everything else, including the body and interiors, was developed by Lotterschmidt. He even showed this car at an auto show as an advertisement of his company – before sending it to a client in Japan.

The car was equipped with a 5.6-litre Mercedes M 117 E56 engine with turbo-chargers Garrett T3 and output 550bhp.

Into the interior were built a telephone and fax, and even a TV. The whereabouts of this vehicle is unknown but perhaps belongs to the same owner that ordered it.

With this car, the company confirmed its ability to fulfil an order of any complexity and Lotec went on to make a few more unique cars on special orders; the peak of work was 1991.

The car turned out with nods to both Jaguar and Bentley, but at the same time it carried the clear features of Japanese cars of those years – as the client wanted.

Widebody

A number of tuning companies built what have been referred to a as 'Widebody'126, when, during the 1980s, cars like Fer-rari, Lamborghini and Porsche had something similar, usually under the brief of getting more airflow to the rear placed engines and brakes.

A widebody 560 SEL created by Koenig (top image) and a Koenig Coupé (bottom image).

ABOVE: **By far one of the prettiest coupé conversions was the AMG widebody, especially beautiful in colour Bornite.**

LEFT: **Front and rear profile shows the subtle styling additional width panelling.**

INTERESTING ODDITIES

MERCEDES
CHAMELEON

ABOVE: **The Chameleon Car Company is mostly known for their very luxurious and reworked conversions on Mercedes-Benz vehicles sold mainly to Middle East clients. Versions called Mercedes 1000 SEL, Typhoon, Tornado and Cyclone with very luxurious interiors and, sometimes to the extreme, exteriors.**

ABOVE: **Two versions of the Gemballa: top image with an unusual saloon bonnet.**

RIGHT: **Someone decided to 'enhance' this Mercedes-Benz with felt-tip pens and a few extra wings and metalwork.**

Rainbow colours are a popular 'upgrade'. This artist-designed **SEC** was by K. Tiroch.

Good old Americans will make a pickup from anything.

CELEBRITY OWNERS

Keke Rosberg (top left), Ayton Senna (top right), Jody Scheckter (bottom left), Emerson Fittipaldi (bottom right).

Necmettin Erbakan, Turkish Prime Minister, loved his Mercedes so much he demanded they be worshiped.

ABOVE: **Michael Jackson.**

ABOVE RIGHT: **Nigel Mansell (top left), Andrea de Cesaris (top right), Nelson Piquet (bottom left) and James Hunt (bottom right).**

RIGHT: **Clint Eastwood.**

SPECIFICATIONS: GENERATION ONE SALOON

280 S

Model   **W 126 V 28**

Description	126.021
Pre-production	Apr 1979
Production	Dec 1979 to Nov 1985

Engine

Combustion principle	four-stroke Otto
Configuration	front, longitudinal; vertical
Engine type	M 110 V 28/110.924; from Oct 1981: 110.926
Number of cylinders/arrangement	6/in-line
Bore x stroke	86.0 x 78.8mm
Total displacement	2746cc (tax classification: 2717cc)
Compression ratio	9.0
Crankshaft bearings	7
Rated output	156bhp/115kW at 5,500rpm
Rated torque	223Nm at 4,000rpm
Number of valves/arrangement	1 intake, 1 exhaust/V-shaped overhead
Valve operation	2 overhead camshafts
Camshaft drive	double roller chain
Fuel system	1 Solex 4 A dual compound downdraught carburettor
Cooling	water cooling/pump; 12ltr water
Lubrication	pressure feed lubrication/6ltr oil
Electric system	12V
Battery	55Ah; from August 1983: 62Ah/in the engine compartment
Generator	three-phase AC/910W; from Aug 1983: 1,120W
Starter	electrical/1.5kW
Ignition	battery ignition

Fuel tank:	position/capacity	above the rear axle/90ltr
Fuel supply	diaphragm pump	

Chassis and Drivetrain

Frame design	steel unit body
Front-wheel suspension	double wishbone
Rear-wheel suspension	semi-trailing arm axle (hydro-pneumatic level control optional)
Front springs	coil springs, supplementary rubber suspension, torsion bar stabilizer
Rear springs	coil springs, supplementary rubber suspension, torsion bar stabilizer
Shock absorber front/rear	gas-pressure shock absorbers
Steering	recirculating-ball power steering
Steering ratio	14.35:1/2.75 turns lock-to-lock; from Oct 1981: 15.06:1/2.89 turns
Brake system (foot brake)	hydraulic dual-circuit brake system with vacuum booster, antilock system optional; disc brakes front (internally ventilated) and rear
Parking brake (hand brake)	mechanical (foot-operated), acting on rear wheels
Diameter of brake discs	brake discs front/rear: 278/279mm
Wheels	sheet-steel wheels (light-alloy wheels optional)
Wheel rims	6 J 14 x H 2
Tyres	195/70 HR 14 90 H
Driven wheels	rear wheels
Drivetrain	divided cardan shaft

Transmission and Drivetrain (as Standard)

Gearing	four-speed manual transmission
Shifting	central floor gear shift lever
Clutch	dry single-disc clutch

Transmission type	change-speed gear
Synchromesh gears	I–IV
Gear ratios	I. 3.98; II. 2.29; III. 1.45; IV. 1.0; R. 3.74
Final drive ratio	3.46
Maximum speed	200km/h (124mph)
Acceleration 0–100km/h	10.1sec
Comments	acceleration by shifting through 0–100km/h (two occupants)
Fuel consumption	8.9/11.1/16.9ltr; from Oct 1981: 8.9/10.9/14.5ltr
by Guideline	80/1268/EEC: figures apply to 90km/h–120km/h/urban cycle

Transmission and Drivetrain (option from Oct 1981)

Gearing	five-speed manual transmission
Shifting	central floor gear shift lever
Clutch	dry single-disc clutch
Transmission type	change-speed gear
Synchromesh gears	I–V
Gear ratios	I. 3.82; II. 2.20; III. 1.40; IV. 1.0;V. 0.81; R. 3.71
Final drive ratio	3.46
Maximum speed	200km/h (124mph)
Acceleration	0–100km/h 10.1sec
Comments	acceleration by shifting through 0–100km/h (two occupants)
Fuel consumption	8.0/9.9/14.5ltr
by Guideline	80/1268/EEC: figures apply to 90km/h–120km/h/urban cycle

Transmission and Drivetrain (Standard Auto)

Gearing	four-speed automatic transmission
Shifting	central floor gear shift lever
Clutch	dry single-disc clutch
Transmission type	planetary gear system
Gear ratios	I. 3.68; II. 2.41; III. 1.44; IV. 1.0; R. 5.14
Final drive ratio	3.46
Maximum speed	195km/h (121mph)
Acceleration	0–100km/h 11.8sec

Comments	acceleration by shifting through 0–100km/h (two occupants)
Fuel consumption	9.2/11.6/16.4ltr; from Oct 1981: 9.2/11.5/14.3ltr
by Guideline	80/1268/EEC: figures apply to 90km/h–120km/h/urban cycle

Dimensions and Weights

Wheelbase	2,930mm
Front/rear track	1,545/1,517mm
Length	4,995mm
Width	1,820mm
Height	1,430mm
Turning circle diameter	11.8m
Kerb weight	1,560kg (3,432lb)
by Guideline	DIN 70020 (ready to drive, including fuel, spare wheel and tool kit)
Gross weight	2,080kg (4,576lb)
Gross axle weight; front	1,000kg (2,200lb)
Gross axle weight; rear	1,080kg (2,376lb)
Payload	520kg (1,144lb)
Permissible trailer weight; braked	1,500kg (3,300lb)
Permissible trailer weight; unbraked	750kg (1,650lb)
Units produced	42,996
Prices	

Sept 1979:	DM 35,877.50
March1980:	DM 37,290.00
Aug 1980:	DM 37,990.60
Jly 1981:	DM 39,290.10
Sept 1981:	DM 39,437.00
Jan 1982:	DM 40,510.50
Jly 982:	DM 41,776.10
Sept 1982:	DM 42,262.00
Jly 1983:	DM 42,636.00
Aug 1983:	DM 43,890.00
Jan 1984:	DM 45,030.00
Sept 1984:	DM 46,341.00
Apr 1985:	DM 47,743.20

280 SE

Model	**W 126 E 28**
Description	126.022
Pre-production	Feb 1979
Production	Dec 1979 to Sept 1985

Engine

Combustion principle	four-stroke Otto (with manifold-injection)
Configuration	front, longitudinal; vertical
Engine type	M 110 E 28/110.987; from Oct 1981: 110.989
Number of cylinders/arrangement	6/in-line
Bore x stroke	86.0 x 78.8mm
Total displacement	2746cc (tax classification: 2717cc)
Compression ratio	9.0
Crankshaft bearings	7
Rated output	185bhp/136kW at 5,800rpm
Rated torque	240Nm at 4,500rpm
Number of valves/arrangement	1 intake, 1 exhaust/V-shaped overhead
Valve operation	2 overhead camshafts
Camshaft drive	double roller chain
Fuel system	manifold injection, mechanically controlled (Bosch K-Jetronic)
Cooling	water cooling/pump; 12ltr water
Lubrication	pressure feed lubrication/6ltr oil
Electric system	12V
Battery	55Ah; from 08.1983: 62Ah/in the engine compartment
Generator	three-phase AC/910W; from Aug 1983: 1,120W
Starter	electrical/1.5kW
Ignition	transistor ignition
Fuel tank: position/capacity	above the rear axle/90ltr
Fuel supply	electric delivery pump

Chassis and Drivetrain

Frame design	steel unit body
Front-wheel suspension	double wishbone
Rear-wheel suspension	semi-trailing arm axle (hydro-pneumatic level control optional)
Front springs	coil springs, supplementary rubber suspension, torsion bar stabilizer
Rear springs	coil springs, supplementary rubber suspension, torsion bar stabilizer
Shock absorber front/rear	gas-pressure shock absorbers
Steering	recirculating-ball power steering
Steering ratio	14.35:1/2.75 turns lock-to-lock; from Oct 1981: 15.06:1/2.89 turns
Brake system (foot brake)	hydraulic dual-circuit brake system with vacuum booster, antilock system optional; disc brakes front (internally ventilated) and rear
Parking brake (hand brake)	mechanical (foot-operated), acting on rear wheels
Diameter of brake discs	brake discs front/rear: 278/279mm
Wheels	sheet-steel wheels (light-alloy wheels optional)
Wheel rims	6 J 14 x H 2
Tyres	195/70VR 14
Driven wheels	rear wheels
Drivetrain	divided cardan shaft

Transmission and Gearing (as standard)

Gearing	four-speed manual transmission
Shifting	central floor gear shift lever
Clutch	dry single-disc clutch
Transmission type	change-speed gear
Synchromesh gears	I–IV
Gear ratios	I. 3.98; II. 2.29; III. 1.45; IV. 1.0; R. 3.74
Final drive ratio	3.46
Maximum speed	210km/h (130mph)
Acceleration	0–100km/h 10.0sec
Comments	acceleration by shifting through 0–100km/h (two occupants)
Fuel consumption	9.1/11.3/17.3ltr; from Oct 1981: 9.0/11.2/14.6ltr
by Guideline	80/1268/EEC: figures apply to 90km/h–120km/h/urban cycle

Transmission and Gearing (option from Oct 1981)

Gearing	five-speed manual transmission
Shifting	central floor gear shift lever
Clutch	dry single-disc clutch
Transmission type	change-speed gear
Synchromesh gears	I–V
Gear ratios	I. 3.82; II. 2.20; III. 1.40; IV. 1.0; V. 0.81; R. 3.71

Final drive ratio	3.46	Height	1,430mm
Maximum speed	210km/h (130mph)	Turning circle diameter	11.8m
Acceleration	0–100km/h 10.0sec	Kerb weight	1,560kg (3,432lb)
Comments	acceleration by shifting through	by Guideline	DIN 70020 (ready to drive,
	0–100km/h (two occupants)		including fuel, spare wheel and tool
Fuel consumption	8.0/10.3/14.6 l		kit)
by Guideline	80/1268/EEC: figures apply to	Gross weight	2,080kg (4,576lb)
	90km/h–120km/h/urban cycle	Gross axle weight; front	1,000kg (2,200lb)
		Gross axle weight; rear	1,080kg (2,376lb)

Transmission and Gearing (Standard Auto)

Gearing	four-speed automatic transmission	Payload	520kg (1,144lb)
Shifting	central floor gear shift lever	Permissible trailer weight;	1,500kg (3,300lb)
Clutch	dry single-disc clutch	braked	
Transmission type	planetary gear system	Permissible trailer weight;	750kg (1,650lb)
Gear ratios	I. 3.68; II. 2.41; III. 1.44; IV. 1.0; R.	unbraked	
	5.14		

General Data

Final drive ratio	3.46	Units produced	133,955
Maximum speed	205km/h (127mph)	Prices	
Acceleration	0–100km/h 10.8sec	Sept 1979:	DM 38,815.50
Comments	acceleration by shifting through	March 1980:	DM 40,341.00
	0–100km/h (two occupants)	Aug 1980:	DM 41,098.10
Fuel consumption	9.4/11.7/16.8ltr; from Oct 1981:	Jly 1981:	DM 42,510.60
	9.5/11.6/14.3ltr	Sept 1981:	DM 42,804.40
by Guideline	80/1268/EEC: figures apply to	Jan 1982:	DM 43,979.60
	90km/h–120km/h/urban cycle	Jly 1982:	DM 45,369.50
		Sept 1982:	DM 45,855.40
		Jly 1983:	DM 46,261.20
		Aug 1983:	DM 47,617.80

Dimensions and Weights

Wheelbase	2,930mm	Jan 1984:	DM 48,849.00
Front/rear track	1,545/1,517mm	Sept 1984:	DM 50,274.00
Length	4,995mm	Apr 1985:	DM 52,041.00
Width	1,820mm		

280 SEL

		Number of cylinders/	6/in-line
		arrangement	
Model	**V 126 E 28**	Bore x stroke	86.0 x 78.8mm
Description	126.023	Total displacement	2746cc (tax classification: 2717cc)
Pre-production	Dec 1979	Compression ratio	9.0
Production	June1980 to Sept 1985	Crankshaft bearings	7
		Rated output	185bhp/136kW at 5,800rpm
		Rated torque	240Nm at 4,500rpm
Engine		Number of valves/	1 intake, 1 exhaust/V-
Combustion principle	four-stroke Otto (with manifold-	arrangement	shaped overhead
	injection)	Valve operation	2 overhead camshafts
Configuration	front, longitudinal; vertical	Camshaft drive	double roller chain
Engine type	M 110 E 28/110.987; from Oct 1981:	Fuel system	manifold injection, mechanically
	110.989		controlled (Bosch K-Jetronic)

Cooling	water cooling/pump; 12ltr water
Lubrication	pressure feed lubrication/6ltr oil
Electric system	12V
Battery	55Ah; from 08.1983: 62Ah/in the engine compartment
Generator	three-phase AC/910W; from Aug 1983: 1,120W
Starter	electrical/1.5kW
Ignition	transistor ignition
Fuel tank: position/capacity	above the rear axle/90ltr
Fuel supply	electric delivery pump

Chassis and Drivetrain

Frame design	steel unit body
Front-wheel suspension	double wishbone
Rear-wheel suspension	semi-trailing arm axle (hydro-pneumatic level control optional)
Front springs	coil springs, supplementary rubber suspension, torsion bar stabilizer
Rear springs	coil springs, supplementary rubber suspension, torsion bar stabilizer
Shock absorber front/rear	gas-pressure shock absorbers
Steering	recirculating-ball power steering
Steering ratio	14.35:1/2.75 turns lock-to-lock; from Oct 1981: 15.06:1/2.89 turns
Brake system (foot brake)	hydraulic dual-circuit brake system with vacuum booster, antilock system optional; disc brakes front (internally ventilated) and rear
Parking brake (hand brake)	mechanical (foot-operated), acting on rear wheels
Diameter of brake discs	brake discs front/rear: 278/279mm
Wheels	sheet-steel wheels (light-alloy wheels optional)
Wheel rims	6 J 14 x H 2
Tyres	195/70VR 14
Driven wheels	rear wheels
Drivetrain	divided cardan shaft

Transmission and Performance (as Standard)

Gearing	four-speed manual transmission
Shifting	central floor gear shift lever
Clutch	dry single-disc clutch
Transmission type	change-speed gear
Synchromesh gears	I–IV
Gear ratios	I. 3.98; II. 2.29; III. 1.45; IV. 1.0; R. 3.74
Final drive ratio	3.46
Maximum speed	210km/h (130mph)
Acceleration	0–100km/h 10.0sec
Comments	acceleration by shifting through 0–100km/h (two occupants)
Fuel consumption	9.1/11.3/17.3ltr; from 10.1981: 9.0/11.2/14.6ltr
by Guideline	80/1268/EEC: figures apply to 90km/h–120km/h/urban cycle

Transmission and Performance (Option from Oct 1981)

Gearing	five-speed manual transmission
Shifting	central floor gear shift lever
Clutch	dry single-disc clutch
Transmission type	change-speed gear
Synchromesh gears	I–V
Gear ratios	I. 3.82; II. 2.20; III. 1.40; IV. 1.0;V. 0.81; R. 3.71
Final drive ratio	3.46
Maximum speed	210km/h (130mph)
Acceleration	0–100km/h 10.0sec
Comments	acceleration by shifting through 0–100km/h (two occupants)
Fuel consumption	8.0/10.3/14.6ltr
by Guideline	80/1268/EEC: figures apply to 90km/h–120km/h/urban cycle

Transmission and Performance (Standard Auto)

Gearing	four-speed automatic transmission
Shifting	central floor gear shift lever
Clutch	dry single-disc clutch
Transmission type	planetary gear system
Gear ratios	I. 3.68; II. 2.41; III. 1.44; IV. 1.0; R. 5.14
Final drive ratio	3.46
Maximum speed	205km/h (127mph)
Acceleration	0–100km/h 10.8sec
Comments	acceleration by shifting through 0–100km/h (two occupants)
Fuel consumption	9.4/11.7/17.1ltr; from 10.1981: 9.5/11.6/14.5ltr
by Guideline	80/1268/EEC: figures apply to 90km/h–120km/h/urban cycle

Dimensions and Weights

Wheelbase	3,070mm
Front/rear track	1,545/1,517mm
Length	5,135mm
Width	1,820mm
Height	1,434mm
Turning circle diameter	12.26m
Kerb weight	1,590kg (3,498lb)
by Guideline	DIN 70020 (ready to drive, including fuel, spare wheel and tool kit)
Gross weight	2,110kg (4,642lb)
Gross axle weight; front	1,010kg (2,222lb)
Gross axle weight; rear	1,100kg (2,420lb)
Payload	520kg (1,144lb)
Permissible trailer weight; braked	1,500kg (3,300lb)

Permissible trailer weight; unbraked   750kg (1,650lb)

General Data

Units produced	20,655
Prices	Sept 1979: DM 41,188.50
March 1980:	DM 42,804.40
Aug 1980:	DM 43,606.70
Jly 1981:	DM 45,098.30
Jan 1982:	DM 46,635.10
Jly 1982:	DM 48,081.50
Sept 1982:	DM 48,567.40
Jly 1983:	DM 48,997.20
Aug 1983:	DM 50,445.00
Jan 1984:	DM 51,756.00
Sept 1984:	DM 53,295.00
Apr 1985:	DM 55,176.00

300SD TURBO-DIESEL

Model   **W 126 D 30 A**

Description	126.120
Pre-production	Sept 1979
Production	Oct 1980 to Aug 1985
Remarks	export model for North America

Engine

Combustion principle	four-stroke diesel (with indirect injection and exhaust turbo-charger)
Configuration	front, longitudinal; vertical
Engine type	OM617 D 30 A/617.951
Number of cylinders/arrangement	5/in-line
Bore x stroke	90.9 x 92.4mm
Total displacement	2998cc
Compression ratio	21,5
Crankshaft bearings	6
Rated output	121bhp/89kW at 4,350rpm; ~from Oct 1982: 125bhp/92kW at 4,350rpm
Rated torque	230Nm at 2,400rpm; from Oct 1982: 250Nm at 2,400rpm
Number of valves/arrangement	1 intake, 1 exhaust/overhead
Valve operation	1 overhead camshaft
Camshaft drive	double roller chain
Fuel system	indirect injection, mechanically controlled; ~Bosch 5-plunger injection pump/exhaust-gas turbo-charger
Cooling	water cooling/pump; 12ltr water
Lubrication	pressure circulation lubrication/8.6ltr oil
Electric system	12V
Battery	90Ah; from 08.1983: 92Ah/in engine compartment
Generator	three-phase AC/770W; from Feb 1984: 910W
Starter	electrical/2.3kW
Ignition	compression ignition
Fuel tank:	position/capacity above the rear axle/77ltr
Fuel supply	mechanically driven delivery pump

Chassis and Drivetrain

Frame design	steel unit body
Front-wheel suspension	double wishbone
Rear-wheel suspension	semi-trailing arm axle (hydro-pneumatic level control optional)
Front springs	coil springs, supplementary rubber suspension, torsion bar stabilizer
Rear springs	coil springs, supplementary rubber suspension, torsion bar stabilizer
Shock absorber front/rear	gas-pressure shock absorbers

Steering	recirculating-ball power steering
Steering ratio	14.35:1/2.75 turns lock-to-lock; from Oct 1981: 15.06:1/2.89 turns
Brake system (foot brake)	hydraulic dual-circuit brake system with vacuum booster, antilock system optional; disc brakes front (internally ventilated) and rear
Parking brake (hand brake)	mechanical (foot-operated), acting on rear wheels
Diameter of brake discs	brake discs front/rear: 278/279mm
Wheels	sheet-steel wheels (light-alloy wheels optional)
Wheel rims	6 J 14 x H 2
Tyres	195/70 HR 14 90 H
Driven wheels	rear wheels
Drivetrain	divided cardan shaft

Transmission and Performance (as Standard)

Gearing	four-speed automatic transmission
Shifting	central floor gear shift lever
Clutch	dry single-disc clutch
Transmission type	planetary gear system
Gear ratios	I. 3.68; II. 2.41; III. 1.44; IV. 1.0; R. 5.14
Final drive ratio	3.07; from Oct 1984: 2.88
Maximum speed	175km/h (109mph)
Acceleration	0–100km/h 15.2sec

Comments	acceleration by shifting through 0–100km/h (two occupants)

Dimensions and Weights

Wheelbase	2,930mm
Front/rear track	1,545/1,517mm
Length	5,145mm
Width	1,820mm
Height	1,430mm; from Oct 1984: 1436mm
Turning circle diameter	11.9m
Kerb weight	1,695–1705kg (3,729–3,751lb), depending on model
by Guideline	DIN 70020 (ready to drive, including fuel, spare wheel and tool kit)
Gross weight	2,155–2,170kg (4,741–4,774lb), depending on model
Gross axle weight; front	1,050–1,070kg (2,310–2,354lb), depending on model
Gross axle weight; rear	1,095–1,115kg (2,409–2,453lb), depending on model
Payload	450–465kg (990–1,023lb), depending on model

General Data

Units produced	78,725
Prices	only available in North America

380 SE

Model	**W 126 E 38**
Description	126.032
Pre-production	May 1979
Production	Jan 1980 to Nov 1985

Engine

Combustion principle	four-stroke Otto (with manifold-injection)
Configuration	front, longitudinal; vertical
Engine type	M 116 E 38/116.961; from Oct 1981: 116.963
Number of cylinders/ arrangement	8/90°V; light-alloy block
Bore x stroke	92.0 x 71.8mm; from Oct 1981: 88.0 x 78.9mm
Total displacement	3818cc (tax 3776cc); from Oct 1981: 3839cc (tax 3793cc)
Compression ratio	9.0; from Oct 1981: 9.4
Crankshaft bearings	5
Rated output	218bhp/160kW at 5,500rpm; ~from Oct 1981: 204bhp/150kW at 5,250rpm
Rated torque	305Nm at 4,000rpm; from Oct 1981: 315Nm at 3,250rpm
Number of valves/ arrangement	1 intake, 1 exhaust/ overhead
Valve operation	1 overhead camshaft per cylinder bank
Camshaft drive	double roller chain
Fuel system	manifold injection, mechanically controlled (Bosch K-Jetronic)
Cooling	water cooling/pump; 12.0ltr water

Lubrication	pressure circulation lubrication/7.5ltr oil
Electric system	12V
Battery	66Ah/in the engine compartment
Generator	three-phase AC/980W; from Aug 1983: 1,120W
Starter	electrical/1.5kW
Ignition	transistor ignition
Fuel tank:	position/capacity above the rear axle/90ltr
Fuel supply	electric delivery pump

Chassis and Drivetrain

Frame design	steel unit body
Front-wheel suspension	double wishbone
Rear-wheel suspension	semi-trailing arm axle (hydro-pneumatic level control optional)
Front springs	coil springs, supplementary rubber suspension, torsion bar stabilizer
Rear springs	coil springs, supplementary rubber suspension, torsion bar stabilizer
Shock absorber front/rear	gas-pressure shock absorbers
Steering	recirculating-ball power steering
Steering ratio	14.35:1/2.75 turns lock-to-lock; from Oct 1981: 15.06:1/2.89 turns
Brake system (foot brake)	hydraulic dual-circuit brake system with vacuum booster, antilock system optional (from Dec 1984 as standard); disc brakes front (internally ventilated) and rear
Parking brake (hand brake)	mechanical (foot-operated), acting on rear wheels
Diameter of brake discs	brake discs front/rear: 278/279mm
Wheels	sheet-steel wheels (light-alloy wheels optional)
Wheel rims	6 1/2 J x 14 H 2
Tyres	205/70VR 14
Driven wheels	rear wheels
Drivetrain	divided cardan shaft

Transmission and Performance (as Standard)

Gearing	four-speed automatic transmission
Shifting	central floor gear shift lever
Clutch	dry single-disc clutch
Transmission type	planetary gear system
Gear ratios	I. 3.68; II. 2.41; III. 1.44; IV. 1.0; R. 5.14

Final drive ratio	3.27; from Oct 1981: 2.47
Maximum speed	215km/h (133mph); from Oct 1981: 210km/h (130mph)
Acceleration 0–100km/h	9.3sec; from Oct 1981: 9.8sec
Comments	acceleration by shifting through 0–100km/h (two occupants)
Fuel consumption	11.1/13.3/18.8ltr; from Oct 1981: 8.7/10.8/13.9ltr
by Guideline	80/1268/EEC: figures apply to 90km/h–120km/h/urban cycle

Dimensions and Weights

Wheelbase	2,930mm
Front/rear track	1,545/1,517mm
Length	4,995mm
Width	1,820mm
Height	1,436mm
Turning circle diameter	11.8m
Kerb weight	1,595kg (3,509lb)
by Guideline	DIN 70020 (ready to drive, including fuel, spare wheel and tool kit)
Gross weight	2,115kg (4.653lb)
Gross axle weight; front	1,020kg (2,244lb)
Gross axle weight; rear	1,095kg (2,409lb)
Payload	520kg (1,144lb)
Permissible trailer weight; braked	1,500kg (3,300lb)
Permissible trailer weight; unbraked	750kg (1,650lb)

General Data

Units produced		58,239
Prices	Sept 1979:	DM 46,669.00
	March 1980:	DM 48,510.90
	Aug 1980:	DM 49,426.20
	Jly 1981:	DM 51,121.20
	Sept 1981:	DM 51,776.60
	Jan 1982:	DM 53,200.40
	Jly 1982:	DM 54,884.10
	Sept 1982:	DM 55,370.00
	Jly 1983:	DM 55,860.00
	Aug 1983:	DM 57,513.00
	Jan 1984:	DM 59,052.00
	Sept 1984:	DM 60,762.00
	Dec 1984:	DM 63,708.90
	Apr 1985:	DM 65,949.00

380 SEL

Model	**V 126 E 38**
Description	126.033
Pre-production	Oct 1979
Production	June1980 to Sept 1985

Engine

Combustion principle	four-stroke Otto (with manifold-injection)
Configuration	front, longitudinal; vertical
Engine type	M 116 E 38/116.961; from Oct 1981: 116.963
Number of cylinders/ arrangement	8/90°V; light-alloy block
Bore x stroke	92.0 x 71.8mm; from Oct 1981: 88.0 x 78.9mm
Total displacement	3818cc (tax 3776cc); from Oct 1981: 3839cc (tax 3793cc)
Compression ratio	9.0; from Oct 1981: 9.4
Crankshaft bearings	5
Rated output	218bhp/160kW at 5,500rpm; ~from Oct 1981: 204bhp/150kW at 5,250rpm
Rated torque	305Nm at 4,000rpm; from Oct 1981: 315Nm at 3,250rpm
Number of valves/ arrangement	1 intake, 1 exhaust/ overhead
Valve operation	1 overhead camshaft per cylinder bank
Camshaft drive	double roller chain
Fuel system	manifold injection, mechanically controlled (Bosch K-Jetronic)
Cooling	water cooling/pump; 12.0ltr water
Lubrication	pressure circulation lubrication/7.5ltr oil
Electric system	12V
Battery	66Ah/in the engine compartment
Generator	three-phase AC/980W; from Aug 1983: 1,120W
Starter	electrical/1.5kW
Ignition	transistor ignition
Fuel tank: position/capacity	above the rear axle/90ltr
Fuel supply	electric delivery pump

Transmission and Performance

Gearing	four-speed automatic transmission
Shifting	central floor gear shift lever
Clutch	dry single-disc clutch
Transmission type	planetary gear system
Gear ratios	I. 3.68; II. 2.41; III. 1.44; IV. 1.0; R. 5.14
Final drive ratio	3.27; from Oct 1981: 2.47
Maximum speed	215km/h (133mph); from Oct 1981: 210km/h (130mph)
Acceleration	0–100km/h 9.3sec; from Oct 1981: 9.8sec
Comments	acceleration by shifting through 0–100km/h (two occupants)
Fuel consumption	11.1/13.3/18.9ltr; from Oct 1981: 8.7/10.8/14.2ltr
by Guideline	80/1268/EEC: figures apply to 90km/h–120km/h/urban cycle

Dimensions and Weights

Wheelbase	3,070mm
Front/rear track	1,545/1,517mm
Length	5,135mm
Width	1,820mm
Height	1,440mm
Turning circle diameter	12.26m
Kerb weight	1,615kg (3,553lb)
by Guideline	DIN 70020 (ready to drive, including fuel, spare wheel and tool kit)
Gross weight	2,135kg (4,697lb)
Gross axle weight; front	1,025kg (2,255lb)
Gross axle weight; rear	1,050kg (2,310lb)
Payload	520kg (1,144lb)
Permissible trailer weight; braked	1,500kg (3,300lb)
Permissible trailer weight; unbraked	750kg (1,650lb)

General Data

Units produced	27,014
Prices	Sept 1979: DM 49,042.00
	March 1980: DM 50,974.30
	Aug 1980: DM 51,934.80
	Jly 1981: DM 53,708.90
	Sept 1981: DM 54,364.30
	Jan 1982: DM 55,855.90
	Jly 1982: DM 57,596.10

Sept 1982: DM 58,082.00

Jly 1983: DM 58,596.00

Aug 1983: DM 60,340.20

Jan 1984: DM 61,959.00

Sept 1984: DM 63,783.00

Dec 1984: DM 66,729.90

Apr 1985: DM 69,084.00

500 SE

Model	**W 126 E 50**
Description	126.036
Pre-production	Sept 1979
Production	Jan 1980 to Sept 1985

Engine

Combustion principle	four-stroke Otto (with manifold-injection)
Configuration	front, longitudinal; vertical
Engine type	M 117 E 50/117.961; from Oct 1981: 117.963
Number of cylinders/ arrangement	8/90°V; light-alloy block
Bore x stroke	96.5 x 85.0mm
Total displacement	4973cc (tax classification: 4939cc)
Compression ratio	8.8; from Oct 1981: 9.2
Crankshaft bearings	5
Rated output	240bhp/177kW at 4,750rpm; ~from Oct 1981: 231bhp/170kW at 4,750rpm
Rated torque	404Nm at 3200rpm; from Oct 1981: 405Nm at 3000rpm
Number of valves/ arrangement	1 intake, 1 exhaust/ overhead
Valve operation	1 overhead camshaft per cylinder bank
Camshaft drive	double roller chain
Fuel system	manifold injection, mechanically controlled (Bosch K-Jetronic)
Cooling	water cooling/pump; 13ltr water
Lubrication	pressure circulation lubrication/ 7.5ltr oil
Electric system	12V
Battery	66Ah/in the engine compartment
Generator	three-phase AC/980W; from Aug 1983: 1,120W
Starter	electrical/1.5kW
Ignition	transistor ignition
Fuel tank: position/capacity	above the rear axle/90ltr

Fuel supply	electric delivery pump

Chassis and Drivetrain

Frame design	steel unit body
Front-wheel suspension	double wishbone
Rear-wheel suspension	twist-beam axle (semi-trailing arm axle with starting- and braking-torque compensation), hydro-pneumatic level control optional
Front springs	coil springs, supplementary rubber suspension, torsion bar stabilizer
Rear springs	coil springs, supplementary rubber suspension, torsion bar stabilizer
Shock absorber front/rear	gas-pressure shock absorbers
Steering	recirculating-ball power steering
Steering ratio	14.35:1/2.75 turns lock-to-lock; from Oct 1981: 15.06:1/2.89 turns
Brake system (foot brake)	hydraulic dual-circuit brake system with vacuum booster, antilock system optional (from 12.1984 as standard); disc brakes front (internally ventilated) and rear
Parking brake (hand brake)	mechanical (foot-operated), acting on rear wheels
Diameter of brake discs	brake discs front/rear: 278/279mm
Wheels	sheet-steel wheels (light-alloy wheels optional)
Wheel rims	6 1/2 J x 14 H 2
Tyres	205/70VR 14
Driven wheels	rear wheels
Drivetrain	divided cardan shaft

Transmission and Drivetrain (as Standard)

Gearing	four-speed automatic transmission
Shifting	central floor gear shift lever
Clutch	dry single-disc clutch
Transmission type	planetary gear system
Gear ratios	I. 3.68; II. 2.41; III. 1.44; IV. 1.0; R. 5.14
Final drive ratio	2.82; from Oct 1981: 2.24

Maximum speed	225km/h (140mph)	Gross axle weight; rear	1,050kg (2,310lb)
Acceleration	0–100km/h 8.1sec	Payload	520kg (1,144lb)
Comments	acceleration by shifting through	Permissible trailer weight;	1,500kg (3,300lb)
	0–100km/h (two occupants)	braked	
Fuel consumption	11.3/13.5/21.2ltr; from Oct 1981:	Permissible trailer weight;	750kg (1,650lb)
	9.1/11.4/15.2ltr	unbraked	
by Guideline	80/1268/EEC: figures apply to		
	90km/h–120km/h/urban cycle		

General Data

Units produced	a total of 33,418 (until Aug 1991)
Prices	Sept 1979: DM 50,680.50

Dimensions and Weights

Wheelbase	2,930mm		March 1980: DM 52,680.60
Front/rear track	1,545/1,517mm		Aug 1980: DM 54,127.00
Length	4,995mm		Jly 1981: DM 55,980.20
Width	1,820mm		Sept 1981: DM 56,635.60
Height	1,436mm		Jan 1982: DM 58,195.00
Turning circle diameter	11.8m		Jly 1982: DM 60,342.00
Kerb weight	1,620kg (3,564lb)		Jly 1983: DM 60,876.00
by Guideline	DIN 70020 (ready to drive, including		Aug 1983: DM 62,643.00
	fuel, spare wheel and tool kit)		Jan 1984: DM 64,296.00
Gross weight	2,140kg (4,708lb)		Sept 1984: DM 66,747.00
Gross axle weight; front	1,030kg (2,266lb)		Apr 1985: DM 72,162.00

500 SEL

		Number of valves/	1 intake, 1 exhaust/overhead
Model	**V 126 E 50**	Valve operation	1 overhead camshaft per cylinder
Description	126.037		bank
Pre-production	Sept 1979	Camshaft drive	double roller chain
Production	June1980 to Sept 1985	Fuel system	manifold injection, mechanically
			controlled (Bosch K-Jetronic)
Engine		Cooling	water cooling/pump; 13ltr water
Combustion principle	four-stroke Otto (with manifold-	Lubrication	pressure circulation
	injection)		lubrication/7.5ltr oil
Configuration	front, longitudinal; vertical	Electric system	12V
Engine type	M 117 E 50/117.961; from Oct 1981:	Battery	66Ah/in the engine compartment
	117.963	Generator	three-phase AC/980W; from Aug
Number of cylinders/	8/90°V; light-alloy block		1983: 1,120W
arrangement		Starter	electrical/1.5kW
Bore x stroke	96.5 x 85.0mm	Ignition	transistor ignition
Total displacement	4973cc (tax classification: 4939cc)	Fuel tank: position/capacity	above the rear axle/90ltr
Compression ratio	8.8; from Oct 1981: 9.2	Fuel supply	electric delivery pump
Crankshaft bearings	5		
Rated output	240bhp/177kW at 4,750rpm; ~from	**Chassis and Drivetrain**	
	Oct 1981: 231bhp/170kW at	Frame design	steel unit body
	4,750rpm	Front-wheel suspension	double-wishbone front axle with
Rated torque	404Nm at 3,200rpm; from Oct		hydro-pneumatic level control
	1981: 405Nm at 3,000rpm		system as an option

Rear-wheel suspension	twist-beam axle (semi-trailing arm axle with starting- and braking-torque compensation), hydro-pneumatic level control optional
Front springs	coil springs, supplementary rubber suspension, fully supporting hydro-pneumatic suspension optional; torsion bar stabilizer
Rear springs	coil springs, supplementary rubber suspension, fully supporting hydro-pneumatic suspension optional; torsion bar stabilizer
Shock absorber front/rear	gas-pressure shock absorbers
Steering	recirculating-ball power steering
Steering ratio	14.35:1/2.75 turns lock-to-lock; from Oct 1981: 15.06:1/2.89 turns
Brake system (foot brake)	hydraulic dual-circuit brake system with vacuum booster, antilock system optional (from Dec 1984 as standard); disc brakes front (internally ventilated) and rear
Parking brake (hand brake)	mechanical (foot-operated), acting on rear wheels
Diameter of brake discs	brake discs front/rear: 278/279mm
Wheels	sheet-steel wheels (light-alloy wheels optional)
Wheel rims	6 1/2 J x 14 H 2
Tyres	205/70VR 14
Driven wheels	rear wheels
Drivetrain	divided cardan shaft

Transmission and Performance (as Standard)

Gearing	four-speed automatic transmission
Shifting	central floor gear shift lever
Clutch	dry single-disc clutch
Transmission type	planetary gear system
Gear ratios	I. 3.68; II. 2.41; III. 1.44; IV. 1.0; R. 5.14
Final drive ratio	2.82; from Oct 1981: 2.24
Maximum speed	225km/h (140mph)
Acceleration	0–100km/h 8.1sec

Comments	acceleration by shifting through 0–100km/h (two occupants)
Fuel consumption	11.3/13.5/21.2ltr; from Oct 1981: 9.1/11.4/15.2ltr
by Guideline	80/1268/EEC: figures apply to 90km/h–120km/h/urban cycle

Dimensions and Weights

Wheelbase	3,070mm
Front/rear track	1,545/1,517mm
Length	5,135mm
Width	1,820mm
Height	1,440mm
Turning circle diameter	12.26m
Kerb weight	1,655kg (3,641lb)
by Guideline	DIN 70020 (ready to drive, including fuel, spare wheel and tool kit)
Gross weight	2,175kg (4,785lb)
Gross axle weight; front	1,015kg (2,233lb)
Gross axle weight; rear	1,135kg (2,497lb)
Payload	520kg (1,144lb)
Permissible trailer weight; braked	1,500kg (3,300lb)
Permissible trailer weight; unbraked	750kg (1,650lb)

General Data

Units produced	a total of 72,693 (until Feb 1992)
Prices	
	Sept 1979: DM 56,161.00
	March 1980: DM 58,364.50
	Aug 1980: DM 59,460.60
	Jly 1981: DM 61,505.90
	Sept 1981: DM 62,161.30
	Jan 1982: DM 63,845.00
	Jly 1982: DM 66,218.00
	Jly 1983: DM 66,804.00
	Aug 1983: DM 68,742.00
	Jan 1984: DM 70,566.00
	Apr 1985: DM 78,831.00

SPECIFICATIONS: GENERATION ONE COUPÉ

380 SEC

Model	**C 126 E 38**
Description	126.043
Pre-production	Sept 1980
Production	Oct 1981to Sept 1985

Engine

Combustion principle	four-stroke Otto (with manifold-injection)
Configuration	front, longitudinal; vertical
Engine type	M 116 E 38/116.963
Number of cylinders/arrangement	8/90°V; light-alloy block
Bore x stroke	88.0 x 78.9mm
Total displacement	3839cc (tax classification: 3793cc)
Compression ratio	9.4
Crankshaft bearings	5
Rated output	204bhp/150kW at 5,250rpm
Rated torque	315Nm at 3,250rpm
Number of valves/arrangement	1 intake, 1 exhaust/overhead
Valve operation	1 overhead camshaft per cylinder bank
Camshaft drive	double roller chain
Fuel system	manifold injection, mechanically controlled (Bosch K-Jetronic)
Cooling	water cooling/pump; 12.0ltr water
Lubrication	pressure circulation lubrication/7.5ltr oil
Electric system	12V
Battery	66Ah/in the engine compartment
Generator	three-phase AC/980W; from Aug 1983: 1,120W
Starter	electrical/1.5kW
Ignition	transistor ignition
Fuel tank: position/capacity	above the rear axle/90ltr
Fuel supply	electric delivery pump

Chassis and Drivetrain

Frame design	steel unit body
Front-wheel suspension	double wishbone
Rear-wheel suspension	semi-trailing arm axle (hydro-pneumatic level control optional)
Front springs	coil springs, supplementary rubber suspension, torsion bar stabilizer
Rear springs	coil springs, supplementary rubber suspension, torsion bar stabilizer
Shock absorber front/rear	gas-pressure shock absorbers
Steering	recirculating-ball power steering
Steering ratio	15.06:1/2.89 turns lock-to-lock
Brake system (foot brake)	hydraulic dual-circuit brake system with vacuum booster, antilock system optional (from Dec 1984 as standard); disc brakes front (internally ventilated) and rear
Parking brake (hand brake)	mechanical (foot-operated), acting on rear wheels
Diameter of brake discs	brake discs front/rear: 286/279mm
Wheels	sheet-steel wheels (light-alloy wheels optional)
Wheel rims	6 1/2 J x 14 H 2
Tyres	205/70VR 14
Driven wheels	rear wheels
Drivetrain	divided cardan shaft

Transmission and Performance

Gearing	four-speed automatic transmission
Shifting	central floor gear shift lever
Clutch	dry single-disc clutch

Transmission type	planetary gear system
Gear ratios	I. 3.68; II. 2.41; III. 1.44; IV. 1.0; R. 5.14
Final drive ratio	2.47
Maximum speed	210km/h (130mph)
Acceleration	0–100km/h 9.8sec
Comments	acceleration by shifting through 0–100km/h (two occupants)
Fuel consumption	8.7/10.8/13.9ltr
by Guideline	80/1268/EEC: figures apply to 90km/h–120km/h/urban cycle

Dimensions and Weights

Wheelbase	2,850mm
Front/rear track	1,545/1,517mm
Length	4,910mm
Width	1,828mm
Height	1,406mm
Turning circle diameter	11.53m
Kerb weight	1,585kg (3,487lb)
by Guideline	DIN 70020 (ready to drive, including fuel, spare wheel and tool kit)

Gross weight	2,105kg (4,631lb)
Gross axle weight; front	1,000kg (2,200lb)
Gross axle weight; rear	1,085kg (2,387lb)
Payload	520kg (1,144lb)
Permissible trailer weight; braked	1,500kg (3,300lb)
Permissible trailer weight; unbraked	750kg (1,650lb)

General Data

Units produced	11,267
Prices	
Sept 1981:	DM 69,495.00
Jan 1982:	DM 71,416.00
Jly 1982:	DM 74,071.50
Jly 1983:	DM 74,727.00
Aug 1983:	DM 77,292.00
Jan 1984:	DM 80,142.00
Sept 1984:	DM 83,049.00
Dec 1984:	DM 85,995.90
Apr 1985:	DM 89,034.00

500 SEC

Model

	C 126 E 50
Description	126.044
Pre-production	Jly 1980
Production	Oct 1981to Sept 1985

Engine

Combustion principle	four-stroke Otto (with manifold-injection)
Configuration	front, longitudinal; vertical
Engine type	M 117 E 50/117.963
Number of cylinders/ arrangement	8/90°V; light-alloy block
Bore x stroke	96.5 x 85.0mm
Total displacement	4973cc (tax classification: 4939cc)
Compression ratio	9.2
Crankshaft bearings	5
Rated output	231bhp/170kW at 4,750rpm
Rated torque	405Nm at 3,000rpm

Number of valves/ arrangement	1 intake, 1 exhaust/overhead
Valve operation	1 overhead camshaft per cylinder bank
Camshaft drive	double roller chain
Fuel system	manifold injection, mechanically controlled (Bosch K-Jetronic)
Cooling	water cooling/pump; 13ltr water
Lubrication	pressure circulation lubrication/7.5ltr oil
Electric system	12V
Battery	66Ah/in the engine compartment
Generator	three-phase AC/980W; from Aug 1983: 1,120W
Starter	electrical/1.5kW
Ignition	transistor ignition
Fuel tank:	position/capacity above the rear axle/90ltr
Fuel supply	electric delivery pump

Transmission and Performance

Gearing	four-speed automatic transmission
Shifting	central floor gear shift lever
Clutch	dry single-disc clutch
Transmission type	planetary gear system
Gear ratios	I. 3.68; II. 2.41; III. 1.44; IV. 1.0; R. 5.14
Final drive ratio	2.24
Maximum speed	225km/h (140mph)
Acceleration	0–100km/h 8.1sec
Comments	acceleration by shifting through 0–100km/h (two occupants)
Fuel consumption	9.1/11.4/15.2ltr
by Guideline	80/1268/EEC: figures apply to 90km/h–120km/h/urban cycle

Dimensions and Weights

Wheelbase	2,845mm
Front/rear track	1,545/1,517mm
Length	4,910mm
Width	1,828mm
Height	1,406mm
Turning circle diameter	11.53m
Kerb weight	1,610kg (3,542lb)

by Guideline	DIN 70020 (ready to drive, including fuel, spare wheel and tool kit)
Gross weight	2,130kg (4,686lb)
Gross axle weight; front	1,010kg (2,222lb)
Gross axle weight; rear	1,120kg (2,464lb)
Payload	520kg (1,144lb)
Permissible trailer weight; braked	1,500kg (3,300lb)
Permissible trailer weight; unbraked	750kg (1,650lb)

General Data

Units produced	a total of 30,184 (until Sept 1991)
Prices	
	Sept 1981: DM 73,902.00
	Jan 1982: DM 75,936.00
	Jly 1982: DM 79,043.50
	Jly 1983: DM 79,743.00
	Aug 1983: DM 82,422.00
	Jan 1984: DM 85,386.00
	Sept 1984: DM 88,464.00
	Dec 1984: DM 91,410.90
	Apr 1985: DM 94,620.00

GENERATION ONE SALES PER YEAR

Model	Type	1979	1980	1981	1982	1983	1984	1985	Total
280 S	126021	408	6,348	7,212	8,761	8,568	6,203	5,496	**42,996**
280 SE	126022	812	22,482	26,654	23,287	25,229	22,656	12,835	**133,955**
280 SEL	126023	1	887	2,423	3,843	4,302	4,598	4,601	**20,655**
380 SE	126032	217	7,935	8,603	7,429	8,147	14,618	11,290	**58,239**
380 SEL	126033	1	1,648	6,726	8,496	6,270	2,016	1,857	**27,014**
500 SE	126036	149	5,312	3,308	3,349	3,646	2,790	3,194	**21,748**
500 SEL	126037	2	2,206	5,942	8,966	12,095	14,808	17,251	**61,270**
380 SEC	126043		3	945	4,393	3,829	1,310	787	**11,267**
500 SEC	126044		1	726	4,059	6,058	6,664	5,865	**23,373**
300 SD	126120	3	4,857	16,595	18,122	20,291	12,546	6,311	**78,725**
Total by Year		**1,593**	**51,679**	**79,134**	**90,705**	**98,435**	**88,209**	**69,487**	**479,242**

SPECIFICATIONS: GENERATION TWO SALOONS

300 SDL TURBO-DIESEL

Model	**V 126 D 30 A**
Description	126.125
Production	Feb 1985 to Sept 1987
Remarks	export model for North America

Engine

Combustion principle	four-stroke diesel (with indirect injection and exhaust turbo-charger)
Configuration	front, longitudinal; vertical
Engine type	OM603 D 30 A/603.961
Number of cylinders/ arrangement	6/in-line; 15-degree inclination to the right
Bore x stroke	87.0 x 84.0mm
Total displacement	2996cc
Compression ratio	22.0
Crankshaft bearings	6
Rated output	150bhp/110kW at 4,600rpm
Rated torque	273Nm at 2,400rpm
Number of valves/ arrangement	1 intake, 1 exhaust/overhead
Valve operation	1 overhead camshaft
Camshaft drive	double roller chain
Fuel system	indirect injection, mechanically controlled; Bosch 6-plunger injection pump/exhaust-gas turbo-charger
Cooling	water cooling/pump; 12ltr water
Lubrication	pressure circulation lubrication/8.6ltr oil
Electric system	12V
Battery	92Ah/in the engine compartment
Generator	three-phase AC/980W
Starter	electrical/2.2kW
Ignition	compression ignition
Fuel tank: position/capacity	above the rear axle/90ltr
Fuel supply	mechanically driven delivery pump

Chassis and Drivetrain

Frame design	steel unit body
Front-wheel suspension	double wishbone
Rear-wheel suspension	semi-trailing arm axle (hydro-pneumatic level control optional)
Front springs	coil springs, supplementary rubber suspension, torsion bar stabilizer
Rear springs	coil springs, supplementary rubber suspension, torsion bar stabilizer
Shock absorber front/rear	gas-pressure shock absorbers
Steering	recirculating-ball power steering
Steering ratio	15.06:1/3.03 turns lock-to-lock
Brake system (foot brake)	hydraulic dual-circuit brake system with vacuum booster and antilock system; ~disc brakes front (internally ventilated) and rear
Parking brake (hand brake)	mechanical (foot-operated), acting on rear wheels
Diameter of brake discs	brake discs front/rear: 300/279mm
Wheels	light-alloy wheels
Wheel rims	7 J x 15 H 2
Tyres	205/65 R 15 93 H
Driven wheels	rear wheels
Drivetrain	divided cardan shaft

Transmission and Performance

Gearing	four-speed automatic transmission
Shifting	central floor gear shift lever
Clutch	dry single-disc clutch
Transmission type	planetary gear system

Gear ratios	I. 3.68; II. 2.41; III. 1.44; IV. 1.0; R. 5.14
Final drive ratio	2.88
Maximum speed	195km/h (121mph)

Dimensions and Weights

Wheelbase	3,070mm
Front/rear track	1,555/1,527mm
Length	5,285mm
Width	1,820mm
Height	1,441mm
Turning circle diameter	12.4m

Kerb weight	1,740kg (3,828lb)
by Guideline	DIN 70020 (ready to drive, including fuel, spare wheel and tool kit)
Gross weight	1,980kg (4,356lb)
Gross axle weight; front	1,040kg (2,288lb)
Gross axle weight; rear	1,145kg (2,519lb)
Payload	470kg (1,034lb)

General Data

Units produced	13,830
Prices	Only available in North America

350 SD TURBO-DIESEL

Model

Model	**W 126 D 35 A**
Description	126.134
Production	June 1990to Aug 1991

Engine

Combustion principle	four-stroke diesel (with indirect injection and exhaust turbo-charger; emission control device with oxidizing catalyst)
Configuration	front, longitudinal; vertical
Engine type	OM603 D 35 A/603.970
Number of cylinders/ arrangement	6/in-line; 15-degree inclination to the right
Bore x stroke	89.0 x 62.4mm
Total displacement	3449cc
Compression ratio	22.0
Crankshaft bearings	6
Rated output	136bhp/100kW at 4,000rpm
Rated torque	310Nm at 2,000rpm
Number of valves/ arrangement	1 intake, 1 exhaust/overhead
Valve operation	1 overhead camshaft
Camshaft drive	double roller chain
Fuel system	indirect injection, mechanically controlled; ~Bosch 6-plunger injection pump/exhaust-gas turbo-charger
Cooling	water cooling/pump; 12ltr water pressure circulation
Lubrication	lubrication/8.6ltr oil
Electric system	12V
Battery	92Ah/in the engine compartment
Generator	three-phase AC/1,120W
Starter	electrical/2.2kW
Ignition	compression ignition
Fuel tank: position/capacity	above the rear axle/90ltr
Fuel supply	mechanically driven delivery pump

Chassis and Drivetrain

Frame design	steel unit body
Front-wheel suspension	double wishbone
Rear-wheel suspension	semi-trailing arm axle (hydro-pneumatic level control optional)
Front springs	coil springs, supplementary rubber suspension, torsion bar stabilizer
Rear springs	coil springs, supplementary rubber suspension, torsion bar stabilizer
Shock absorber front/rear	gas-pressure shock absorbers
Steering	recirculating-ball power steering
Steering ratio	15.06:1/3.03 turns lock-to-lock
Brake system (foot brake)	hydraulic dual-circuit brake system with vacuum booster and antilock system; ~disc brakes front (internally ventilated) and rear
Parking brake (hand brake)	mechanical (foot-operated), acting on rear wheels
Diameter of brake discs	brake discs front/rear: 300/279mm
Wheels	sheet-steel wheels (light-alloy wheels optional)
Wheel rims	6 1/2 J x 15 H 2

Tyres	205/65 R 15 94 H
Driven wheels	rear wheels
Drivetrain	divided cardan shaft

Transmission and Performance

Gearing	four-speed automatic transmission
Shifting	central floor gear shift lever
Clutch	dry single-disc clutch
Transmission type	planetary gear system
Gear ratios	I. 3.87; II. 2.25; III. 1.44; IV. 1.0; R. 5.59
Final drive ratio	2.82
Maximum speed	175km/h (109mph)

Dimensions and Weights

Wheelbase	2,930mm
Front/rear track	1,562/1,534mm

Length	5,145mm
Width	1,820mm
Height	1,438mm
Turning circle diameter	11.9m
Kerb weight	1,770kg (3,894lb)
by Guideline	DIN 70020 (ready to drive, including fuel, spare wheel and tool kit)
Gross weight	2,240kg (4,928lb)
Gross axle weight; front	1,090kg (2,398lb)
Gross axle weight; rear	1,150kg (2,530lb)
Payload	470kg (1,034lb)

General Data

Units produced	2,066
Prices	Only available in North America

350 SDL TURBO-DIESEL

Model	**V 126 D 35 A**
Description	126.135
Production	June 1990 to Aug 1991

Engine

Combustion principle	four-stroke diesel (with indirect injection and exhaust turbo-charger; emission control device with oxidizing catalyst)
Configuration	front, longitudinal; vertical
Engine type	OM603 D 35 A/603.970
Number of cylinders/ arrangement	6/in-line; 15-degree inclination to the right
Bore x stroke	89.0 x 62.4mm
Total displacement	3449cc
Compression ratio	22.0
Crankshaft bearings	6
Rated output	136bhp/100kW at 4,000rpm
Rated torque	310Nm at 2,000rpm
Number of valves/ arrangement	1 intake, 1 exhaust/overhead
Valve operation	1 overhead camshaft
Camshaft drive	double roller chain
Fuel system	indirect injection, mechanically controlled; ~Bosch 6-plunger injection pump/exhaust-gas turbo-charger
Cooling	water cooling/pump; 12ltr water
Lubrication	pressure circulation lubrication/8.6ltr oil
Electric system	12V
Battery	92Ah/in the engine compartment
Generator	three-phase AC/1,120W
Starter	electrical/2.2kW
Ignition	compression ignition
Fuel tank: position/capacity	above the rear axle/90ltr
Fuel supply	mechanically driven delivery pump

Chassis and Drivetrain

Frame design	steel unit body
Front-wheel suspension	double wishbone
Rear-wheel suspension	semi-trailing arm axle (hydro-pneumatic level control optional)
Front springs	coil springs, supplementary rubber suspension, torsion bar stabilizer
Rear springs	coil springs, supplementary rubber suspension, torsion bar stabilizer
Shock absorber front/rear	gas-pressure shock absorbers
Steering	recirculating-ball power steering
Steering ratio	15.06:1/3.03 turns lock-to-lock
Brake system (foot brake)	hydraulic dual-circuit brake system with vacuum booster and

Parking brake (hand brake)	antilock system; ~disc brakes front (internally ventilated) and rear mechanical (foot-operated), acting on rear wheels
Diameter of brake discs	brake discs front/rear: 300/279mm
Wheels	sheet-steel wheels (light-alloy wheels optional)
Wheel rims	6 1/2 J x 15 H 2
Tyres	205/65 R 15 94 H
Driven wheels	rear wheels
Drivetrain	divided cardan shaft

Transmission and Drivetrain

Gearing	four-speed automatic transmission
Shifting	central floor gear shift lever
Clutch	dry single-disc clutch
Transmission type	planetary gear system
Gear ratios	I. 3.87; II. 2.25; III. 1.44; IV. 1.0; R. 5.59
Final drive ratio	2.82
Maximum speed	175km/h (109mph)

Dimensions and Weights

Wheelbase	3,070mm
Front/rear track	1,562/1,534mm
Length	5,285mm
Width	1,820mm
Height	1,441mm
Turning circle diameter	12.4m
Kerb weight	1,790kg (3,938lb)
by Guideline	DIN 70020 (ready to drive, including fuel, spare wheel and tool kit)
Gross weight	2,270kg (4,994lb)
Gross axle weight; front	1,100kg (2,420lb)
Gross axle weight; rear	1,160kg (2,552lb)
Payload	470kg (1,034lb)

General Data

Units produced	2,925
Prices	Only available in North America

260 SE

Model

	W 126 E 26
Description	126.020
Production	June 1985/Oct 1985to Feb 1991

Engine

Combustion principle	four-stroke Otto (with manifold-injection; emission control device with 3-way catalyst optional, from 09.1986 as standard)
Configuration	front, longitudinal; vertical
Engine type	M 103 E 26/103.941
Number of cylinders/ arrangement	6/in-line; 15-degree inclination to the right
Bore x stroke	82.9 x 80.25mm
Total displacement	2599cc (tax classification: 2548cc)
Compression ratio	9.2
Crankshaft bearings	7
Rated output	166bhp/122kW (with catalyst 160bhp/118kW) at 5,800rpm
Rated torque	228Nm (with catalyst 220Nm) at 4,600rpm
Number of valves/ arrangement	1 intake, 1 exhaust/V-shaped overhead
Valve operation	1 overhead camshaft
Camshaft drive	single roller chain
Fuel system	manifold injection, mechanically-electronically controlled~(Bosch KE-Jetronic)
Cooling	water cooling/pump; 8.5ltr water
Lubrication	pressure feed lubrication/6ltr oil
Electric system	12V
Battery	62Ah/in the engine compartment
Generator	three-phase AC/1,120W
Starter	electrical/1.5bhp; from 01.1988: 1.7kW
Ignition	electronic ignition system
Fuel tank: position/capacity	above the rear axle/90ltr
Fuel supply	electric delivery pump

Chassis and Drivetrain

Frame design	steel unit body
Front-wheel suspension	double wishbone
Rear-wheel suspension	semi-trailing arm axle (hydro-pneumatic level control optional)

Front springs	coil springs, supplementary rubber suspension, torsion bar stabilizer
Rear springs	coil springs, supplementary rubber suspension, torsion bar stabilizer
Shock absorber front/rear	gas-pressure shock absorbers
Steering	recirculating-ball power steering
Steering ratio	15.06:1/3.03 turns lock-to-lock
Brake system (foot brake)	hydraulic dual-circuit brake system with vacuum booster, antilock system optional (from 09.1986 as standard); disc brakes front (internally ventilated) and rear
Parking brake (hand brake)	mechanical (foot-operated), acting on rear wheels
Diameter of brake discs	brake discs front/rear: 300/279mm
Wheels	sheet-steel wheels (light-alloy wheels optional)
Wheel rims	7 J x 15 H 2
Tyres	205/65 R 15 93 H
Driven wheels	rear wheels
Drivetrain	divided cardan shaft

Transmission and Performance (Manual Transmission)

Gearing	five-speed manual transmission
Shifting	central floor gear shift lever
Clutch	dry single-disc clutch
Transmission type	change-speed gear
Synchromesh gears	I–V
Gear ratios	I. 3.86; II. 2.18; III. 1.38; IV. 1.0;V. 0.80; R. 4.22
Final drive ratio	3.46
Maximum speed	205km/h (127mph); with catalyst 200km/h (124mph)
Acceleration 0–100km/h	10.2sec (with catalyst 10.5sec)
Comments	acceleration by shifting through 0–100km/h (two occupants)
Fuel consumption	7.4/9.6/13.8ltr (with catalyst 7.7/10.1/14.3ltr)
by Guideline	80/1268/EEC: figures apply to 90km/h–120km/h/urban cycle

Transmission and Performance (Auto Transmission)

Gearing	four-speed automatic transmission
Shifting	central floor gear shift lever
Clutch	dry single-disc clutch
Transmission type	planetary gear system

Gear ratios	I. 4.25; II. 2.41; III. 1.49; IV. 1.0; R. 5.67
Final drive ratio	3.46
Maximum speed	200km/h (124mph); with catalyst 195km/h (121mph))
Acceleration 0–100km/h	10.5sec (with catalyst 10.9sec)
Comments	acceleration by shifting through 0–100km/h (two occupants)
Fuel consumption	8.8/11.0/13.3ltr (with catalyst 9.1/11.5/13.8ltr)
by Guideline	80/1268/EEC: figures apply to 90km/h–120km/h/urban cycle

Dimensions and Weights

Wheelbase	2,930mm
Front/rear track	1,555/1,527mm
Length	5,020mm
Width	1,820mm
Height	1,437mm
Turning circle diameter	11.8m
Kerb weight	1,520kg (1,144lb); from Sept 1987: 1,570kg (3,454lb)
by Guideline	DIN 70020 (ready to drive, including fuel, spare wheel and tool kit)
Gross weight	2,040kg (4,488lb); from Sept 1987: 2,090kg (4,598lb)
Gross axle weight; front	975kg (2,145lb); from Sept 1987: 990kg (2,178lb)
Gross axle weight; rear	1,065kg (2,343lb); from Sept 1987: 1,100kg (2,420lb)
Payload	520kg (1,144lb)
Permissible trailer weight; braked	1,500kg (3,300lb); from March 1989: 1,900kg (4,180lb)
Permissible trailer weight; unbraked	750kg (1,650lb)

General Data

Units produced	20,836
Prices	Sept 1985: DM 50,673.00
	Dec 1985: DM 51,585.00
	Sept 1986: DM 56,373.00
	June 1987: DM 57,969.00
	Feb 1988: DM 59,337.00
	Sept 1988: DM 61,047.00
	Feb 1989: DM 62,301.00
	Jan 1990: DM 64,068.00
	Oct 1990: DM 66,177.00

300 SE

Model	**W 126 E 30**
Description	126.024
Production	Aug 1985/Sept 1985to Oct 1991

Engine

Combustion principle	four-stroke Otto (with manifold-injection; emission control device with 3-way catalyst optional, from Sept 1986 as standard)
Configuration	front, longitudinal; vertical
Engine type	M 103 E 30/103.981
Number of cylinders/arrangement	6/in-line; 15-degree inclination to the right
Bore x stroke	88.5 x 80.25mm
Total displacement	2962cc (tax classification: 2932cc)
Compression ratio	9.2
Crankshaft bearings	7
Rated output	188bhp/138kW (with catalyst 179bhp/132kW) at 5,700rpm
Rated torque	260Nm (with catalyst 255Nm) at 4,400rpm
Number of valves/arrangement	1 intake, 1 exhaust/V-shaped overhead
Valve operation	1 overhead camshaft
Camshaft drive	single roller chain
Fuel system	manifold injection, mechanically-electronically controlled~(Bosch KE-Jetronic)
Cooling	water cooling/pump; 8.5ltr water
Lubrication	pressure feed lubrication/6ltr oil
Electric system	12V
Battery	62Ah/in the engine compartment
Generator	three-phase AC/1,120W
Starter	electrical/1.5bhp; from 01.1988: 1.7kW
Ignition	electronic ignition system
Fuel tank: position/capacity	above the rear axle/90ltr
Fuel supply	electric delivery pump

Chassis and Drivetrain

Frame design	steel unit body
Front-wheel suspension	double wishbone
Rear-wheel suspension	semi-trailing arm axle (hydro-pneumatic level control optional)
Front springs	coil springs, supplementary rubber suspension, torsion bar stabilizer
Rear springs	coil springs, supplementary rubber suspension, torsion bar stabilizer
Shock absorber front/rear	gas-pressure shock absorbers
Steering	recirculating-ball power steering
Steering ratio	15.06:1/3.03 turns lock-to-lock
Brake system (foot brake)	hydraulic dual-circuit brake system with vacuum booster, antilock system optional (from Sept 1986 as standard); disc brakes front (internally ventilated) and rear
Parking brake (hand brake)	mechanical (foot-operated), acting on rear wheels
Diameter of brake discs	brake discs front/rear: 300/279mm
Wheels	sheet-steel wheels (light-alloy wheels optional)
Wheel rims	7 J x 15 H 2
Tyres	205/65VR 15
Driven wheels	rear wheels
Drivetrain	divided cardan shaft

Transmission and Performance (Manual Transmission)

Gearing	five-speed manual transmission
Shifting	central floor gear shift lever
Clutch	dry single-disc clutch
Transmission type	change-speed gear
Synchromesh gears	I–V
Gear ratios	I. 3.86; II. 2.18; III. 1.38; IV. 1.0;V. 0.80; R. 4.22
Final drive ratio	3.46
Maximum speed	210km/h (130mph); with catalyst 205km/h (127mph)
Acceleration 0–100km/h	9.1sec (with catalyst 9.3sec)
Comments	acceleration by shifting through 0–100km/h (two occupants)
Fuel consumption by Guideline	7.6/9.7/14.1ltr (with catalyst 8.0/10.3/14.5ltr) 80/1268/EEC: figures apply to 90km/h–120km/h/urban cycle

Transmission and Performance (Auto Transmission until Sept 1988)

Gearing	four-speed automatic transmission
Shifting	central floor gear shift lever
Clutch	dry single-disc clutch
Transmission type	planetary gear system
Gear ratios	I. 3.68; II. 2.41; III. 1.44; IV. 1.0; R. 5.14

Final drive ratio	3.46		Length	5,020mm
Maximum speed	205km/h (127mph); (127mph); with catalyst 200km/h (124mph) (124mph)		Width	1,820mm
			Height	1,437mm
			Turning circle diameter	11.8m
Acceleration 0–100km/h	9.1sec (with catalyst 9.4sec)		Kerb weight	1,520kg (1,144lb); from Sept 1987: 1,570kg
Comments	acceleration by shifting through 0–100km/h (two occupants)			
			by Guideline	DIN 70020 (ready to drive, including fuel, spare wheel and tool kit)
Fuel consumption	9.1/11.2/13.5ltr (with catalyst 9.4/11.8/13.9ltr)			
			Gross weight	2,040kg (4,488lb); from Sept 1987: 2090kg (4,598lb)
by Guideline	80/1268/EEC: figures apply to 90km/h–120km/h/urban cycle			
			Gross axle weight; front	975kg (2,145lb); from Sept 1987: 990kg (2,178lb)

Transmission and Performance (Auto Transmission after Sept 1988)

			Gross axle weight; rear	1,065kg (2,343lb); from Sept 1987: 1,100kg (2,420lb)
Gearing	four-speed automatic transmission			
Shifting	central floor gear shift lever		Payload	520kg (1,144lb)
Clutch	dry single-disc clutch		Permissible trailer weight; braked	1,500kg (3,300lb); from March 1989: 1,900kg (4,180lb)
Transmission type	planetary gear system			
Gear ratios	I. 3.87; II. 2.25; III. 1.44; IV. 1.0; R. 5.59			
Final drive ratio	3.46		Permissible trailer weight; unbraked	750kg (1,650lb)
Maximum speed	205km/h (127mph); (with catalyst 200km/h (124mph)			

General Data

Acceleration 0–100km/h	9.1sec (with catalyst 9.4sec)		Units produced	105,422
Comments	acceleration by shifting through 0–100km/h (two occupants)		Prices	
				Sept 1985: DM 54,891.00
Fuel consumption	9.1/11.2/13.5ltr (with catalyst 9.4/11.8/13.9ltr)			Dec 1985: DM 55,860.00
				Sept 1986: DM 60,648.00
by Guideline	80/1268/EEC: figures apply to 90km/h–120km/h/urban cycle			June 1987: DM 62,358.00
				Feb 1988: DM 63,840.00
				Sept 1988: DM 65,550.00

Dimensions and Weights

				Feb 1989: DM 66,918.00
Wheelbase	2,930mm			Jan 1990: DM 68,856.00
Front/rear track	1,555/1,527mm			Oct 1990: DM 71,136.00

---

300 SEL

			Engine type	M 103 E 30/103.981
Model	**V 126 E 30**		Number of cylinders/ arrangement	6/in-line; 15-degree inclination to the right
Description	126.025			
Production	Aug 1985/Sept 1985 to Aug 1991		Bore x stroke	88.5 x 80.25mm
			Total displacement	2962cc (tax classification: 2932cc)
			Compression ratio	9.2
Engine			Crankshaft bearings	7
Combustion principle	four-stroke Otto (with manifold-injection; emission control device with 3-way catalyst optional, from Sept 1986 as standard)		Rated output	188bhp/138kW (with catalyst 179bhp/132kW) at 5,700rpm
			Rated torque	260Nm (with catalyst 255Nm) at 4,400rpm
Configuration	front, longitudinal; vertical		Number of valves/arrangement	1 intake, 1 exhaust/V-shaped overhead

Valve operation	I overhead camshaft
Camshaft drive	single roller chain
Fuel system	manifold injection, mechanically-electronically controlled~(Bosch KE-Jetronic)
Cooling	water cooling/pump; 8.5ltr water
Lubrication	pressure feed lubrication/6ltr oil
Electric system	12V
Battery	62Ah/in the engine compartment
Generator	three-phase AC/1,120W
Starter	electrical/1.5bhp; from 01.1988: 1.7kW
Ignition	electronic ignition system
Fuel tank: position/capacity	above the rear axle/90ltr
Fuel supply	electric delivery pump

Chassis and Drivetrain

Frame design	steel unit body
Front-wheel suspension	double wishbone
Rear-wheel suspension	semi-trailing arm axle (hydro-pneumatic level control optional)
Front springs	coil springs, supplementary rubber suspension, torsion bar stabilizer
Rear springs	coil springs, supplementary rubber suspension, torsion bar stabilizer
Shock absorber front/rear	gas-pressure shock absorbers
Steering	recirculating-ball power steering
Steering ratio	15.06:1/3.03 turns lock-to-lock
Brake system (foot brake)	hydraulic dual-circuit brake system with vacuum booster, antilock system optional (from Sept 1986 as standard); disc brakes front (internally ventilated) and rear
Parking brake (hand brake)	mechanical (foot-operated), acting on rear wheels
Diameter of brake discs	brake discs front/rear: 300/279mm
Wheels	sheet-steel wheels (light-alloy wheels optional)
Wheel rims	7 J x 15 H 2
Tyres	205/65VR 15
Driven wheels	rear wheels
Drivetrain	divided cardan shaft

Transmission and Performance (Manual Transmission)

Gearing	five-speed manual transmission
Shifting	central floor gear shift lever
Clutch	dry single-disc clutch
Transmission type	change-speed gear
Synchromesh gears	I–V
Gear ratios	I. 3.86; II. 2.18; III. 1.38; IV. 1.0;V. 0.80; R. 4.22
Final drive ratio	3.46
Maximum speed	210km/h (130mph); with catalyst 205km/h (127mph)
Acceleration 0–100km/h	9.1sec (with catalyst 9.3sec)
Comments	acceleration by shifting through 0–100km/h (two occupants)
Fuel consumption	7.6/9.7/14.1ltr (with catalyst 8.0/10.3/14.5ltr)
by Guideline	80/1268/EEC: figures apply to 90km/h–120km/h/urban cycle

Transmission and Performance (Auto Transmission until Sept 1988)

Gearing	four-speed automatic transmission
Shifting	central floor gear shift lever
Clutch	dry single-disc clutch
Transmission type	planetary gear system
Gear ratios	I. 3.68; II. 2.41; III. 1.44; IV. 1.0; R. 5.14
Final drive ratio	3.46
Maximum speed	205km/h (127mph); with catalyst 200km/h (124mph)
Acceleration 0–100km/h	9.1sec (with catalyst 9.4sec)
Comments	acceleration by shifting through 0–100km/h (two occupants)
Fuel consumption	9.1/11.2/13.5ltr (with catalyst 9.4/11.8/13.9ltr)
by Guideline	80/1268/EEC: figures apply to 90km/h–120km/h/urban cycle

Transmission and Performance (Auto Transmission after Sept 1988)

Gearing	four-speed automatic transmission
Shifting	central floor gear shift lever
Clutch	dry single-disc clutch
Transmission type	planetary gear system
Gear ratios	I. 3.87; II. 2.25; III. 1.44; IV. 1.0; R. 5.59
Final drive ratio	3.46
Maximum speed	205km/h (127mph); with catalyst 200km/h (124mph)
Acceleration 0–100km/h	9.1sec (with catalyst 9.4sec)
Comments	acceleration by shifting through

0–100km/h (two occupants)

Fuel consumption 9.1/11.2/13.5ltr (with catalyst 9.4/11.8/13.9ltr)
by Guideline 80/1268/EEC: figures apply to 90km/h–
120km/h/urban cycle

Dimensions and Weights

Wheelbase	3,070mm
Front/rear track	1,555/1,527mm
Length	5,160mm
Width	1,820mm
Height	1,441mm
Turning circle diameter	12.3m
Kerb weight	1550kg; from Sept 1987: 1,590kg (3,498lb)
by Guideline	DIN 70020 (ready to drive, including fuel, spare wheel and tool kit)
Gross weight	2,070kg (4,554lb); from Sept 1987: 2,110kg (4,642lb)
Gross axle weight; front	995kg (2,189lb); from Sept 1987: 1,010kg (2,222lb)
Gross axle weight; rear	1,075kg (2,365lb); from Sept 1987: 1,100kg (2,420lb)
Payload	520kg (1,144lb)
Permissible trailer weight; braked	1,500kg (3,300lb); from March 1989: 1,900kg (4,180lb)
Permissible trailer weight; unbraked	750kg (1,650lb)

General Data

Units produced	40,956
Prices	
	Sept 1985: DM 58,596.00
	Dec 1985: DM 59,679.00
	Sept 1986: DM 64,467.00
	June 1987: DM 66,291.00
	Feb 1988: DM 67,887.00
	Sept 1988: DM 69,426.00
	Feb 1989: DM 70,908.00
	Jan 1990: DM 72,960.00
	Oct 1990: DM 75,354.00

420 SE

Model	**W 126 E 42**
Description	126.034
Production	June 1985/Sept 1985 to Dec 1991

Engine

Combustion principle	four-stroke Otto (with manifold-injection; emission control device with 3-way catalyst optional, from Sept 1986 as standard)
Configuration	front, longitudinal; vertical
Engine type	M 116 E 42/116.965
Number of cylinders/ arrangement	8/90°V; light-alloy block
Bore x stroke	92.0 x 78.9mm
Total displacement	4196cc (tax classification: 4146cc)
Compression ratio	9.0; from Sept 1987: 10.0
Crankshaft bearings	5
Rated output	218bhp/160kW (with catalyst 204bhp/150kW) at 5,200rpm; ~from Sept 1987: 231bhp/170kW (with catalyst 224bhp/165kW) at 5,400rpm
Rated torque	330Nm at 3,750rpm (with catalyst 310Nm at 3,600rpm); ~from Sept 1987: 335Nm (with catalyst 325Nm) at 4,000rpm
Number of valves/ arrangement	1 intake, 1 exhaust/overhead
Valve operation	1 overhead camshaft per cylinder bank
Camshaft drive	double roller chain
Fuel system	manifold injection, mechanically-electronically controlled~(Bosch KE-Jetronic)
Cooling	water cooling/pump; 12.0ltr water
Lubrication	pressure circulation lubrication/8ltr oil
Electric system	12V
Battery	66Ah; from Sept 1990: 74Ah/in the engine compartment
Generator	three-phase AC/1,120W
Starter	electrical/1.5bhp; from 01.1988: 1.7kW
Ignition	electronic ignition system
Fuel tank: position/capacity	above the rear axle/90ltr
Fuel supply	electric delivery pump

Chassis and Drivetrain

Frame design	steel unit body
Front-wheel suspension	double wishbone
Rear-wheel suspension	semi-trailing arm axle (hydro-pneumatic level control optional)
Front springs	coil springs, supplementary rubber suspension, torsion bar stabilizer
Rear springs	coil springs, supplementary rubber suspension, torsion bar stabilizer
Shock absorber front/rear	gas-pressure shock absorbers
Steering	recirculating-ball power steering
Steering ratio	15.06:1/3.03 turns lock-to-lock
Brake system (foot brake)	hydraulic dual-circuit brake system with vacuum booster and antilock system; disc brakes front (internally ventilated) and rear
Parking brake (hand brake)	mechanical (foot-operated), acting on rear wheels
Diameter of brake discs	brake discs front/rear: 300/279mm
Wheels	sheet-steel wheels (light-alloy wheels optional)
Wheel rims	7 J x 15 H 2
Tyres	205/65VR 15
Driven wheels	rear wheels
Drivetrain	divided cardan shaft

Transmission and Performance (as standard until Sept 1988)

Gearing	four-speed automatic transmission
Shifting	central floor gear shift lever
Clutch	dry single-disc clutch
Transmission type	planetary gear system
Gear ratios	I. 3.68; II. 2.41; III. 1.44; IV. 1.0; R. 5.14
Final drive ratio	2.47
Maximum speed	218km/h (135mph); with catalyst 210km/h (130mph); ~from Sept 1987: 222km/h (138mph); with catalyst 220km/h (136mph)
Acceleration 0–100km/h	8.3sec (with catalyst 8.7sec); from Sept 1987: 8.2sec (with catalyst 8.3sec)
Comments	acceleration by shifting through 0–100km/h (two occupants)
Fuel consumption	8.9/11.0/14.6ltr (with catalyst 9.3/11.6/14.9 l); ~from Sept 1987: 8.7/10.7/15.1ltr (with catalyst 9.1/11.3/15.4ltr)
by Guideline	80/1268/EEC: figures apply to 90km/h–120km/h/urban cycle

Transmission and Performance (as Standard after Sept 1988)

Gearing	four-speed automatic transmission
Shifting	central floor gear shift lever
Clutch	dry single-disc clutch
Transmission type	planetary gear system
Gear ratios	I. 3.87; II. 2.25; III. 1.44; IV. 1.0; R. 5.59
Final drive ratio	2.47
Maximum speed	222km/h (138mph); with catalyst 220km/h (136mph)
Acceleration 0–100km/h	8.2sec (with catalyst 8.3sec)
Comments	acceleration by shifting through 0–100km/h (two occupants)
Fuel consumption	8.7/10.7/15.1ltr (with catalyst 9.1/11.3/15.4ltr)
by Guideline	80/1268/EEC: figures apply to 90km/h–120km/h/urban cycle

Dimensions and Weights

Wheelbase	2,930mm
Front/rear track	1,555/1,527mm
Length	5,020mm
Width	1,820mm
Height	1,437mm
Turning circle diameter	11.8m
Kerb weight	1,600kg (3,520lb); from Sept 1987: 1,640kg (3,608lb
by Guideline	DIN 70020 (ready to drive, including fuel, spare wheel and tool kit)
Gross weight	2,120kg (4,664lb); from Sept 1987: 2,160kg (4,752lb)
Gross axle weight; front	1,030kg (2,266lb); from Sept 1987: 1,015kg (2,233lb)
Gross axle weight; rear	1,090kg (2,398lb); from Sept 1987: 1,120kg (2,464lb)
Payload	520kg (1,144lb)
Permissible trailer weight; braked	1,500kg (3,300lb); from March 1989: 1,900kg (4,180lb)
Permissible trailer weight; unbraked	750kg (1,650lb)

General Data

Units produced	13,996

Prices

Sept 1985: DM 70,623.00	Dec 1988: DM 78,318.00
Dec 1985: DM 71,877.00	Sept 1988: DM 80,028.00
Sept 1986: DM 74,385.00	Feb 1989: DM 81,681.00
June 1987: DM 76,494.00	Jan 1990: DM 84,075.00
	Oct 1990: DM 86,868.00

420 SEL

Model	**V 126 E 42**
Description	126.035
Production	June 1985/Oct 1985 to Oct 1991

Engine

Combustion principle	four-stroke Otto (with manifold-injection; emission control device with 3-way catalyst optional, from Sept 1986 as standard)
Configuration	front, longitudinal; vertical
Engine type	M 116 E 42/116.965
Number of cylinders/arrangement	8/90°V; light-alloy block
Bore x stroke	92.0 x 78.9mm
Total displacement	4196cc (tax classification: 4146cc)
Compression ratio	9.0; from Sept 1987: 10.0
Crankshaft bearings	5
Rated output	218bhp/160kW (with catalyst 204bhp/150kW) at 5,200rpm; ~from Sept 1987: 231bhp/170kW (with catalyst 224bhp/165kW) at 5,400rpm
Rated torque	330Nm at 3,750rpm (with catalyst 310Nm at 3,600rpm); ~from Sept 1987: 335Nm (with catalyst 325Nm) at 4,000rpm
Number of valves/arrangement	1 intake, 1 exhaust/overhead
Valve operation	1 overhead camshaft per cylinder bank
Camshaft drive	double roller chain
Fuel system	manifold injection, mechanically-electronically controlled~(Bosch KE-Jetronic)
Cooling	water cooling/pump; 12.0ltr water
Lubrication	pressure circulation lubrication/8ltr oil

Electric system	12V
Battery	66Ah; from Sept 1990: 74Ah/in the engine compartment
Generator	three-phase AC/1,120W
Starter	electrical/1.5bhp; from 01.1988: 1.7kW
Ignition	electronic ignition system
Fuel tank: position/capacity	above the rear axle/90ltr
Fuel supply	electric delivery pump

Chassis and Drivetrain

Frame design	steel unit body
Front-wheel suspension	double-wishbone front axle with hydro-pneumatic level control system as an option
Rear-wheel suspension	semi-trailing arm axle (hydro-pneumatic level control optional)
Front springs	coil springs, supplementary rubber suspension, fully supporting hydro-pneumatic suspension optional; torsion bar stabilizer
Rear springs	coil springs, supplementary rubber suspension, fully supporting hydro-pneumatic suspension optional; torsion bar stabilizer
Shock absorber front/rear	gas-pressure shock absorbers
Steering	recirculating-ball power steering
Steering ratio	15.06:1/3.03 turns lock-to-lock
Brake system (foot brake)	hydraulic dual-circuit brake system with vacuum booster and antilock system; ~disc brakes front (internally ventilated) and rear
Parking brake (hand brake)	mechanical (foot-operated), acting on rear wheels
Diameter of brake discs	brake discs front/rear: 300/279mm
Wheels	sheet-steel wheels (light-alloy wheels optional)
Wheel rims	7 J x 15 H 2
Tyres	205/65VR 15
Driven wheels	rear wheels
Drivetrain	divided cardan shaft

Transmission and Performance (as Standard until Sept 1988)

Gearing	four-speed automatic transmission
Shifting	central floor gear shift lever
Clutch	dry single-disc clutch
Transmission type	planetary gear system
Gear ratios	I. 3.68; II. 2.41; III. 1.44; IV. 1.0; R. 5.14
Final drive ratio	2.47
Maximum speed	218km/h (135mph); with catalyst 210km/h (130mph); ~from Sept 1987: 222km/h (138mph); with catalyst 220km/h (136mph)
Acceleration 0–100km/h	8.3sec (with catalyst 8.7sec); from Sept 1987: 8.2sec (with catalyst 8.3sec)
Comments	acceleration by shifting through 0–100km/h (two occupants)
Fuel consumption	8.9/11.0/14.9ltr (with catalyst 9.3/11.6/15.2 l); ~from Sept 1987: 8.7/10.7/15.1ltr (with catalyst 9.1/11.3/15.4 l)
by Guideline	80/1268/EEC: figures apply to 90km/h–120km/h/urban cycle

Transmission and Performance (as Standard after Sept 1988)

Gearing	four-speed automatic transmission
Shifting	central floor gear shift lever
Clutch	dry single-disc clutch
Transmission type	planetary gear system
Gear ratios	I. 3.87; II. 2.25; III. 1.44; IV. 1.0; R. 5.59
Final drive ratio	2.47
Maximum speed	222km/h (138mph); with catalyst 220km/h (136mph)
Acceleration 0–100km/h	8.2sec (with catalyst 8.3sec)
Comments	acceleration by shifting through 0–100km/h (two occupants)
Fuel consumption	8.7/10.7/15.1ltr (with catalyst 9.1/11.3/15.4ltr)

by Guideline	80/1268/EEC: figures apply to 90km/h–120km/h/urban cycle

Dimensions and Weights

Wheelbase	3,070mm
Front/rear track	1,555/1,527mm
Length	5,160mm
Width	1,820mm
Height	1,441mm
Turning circle diameter	12.3m
Kerb weight	1,630kg (3,586lb); from Sept 1987: 1,660kg (3,652lb)
by Guideline	DIN 70020 (ready to drive, including fuel, spare wheel and tool kit)
Gross weight	2,150kg (4,730lb); from Sept 1987: 2,180kg (4,796lb)
Gross axle weight; front	1,050kg (2,310lb); from Sept 1987: 1,060kg (2,332lb)
Gross axle weight; rear	1,100kg (2,420lb); from Sept 1987: 1,120kg (2,464lb)
Payload	520kg (1,144lb)
Permissible trailer weight; braked	1,500kg (3,300lb); from March 1989: 1,900kg (4,180lb)
Permissible trailer weight; unbraked	750kg (1,650lb)

General Data

Units produced	74,017
Prices	
	Sept 1985: DM 74,328.00
	Dec 1985: DM 75,696.00
	Sept 1986: DM 78,204.00
	June 1987: DM 80,427.00
	Feb 1988: DM 82,365.30
	Sept 1988: DM 83,904.00
	Feb 1989: DM 85,671.00
	Jan 1990: DM 88,179.00
	Oct 1990: DM 91,086.00

500 SE

Model	**W 126 E 50**
Description	126.036
Production	Sept 1985 to Aug 1991

Engine

Combustion principle	four-stroke Otto (with manifold-injection; emission control device with 3-way catalyst optional, from Sept 1986 as standard)
Configuration	front, longitudinal; vertical

Engine type	M 117 E 50/117.965
Number of cylinders/ arrangement	8/90°V; light-alloy block
Bore x stroke	96.5 x 85.0mm
Total displacement	4973cc (tax classification: 4939cc)
Compression ratio	9.0; from Sept 1987: 10.0
Crankshaft bearings	5
Rated output	245bhp/180kW at 4,750rpm (with catalyst 223bhp/164kW at 4,700rpm); from Sept 1987: 265bhp/195kW (with catalyst 252bhp/185kW) at 5,200rpm
Rated torque	400Nm at 3,750rpm (with catalyst 365Nm at 2,500rpm); from ~Sept 1987: 405Nm at 4,000rpm (with catalyst 390Nm at 3,750rpm)
Number of valves/ arrangement	1 intake, 1 exhaust/overhead
Valve operation	1 overhead camshaft per cylinder bank
Camshaft drive	double roller chain
Fuel system	manifold injection, mechanically-electronically controlled~(Bosch KE-Jetronic)
Cooling	water cooling/pump; 13ltr water
Lubrication	pressure circulation lubrication/ 8ltr oil
Electric system	12V
Battery	66Ah; from Sept 1990: 74Ah/in the engine compartment
Generator	three-phase AC/1,120W
Starter	electrical/1.5bhp; from Jan 1988: 1.7kW
Ignition	electronic ignition system
Fuel tank: position/capacity	above the rear axle/90ltr
Fuel supply	electric delivery pump

Chassis and Drivetrain

Frame design	steel unit body
Front-wheel suspension	double wishbone
Rear-wheel suspension	twist-beam axle (semi-trailing arm axle with starting- and braking-torque compensation), hydro-pneumatic level control optional
Front springs	coil springs, supplementary rubber suspension, torsion bar stabilizer
Rear springs	coil springs, supplementary rubber suspension, torsion bar stabilizer
Shock absorber front/rear	gas-pressure shock absorbers
Steering	recirculating-ball power steering
Steering ratio	15.06:1/3.03 turns lock-to-lock
Brake system (foot brake)	hydraulic dual-circuit brake system with vacuum booster and antilock system; disc brakes front (internally ventilated) and rear
Parking brake (hand brake)	mechanical (foot-operated), acting on rear wheels
Diameter of brake discs	brake discs front/rear: 300/279mm
Wheels	sheet-steel wheels (light-alloy wheels optional)
Wheel rims	7 J x 15 H 2
Tyres	205/65VR 15
Driven wheels	rear wheels
Drivetrain	divided cardan shaft

Transmission and Performance (as Standard until Sept 1988)

Gearing	four-speed automatic transmission
Shifting	central floor gear shift lever
Clutch	dry single-disc clutch
Transmission type	planetary gear system
Gear ratios	I. 3.68; II. 2.41; III. 1.44; IV. 1.0; R. 5.14
Final drive ratio	2.24
Maximum speed	230km/h (143mph); with catalyst 220km/h (136mph); ~from Sept 1987: 235km/h 146mph); with catalyst 230km/h (143mph)
Acceleration 0–100km/h	7.3sec (with catalyst 8.0sec); from 09.87: 7.2sec (with catalyst 7.5sec)
Comments	acceleration by shifting through 0–100km/h (two occupants)
Fuel consumption	9.1/11.4/15.4ltr (with catalyst 9.6/12.0/15.9ltr); ~from Sept 1987: 8.8/11.1/15.8ltr (with catalyst 9.4/11.7/16.2ltr)
by Guideline	80/1268/EEC: figures apply to 90km/h–120km/h/urban cycle

Transmission and Performance (as Standard after Sept 1988)

Gearing	four-speed automatic transmission
Shifting	central floor gear shift lever
Clutch	dry single-disc clutch
Transmission type	planetary gear system

Gear ratios	I. 3.87; II. 2.25; III. 1.44; IV. 1.0; R. 5.59	Gross weight	2,140kg (4,708lb); from Sept 1987: 2,190kg (4,818lb)
Final drive ratio	2.24		
Maximum speed	235km/h (146mph); with catalyst 230km/h (143mph)	Gross axle weight; front	1,040kg (2,288lb); from Sept 1987: 1,050kg (2,310lb)
Acceleration 0–100km/h	7.2sec (with catalyst 7.5sec)	Gross axle weight; rear	1,100kg (2,420lb); from Sept 1987: 1,140kg (2,420lb)
Comments	acceleration by shifting through 0–100km/h (two occupants)	Payload	520kg (1,144lb)
Fuel consumption	8.8/11.1/15.8ltr (with catalyst 9.4/11.7/16.2ltr)	Permissible trailer weight; braked	1,500kg (3,300lb); from March 1989: 1,900kg (4,180lb)
by Guideline	80/1268/EEC: figures apply to 90km/h–120km/h/urban cycle	Permissible trailer weight; unbraked	750kg (1,650lb)

Dimensions and Weights

Wheelbase	2,930mm
Front/rear track	1,555/1,527mm
Length	5,020mm
Width	1,820mm
Height	1,437mm
Turning circle diameter	11.8m
Kerb weight	1,620kg (3,564lb); from Sept 1987: 1,670kg (3,674lb)
by Guideline	DIN 70020 (ready to drive, including fuel, spare wheel and tool kit)

General Data

Units produced	a total of 33,418 (from Sept 1979)
Prices	
	Sept 1985: DM 76,437.00
	Dec 1985: DM 77,805.00
	Sept 1986: DM 80,199.00
	June 1987: DM 82,536.00
	Feb 1988: DM 84,531.00
	Sept 1988: DM 86,241.00
	Feb 1989: DM 88,065.00
	Jan 1990: DM 90,687.00
	Oct 1990: DM 93,708.00

---

500 SEL

Model

Model	**V 126 E 50**
Description	126.037
Production	Sept 1985 to Feb 1992

Engine

Combustion principle	four-stroke Otto (with manifold-injection; emission control device with 3-way catalyst optional, from Sept 1986 as standard)
Configuration	front, longitudinal; vertical
Engine type	M 117 E 50/117.965
Number of cylinders/ arrangement	8/90°V; light-alloy block
Bore x stroke	96.5 x 85.0mm
Total displacement	4973cc (tax classification: 4939cc)
Compression ratio	9.0; from Sept 1987: 10.0
Crankshaft bearings	5
Rated output	245bhp/180kW at 4,750rpm (with catalyst 223bhp/164kW at 4,700rpm); from Sept 1987: 265bhp/195kW (with catalyst 252bhp/185kW) at 5,200rpm
Rated torque	400Nm at 3,750rpm (with catalyst 365Nm at 2,500rpm); from ~Sept 1987: 405Nm at 4,000rpm (with catalyst 390Nm at 3,750rpm)
Number of valves/ arrangement	1 intake, 1 exhaust/overhead
Valve operation	1 overhead camshaft per cylinder bank
Camshaft drive	double roller chain
Fuel system	manifold injection, mechanically-electronically controlled~(Bosch KE-Jetronic)
Cooling	water cooling/pump; 13ltr water
Lubrication	pressure circulation lubrication/ 8ltr oil
Electric system	12V

Battery	66Ah; from Sept 1990: 74Ah/in the engine compartment
Generator	three-phase AC/1,120W
Starter	electrical/1.5bhp; from Jan 1988: 1.7kW
Ignition	electronic ignition system
Fuel tank: position/capacity	above the rear axle/90ltr
Fuel supply	electric delivery pump

Transmission and Performance (as Standard until Sept 1988)

Gearing	four-speed automatic transmission
Shifting	central floor gear shift lever
Clutch	dry single-disc clutch
Transmission type	planetary gear system
Gear ratios	I. 3.68; II. 2.41; III. 1.44; IV. 1.0; R. 5.14
Final drive ratio	2.24
Maximum speed	230km/h (143mph); with catalyst 220km/h (136mph); ~from Sept 1987: 235km/h (146mph); with catalyst 230km/h (143mph)
Acceleration 0–100km/h	7.3sec (with catalyst 8.0sec); from Sept 1987: 7.2sec (with catalyst 7.5sec)
Comments	acceleration by shifting through 0–100km/h (two occupants)
Fuel consumption	9.1/11.4/15.4ltr (with catalyst 9.6/12.0/15.9ltr); ~from Sept 1987: 8.8/11.1/15.8ltr (with catalyst 9.4/11.7/16.2ltr)
by Guideline	80/1268/EEC: figures apply to 90km/h–120km/h/urban cycle

Transmission and Performance (as Standard after Sept 1988)

Gearing	four-speed automatic transmission
Shifting	central floor gear shift lever
Clutch	dry single-disc clutch
Transmission type	planetary gear system
Gear ratios	I. 3.87; II. 2.25; III. 1.44; IV. 1.0; R. 5.59
Final drive ratio	2.24
Maximum speed	235km/h (136mph); with catalyst 230km/h (143mph)
Acceleration 0–100km/h	7.2sec (with catalyst 7.5sec)
Comments	acceleration by shifting through 0–100km/h (two occupants)
Fuel consumption	8.8/11.1/15.8ltr (with catalyst 9.4/11.7/16.2ltr)
by Guideline	80/1268/EEC: figures apply to 90km/h–120km/h/urban cycle

Dimensions and Weights

Wheelbase	3,070mm
Front/rear track	1,555/1,527mm
Length	5,160mm
Width	1,820mm
Height	1,441mm
Turning circle diameter	12.3m
Kerb weight	1,670kg (3,674lb); from Sept 1987: 1,690kg (3,718lb)
by Guideline	DIN 70020 (ready to drive, including fuel, spare wheel and tool kit)
Gross weight	2,190kg (4,818lb); from Sept 1987: 1,980kg (4,356lb)
Gross axle weight; front	1,070kg (2,354lb); from Sept 1987: 1,060kg (2,332lb)
Gross axle weight; rear	1,120kg (2,464lb); from Sept 1987: 1,150kg (2,530lb)
Payload	520kg (1,144lb)
Permissible trailer weight; braked	1,500kg (3,300lb); from March 1989: 1,900kg (4,180lb)
Permissible trailer weight; unbraked	750kg (1,650lb)

General Data

Units produced	a total of 72,693 (from Sept 1979)
Prices	
	Sept 1985: DM 83,904.00
	Dec 1985: DM 85,443.00
	Sept 1986: DM 87,837.00
	June 1987: DM 90,345.00
	Feb 1988: DM 92,511.00
	Sept 1988: DM 93,195.00
	Feb 1989: DM 95,133.00
	Jan 1990: DM 97,869.00
	Oct 1990: DM 101,118.00

560 SE

Model	**W 126 E 56**
Description	126.038
Production	Apr 1988 to Jan 1991

Engine

Combustion principle	four-stroke Otto (with manifold-injection; emission control device with 3-way catalyst optional, from Sept 1986 as standard)
Configuration	front, longitudinal; vertical
Engine type	M 117 E 56/117.968
Number of cylinders /arrangement	8/90°V; light-alloy block
Bore x stroke	96.5 x 94.8mm
Total displacement	5547cc (tax classification: 5491cc)
Compression ratio	9.0; from Sept 1987: 10.0
Crankshaft bearings	5
Rated output	300bhp/220kW at 5,000rpm (with catalyst 279bhp/205kW at 5,200rpm)
Rated torque	455Nm (with catalyst 430Nm) at 3,750rpm
Number of valves/ arrangement	1 intake, 1 exhaust/overhead
Valve operation	1 overhead camshaft per cylinder bank
Camshaft drive	double roller chain
Fuel system	manifold injection, mechanically-electronically controlled~(Bosch KE-Jetronic)
Cooling	water cooling/pump; 13ltr water
Lubrication	pressure circulation lubrication/ 8ltr oil
Electric system	12V
Battery	92Ah/in the engine compartment
Generator	three-phase AC/1,120W
Starter	electrical/1.5bhp; from 01.1988: 1.7kW
Ignition	electronic ignition system
Fuel tank: position/capacity	above the rear axle/90ltr
Fuel supply	electric delivery pump

Chassis and Drivetrain

Frame design	steel unit body
Front-wheel suspension	double wishbone
Rear-wheel suspension	twist-beam axle (semi-trailing arm axle with starting- and braking-torque compensation) with hydro-pneumatic level control
Front springs	coil springs, supplementary rubber suspension, torsion bar stabilizer
Rear springs	coil springs, supplementary rubber suspension, torsion bar stabilizer
Shock absorber front/rear	gas-pressure shock absorbers
Steering	recirculating-ball power steering
Steering ratio	15.06:1/3.03 turns lock-to-lock
Brake system (foot brake)	hydraulic dual-circuit brake system with vacuum booster and antilock system; disc brakes front (internally ventilated) and rear
Parking brake (hand brake)	mechanical (foot-operated), acting on rear wheels
Diameter of brake discs	brake discs front/rear: 300/279mm
Wheels	light-alloy wheels
Wheel rims	7 J x 15 H 2
Tyres	215/65VR 15, from 1988: 215/65 ZR 15
Driven wheels	rear wheels
Drivetrain	divided cardan shaft

Transmission and Performance

Gearing	four-speed automatic transmission
Shifting	central floor gear shift lever
Clutch	dry single-disc clutch
Transmission type	planetary gear system
Gear ratios	I. 3.87; II. 2.25; III. 1.44; IV. 1.0; R. 5.59
Final drive ratio	2.65
Maximum speed	250km/h (155mph); with catalyst 240km/h (149mph)
Acceleration 0–100km/h	6.8sec (with catalyst 7.2sec)
Comments	acceleration by shifting through 0–100km/h (two occupants)
Fuel consumption	10.5/12.7/16.8ltr (with catalyst 11.1/13.6/17.6ltr)
by Guideline	80/1268/EEC: figures apply to 90km/h–120km/h/urban cycle

Dimensions and Weights

Wheelbase	2,930mm
Front/rear track	1,555/1,527mm
Length	5,020mm
Width	1,820mm
Height	1,437mm; from Nov 1988: 1,443mm
Turning circle diameter	11.8m
Kerb weight	1,800kg (3,960lb)
by Guideline	DIN 70020 (ready to drive, including fuel, spare wheel and tool kit)
Gross weight	2,260kg (4,972lb)
Gross axle weight; front	1,090kg (2,398lb)
Gross axle weight; rear	1,170kg (2,574lb)

Payload	460kg (1,012lb)
Permissible trailer weight; braked	1,500kg (3,300lb); from March 1989: 1,900kg (4,180lb)
Permissible trailer weight; unbraked	750kg (1,650lb)

General Data

Units produced	1,252
Prices	
	Sept 1988: DM 125,400.00
	Feb 1989: DM 128,022.00
	Jan 1990: DM 131,727.00
	Oct 1990: DM 136,059.00

560 SEL

Model

	V 126 E 56
Description	126.039
Production	Sept 1985/Oct 1985 to Apr 1992

Engine

Combustion principle	four-stroke Otto (with manifold-injection; emission control device with 3-way catalyst optional, from Sept 1986 as standard)
Configuration	front, longitudinal; vertical
Engine type	M 117 E 56/117.968
Number of cylinders/arrangement	8/90°V; light-alloy block
Bore x stroke	96.5 x 94.8mm
Total displacement	5547cc (tax classification: 5491cc)
Compression ratio	9.0; from Sept 1987: 10.0
Crankshaft bearings	5
Rated output	272bhp/200kW at 5,000rpm (with catalyst 242bhp/178kW at 4,800rpm); from Sept 1987: 300bhp/220kW at 5,000rpm (with catalyst 279bhp/205kW at 5,200rpm)
Rated torque	430Nm at 3,750rpm (with catalyst 390Nm at 3,500rpm); from ~Sept 1987: 455Nm (with catalyst 430Nm) at 3750rpm
Number of valves/arrangement	1 intake, 1 exhaust/overhead
Valve operation	1 overhead camshaft per cylinder bank
Camshaft drive	double roller chain
Fuel system	manifold injection, mechanically-electronically controlled~(Bosch KE-Jetronic)
Cooling	water cooling/pump; 13ltr water
Lubrication	pressure circulation lubrication/8ltr oil
Electric system	12V
Battery	92Ah/in the engine compartment
Generator	three-phase AC/1,120W
Starter	electrical/1.5bhp; from 01.1988: 1.7kW
Ignition	electronic ignition system
Fuel tank: position/capacity	above the rear axle/90ltr
Fuel supply	electric delivery pump

Chassis and Drivetrain

Frame design	steel unit body
Front-wheel suspension	double-wishbone front axle with hydro-pneumatic level control system as an option
Rear-wheel suspension	twist-beam axle (semi-trailing arm axle with starting- and braking-torque compensation) with hydro-pneumatic level control
Front springs	coil springs, supplementary rubber suspension, fully supporting hydro-pneumatic suspension optional; torsion bar stabilizer

Rear springs	coil springs, hydro-pneumatic spring struts, torsion bar stabilizer
Shock absorber front/rear	gas-pressure shock absorbers
Steering	recirculating-ball power steering
Steering ratio	15.06:1/3.03 turns lock-to-lock
Brake system (foot brake)	hydraulic dual-circuit brake system with vacuum booster and antilock system; disc brakes front (internally ventilated) and rear
Parking brake (hand brake)	mechanical (foot-operated), acting on rear wheels
Diameter of brake discs	brake discs front/rear: 300/279mm
Wheels	light-alloy wheels
Wheel rims	7 J x 15 H 2
Tyres	215/65VR 15, from 1988: 215/65 ZR 15
Driven wheels	rear wheels
Drivetrain	divided cardan shaft

Transmission and Performance

Gearing	four-speed automatic transmission
Shifting	central floor gear shift lever
Clutch	dry single-disc clutch
Transmission type	planetary gear system
Gear ratios	I. 3.87; II. 2.25; III. 1.44; IV. 1.0; R. 5.59
Final drive ratio	2.65
Maximum speed	238km/h (148mph); with catalyst 228km/h (141mph); ~from Sept 1987: 250km/h (155mph); with catalyst 240km/h (149mph)
Acceleration 0–100km/h	6.9sec (with catalyst 7.6sec); from Sept 1987: 6.8sec (with catalyst 7.2sec)
Comments	acceleration by shifting through 0–100km/h (two occupants)
Fuel consumption	10.6/12.9/17.1ltr (with catalyst 11.4/13.9/18.0ltr); from Sept 1987: 10.5/12.7/16.8ltr (with catalyst 11.1/13.6/17.6ltr)
by Guideline	80/1268/EEC: figures apply to 90km/h–120km/h/urban cycle

Dimensions and Weights

Wheelbase	3,070mm
Front/rear track	1,555/1,527mm
Length	5,160mm
Width	1,820mm
Height	1,446mm
Turning circle diameter	12.3m
Kerb weight	1,810kg (3,982lb); from Sept 1987: 1,830kg (4,026lb)
by Guideline	DIN 70020 (ready to drive, including fuel, spare wheel and tool kit)
Gross weight	2,270kg (4,994lb); from Sept 1987: 2,290kg (5,038lb)
Gross axle weight; front	1,110kg (2,442lb); from Sept 1987: 1,085kg (2,387lb)
Gross axle weight; rear	1,160kg (2,552lb); from Sept 1987: 1,185kg (2,607lb)
Payload	460kg (1,012lb)
Permissible trailer weight; braked	1,500kg (3,300lb); from March 1989: 1,900kg (4,180lb)
Permissible trailer weight; unbraked	750kg (1,650lb)

General Data

Units produced	75,071
Prices	
	Sept 1985: DM 121,410.00
	Sept 1986: DM 123,804.00
	June 1987: DM 127,338.00
	Feb 1988: DM 130,416.00
	Feb 1989: DM 133,152.00
	Jan 1990: DM 137,028.00
	Oct 1990: DM 141,531.00

SPECIFICATIONS: GENERATION TWO COUPÉ

420 SEC

Model	**C 126 E 42**
Description	126.046
Pre-production	Aug 1985
Production	Oct 1985 to Oct 1991

Engine

Combustion principle	four-stroke Otto (with manifold-injection; emission control device with 3-way catalyst optional, from Sept 1986 as standard)
Configuration	front, longitudinal; vertical
Engine type	M 116 E 42/116.965
Number of cylinders/ arrangement	8/90°V; light-alloy block
Bore x stroke	92.0 x 78.9mm
Total displacement	4196cc (tax classification: 4146cc)
Compression ratio	9.0; from Sept 1987: 10.0
Crankshaft bearings	5
Rated output	218bhp/160kW (with catalyst 204bhp/150kW) at 5,200rpm; ~from Sept 1987: 231bhp/170kW (with catalyst 224bhp/165kW) at 5,400rpm
Rated torque	330Nm at 3,750rpm (with catalyst 310Nm at 3,600rpm); ~from Sept 1987: 335Nm (with catalyst 325Nm) at 4,000rpm
Number of valves/ arrangement	1 intake, 1 exhaust/overhead
Valve operation	1 overhead camshaft per cylinder bank
Camshaft drive	double roller chain
Fuel system	manifold injection, mechanically-electronically controlled~(Bosch KE-Jetronic)
Cooling	water cooling/pump; 12.0ltr water
Lubrication	pressure circulation lubrication/ 8ltr oil
Electric system	12V
Battery	66Ah; from Sept 1990: 74Ah/in the engine compartment
Generator	three-phase AC/1,120W
Starter	electrical/1.5bhp; from 01.1988: 1.7kW
Ignition	electronic ignition system
Fuel tank: position/capacity	above the rear axle/90ltr
Fuel supply	electric delivery pump

Chassis and Drivetrain

Frame design	steel unit body
Front-wheel suspension	double wishbone
Rear-wheel suspension	semi-trailing arm axle (hydro-pneumatic level control optional)
Front springs	coil springs, supplementary rubber suspension, torsion bar stabilizer
Rear springs	coil springs, supplementary rubber suspension, torsion bar stabilizer
Shock absorber front/rear	gas-pressure shock absorbers
Steering	recirculating-ball power steering
Steering ratio	15.06:1/3.03 turns lock-to-lock
Brake system (foot brake)	hydraulic dual-circuit brake system with vacuum booster and antilock system; ~disc brakes front (internally ventilated) and rear
Parking brake (hand brake)	mechanical (foot-operated), acting on rear wheels
Diameter of brake discs	brake discs front/rear: 300/279mm

Wheels	sheet-steel wheels (light-alloy wheels optional)
Wheel rims	7 J x 15 H 2
Tyres	205/65VR 15
Driven wheels	rear wheels
Drivetrain	divided cardan shaft

Transmission and Performance (as Standard until Sept 1988)

Gearing	four-speed automatic transmission
Shifting	central floor gear shift lever
Clutch	dry single-disc clutch
Transmission type	planetary gear system
Gear ratios	I. 3.68; II. 2.41; III. 1.44; IV. 1.0; R. 5.14
Final drive ratio	2.47
Maximum speed	218km/h (135mph); with catalyst 210km/h (130mph); ~from Sept 1987: 222km/h (138mph); with catalyst 220km/h (136mph)
Acceleration 0–100km/h	8.3sec (with catalyst 8.7sec); from Sept 1987: 8.2sec (with catalyst 8.3sec)
Comments	acceleration by shifting through 0–100km/h (two occupants)
Fuel consumption	8.9/11.0/14.6ltr (with catalyst 9.3/11.6/14.9ltr); ~from Sept 1987: 8.7/10.7/15.1ltr (with catalyst 9.1/11.3/15.4ltr)
by Guideline	80/1268/EEC: figures apply to 90km/h–120km/h/urban cycle

Transmission and Performance (as Standard after Sept 1988)

Gearing	four-speed automatic transmission
Shifting	central floor gear shift lever
Clutch	dry single-disc clutch
Transmission type	planetary gear system
Gear ratios	I. 3.87; II. 2.25; III. 1.44; IV. 1.0; R. 5.59
Final drive ratio	2.47
Maximum speed	222km/h (138mph); with catalyst 220km/h (136mph)
Acceleration 0–100km/h	8.2sec (with catalyst 8.3sec)
Comments	acceleration by shifting through 0–100km/h (two occupants)

Fuel consumption	8.7/10.7/15.1ltr (with catalyst 9.1/11.3/15.4ltr)
by Guideline	80/1268/EEC: figures apply to 90km/h–120km/h/urban cycle

Dimensions and Weights

Wheelbase	2,850mm
Front/rear track	1,555/1,527mm
Length	4,935mm
Width	1,828mm
Height	1,407mm
Turning circle diameter	11.5m
Kerb weight	1600kg; from Sept 1987: 1,620kg (3,564lb)
by Guideline	DIN 70020 (ready to drive, including fuel, spare wheel and tool kit)
Gross weight	2,120kg (4,664lb); from Sept 1987: 2,140kg (4,708lb)
Gross axle weight; front	1,020kg (2,244lb); from Sept 1987: 1,025kg (2,255lb)
Gross axle weight; rear	1,100kg (2,420lb); from Sept 1987: 1,115kg (2,453lb)
Payload	520kg (1,144lb)
Permissible trailer weight; braked	1,500kg (3,300lb); from March 1989: 1,900kg (4,180lb)
Permissible trailer weight; unbraked	750kg (1,650lb)

General Data

Units produced	3,680
Prices	
	Sept 1985: DM 94,563.00
	Dec 1985: DM 96,273.00
	Sept 1986: DM 98,667.00
	June 1987: DM 101,517.00
	Feb 1988: DM 103,968.00
	Sept 1988: DM 104,652.00
	Feb 1989: DM 106,818.00
	Jan 1990: DM 109,896.00
	Oct 1990: DM 113,544.00
	March 1991: DM 116,964.00

500 SEC

Model	**C 126 E 50**
Description	126.044
Production	Sept 1985 to Sept 1991

Engine

Combustion principle	four-stroke Otto (with manifold-injection; emission control device with 3-way catalyst optional, from Sept 1986 as standard)
Configuration	front, longitudinal; vertical
Engine type	M 117 E 50/117.965
Number of cylinders /arrangement	8/90°V; light-alloy block
Bore x stroke	96.5 x 85.0mm
Total displacement	4973cc (tax classification: 4939cc)
Compression ratio	9.0; from Sept 1987: 10.0
Crankshaft bearings	5
Rated output	245bhp/180kW at 4,750rpm (with catalyst 223bhp/164kW at 4,700rpm); from Sept 1987: 265bhp/195kW (with catalyst 252bhp/185kW) at 5,200rpm
Rated torque	400Nm at 3,750rpm (with catalyst 365Nm at 2,500rpm); from ~Sept 1987: 405Nm at 4,000rpm (with catalyst 390Nm at 3,750rpm)
Number of valves/ arrangement	1 intake, 1 exhaust/overhead
Valve operation	1 overhead camshaft per cylinder bank
Camshaft drive	double roller chain
Fuel system	manifold injection, mechanically-electronically controlled~(Bosch KE-Jetronic)
Cooling	water cooling/pump; 13ltr water
Lubrication	pressure circulation lubrication/ 8ltr oil
Electric system	12V
Battery	66Ah; from Sept 1990: 74Ah/in the engine compartment
Generator	three-phase AC/1,120W
Starter	electrical/1.5bhp; from 01.1988: 1.7kW
Ignition	electronic ignition system
Fuel tank: position/capacity	above the rear axle/90ltr
Fuel supply	electric delivery pump

Chassis and Drivetrain

Frame design	steel unit body
Front-wheel suspension	double wishbone
Rear-wheel suspension	twist-beam axle (semi-trailing arm axle with starting- and braking-torque compensation), hydro-pneumatic level control optional
Front springs	coil springs, supplementary rubber suspension, torsion bar stabilizer
Rear springs	coil springs, supplementary rubber suspension, torsion bar stabilizer
Shock absorber front/rear	gas-pressure shock absorbers
Steering	recirculating-ball power steering
Steering ratio	15.06:1/3.03 turns lock-to-lock
Brake system (foot brake)	hydraulic dual-circuit brake system with vacuum booster and antilock system; ~disc brakes front (internally ventilated) and rear
Parking brake (hand brake)	mechanical (foot-operated), acting on rear wheels
Diameter of brake discs	brake discs front/rear: 300/279mm
Wheels	sheet-steel wheels (light-alloy wheel optional)
Wheel rims	7 J x 15 H 2
Tyres	205/65VR 15
Driven wheels	rear wheels
Drivetrain	divided cardan shaft

Transmission and Performance (as Standard until Sept 1988)

Gearing	four-speed automatic transmission
Shifting	central floor gear shift lever
Clutch	dry single-disc clutch
Transmission type	planetary gear system
Gear ratios	I. 3.68; II. 2.41; III. 1.44; IV. 1.0; R. 5.14
Final drive ratio	2.24
Maximum speed	230km/h (143mph); with catalyst 220km/h (136mph); ~from Sept 1987: 235km/h (146mph); with catalyst 230km/h (143mph)
Acceleration 0–100km/h	7.3sec (with catalyst 8.0sec); from Sept 1987: 7.2sec (with catalyst 7.5sec)

Comments	acceleration by shifting through 0–100km/h (two occupants)
Fuel consumption	9.1/11.4/15.4ltr (with catalyst 9.6/12.0/15.9ltr); ~from Sept 1987: 8.8/11.1/15.8ltr (with catalyst 9.4/11.7/16.2ltr)
by Guideline	80/1268/EEC: figures apply to 90km/h–120km/h/urban cycle

Transmission and performance (as Standard after Sept 1988)

Gearing	four-speed automatic transmission
Shifting	central floor gear shift lever
Clutch	dry single-disc clutch
Transmission type	planetary gear system
Gear ratios	I. 3.87; II. 2.25; III. 1.44; IV. 1.0; R. 5.59
Final drive ratio	2.24
Maximum speed	235km/h (146mph); with catalyst 230km/h (143mph)
Acceleration 0–100km/h	7.2secs (with catalyst 7.5sec)
Comments	acceleration by shifting through 0–100km/h (two occupants)
Fuel consumption	8.8/11.1/15.8ltr (with catalyst 9.4/11.7/16.2ltr)
by Guideline	80/1268/EEC: figures apply to 90km/h–120km/h/urban cycle

Dimensions and Weights

Wheelbase	2,845mm
Front/rear track	1,555/1,527mm
Length	4,935mm
Width	1,828mm
Height	1,407mm
Turning circle diameter	11.5m
Kerb weight	1,620kg (3,564lb); from Sept 1987: 1,650kg (3,564lb)
by Guideline	DIN 70020 (ready to drive, including fuel, spare wheel and tool kit)
Gross weight	2,140kg (4,708lb); from Sept 1987: 2,170kg (4,741lb)
Gross axle weight; front	1,025kg (2,255lb); from Sept 1987: 1,015kg (2,233lb)
Gross axle weight; rear	1,115kg (2,453lb); from Sept 1987: 1,130kg (2,486lb)
Payload	520kg (1,144lb)
Permissible trailer weight; braked	1,500kg (3,300lb); from March 1989: 1,900kg (4,180lb)
Permissible trailer weight; unbraked	750kg (1,650lb)

General Data

Units produced	a total of 30,184 (from Jly 1980)
Prices	Sept 1985: DM 100,377.00
	Dec 1985: DM 102,201.00
	Sept 1986: DM 104,595.00
	June 1987: DM 107,559.00
	Feb 1988: DM 110,181.00
	Sept 1988: DM 110,865.00
	Feb 1989: DM 113,202.00
	Jan 1990: DM 116,508.00
	Oct 1990: DM 120,384.00
	March 1991: DM 123,975.00

560 SEC

Model	**C 126 E 56**
Description	126.045
Pre-production	June 1985
Production	Oct 1985 to Oct 1991

Engine

Combustion principle	four-stroke Otto (with manifold-injection; emission control device with 3-way catalyst optional, from Sept 1986 as standard)
Configuration	front, longitudinal; vertical
Engine type	M 117 E 56/117.968
Number of cylinders/arrangement	8/90°V; light-alloy block
Bore x stroke	96.5 x 94.8mm
Total displacement	5547cc (tax classification: 5491cc)
Compression ratio	9.0; from Sept 1987: 10.0
Crankshaft bearings	5
Rated output	272bhp/200kW at 5,000rpm (with catalyst 242bhp/178kW at 4,800rpm); from Sept 1987: 300bhp/220kW at 5,000rpm (with catalyst 279bhp/205kW at 5,200rpm)
Rated torque	430Nm at 3,750rpm (with catalyst 390Nm at 3,500rpm); from ~Sept 1987: 455Nm (with catalyst 430Nm) at 3,750rpm
Number of valves/arrangement	1 intake, 1 exhaust/overhead
Valve operation	1 overhead camshaft per cylinder bank
Camshaft drive	double roller chain
Fuel system	manifold injection, mechanically-electronically controlled~(Bosch KE-Jetronic)
Cooling	water cooling/pump; 13ltr water
Lubrication	pressure circulation lubrication/8ltr oil
Electric system	12V
Battery	92Ah/in the engine compartment
Generator	three-phase AC/1,120W
Starter	electrical/1.5bhp; from 01.1988: 1.7kW
Ignition	electronic ignition system
Fuel tank: position/capacity	above the rear axle/90ltr
Fuel supply	electric delivery pump

Chassis and Drivetrain

Frame design	steel unit body
Front-wheel suspension	double wishbone
Rear-wheel suspension	twist-beam axle (semi-trailing arm axle with starting- and braking-torque compensation) with hydro-pneumatic level control
Front springs	coil springs, supplementary rubber suspension, torsion bar stabilizer
Rear springs	coil springs, hydro-pneumatic spring struts, torsion bar stabilizer
Shock absorber front/rear	gas-pressure shock absorbers
Steering	recirculating-ball power steering
Steering ratio	15.06:1/3.03 turns lock-to-lock
Brake system (foot brake)	hydraulic dual-circuit brake system with vacuum booster and antilock system; ~disc brakes front (internally ventilated) and rear
Parking brake (hand brake)	mechanical (foot-operated), acting on rear wheels
Diameter of brake discs	brake discs front/rear: 300/279mm
Wheels	light-alloy wheels
Wheel rims	7 J x 15 H 2
Tyres	215/65VR 15, from 1988: 215/65 ZR 15
Driven wheels	rear wheels

Transmission and Performance

Gearing	four-speed automatic transmission
Shifting	central floor gear shift lever
Clutch	dry single-disc clutch
Transmission type	planetary gear system
Gear ratios	I. 3.87; II. 2.25; III. 1.44; IV. 1.0; R. 5.59
Final drive ratio	2.65
Maximum speed	238km/h (148mph); with catalyst 228km/h (141mph); ~from Sept 1987: 250km/h (155mph); with catalyst 240km/h (149mph)
Acceleration 0–100km/h	6.9sec (with catalyst 7.6sec); from Sept 1987: 6.8sec (with catalyst 7.2sec)

Comments	acceleration by shifting through 0–100km/h (two occupants)
Fuel consumption	10.6/12.9/17.1ltr (with catalyst 11.4/13.9/18.0ltr); ~from Sept 1987: 10.6/12.9/17.1ltr (with catalyst 11.4/13.9/18.0ltr)
by Guideline	80/1268/EEC: figures apply to 90km/h–120km/h/urban cycle

Dimensions and Weights

Wheelbase	2,845mm
Front/rear track	1,555/1,527mm
Length	4,935mm
Width	1,828mm
Height	1,402mm
Turning circle diameter	11.5m
Kerb weight	1750kg (1,650lb); from Sept 1987: 1,540kg (3,388lb)
by Guideline	DIN 70020 (ready to drive, including fuel, spare wheel and tool kit)
Gross weight	2,210kg (4,862lb); from Sept 1987: 2,220kg (4,884lb)

Gross axle weight; front	1,070kg (2,354lb); from Sept 1987: 1,070kg (2,354lb)
Gross axle weight; rear	1,140kg (2,420lb); from Sept 1987: 1,150kg (2,530lb)
Payload	460kg (1,012lb)
Permissible trailer weight; braked	1,500kg (3,300lb); from March 1989: 1,900kg (4,180lb)
Permissible trailer weight; unbraked	750kg (1,650lb)

General Data

Units produced	28,929
Prices	
	Sept 1985: DM 133,608.00
	Sept 1986: DM 136,002.00
	June 1987: DM 139,935.00
	Feb 1988: DM 143,298.00
	Sept 1988: DM 143,469.00
	Feb 1989: DM 146,490.00
	Jan 1990: DM 150,765.00
	Oct 1990: DM 155,724.00
	March 1991: DM 160,398.00

GENERATION TWO SALES PER YEAR

Model	Type	1985	1986	1987	1988	1989	1990	1991	1992	Total
260 SE	126020	2,222	6,198	4,657	3,120	2,455	2,100	84		**20,836**
300 SE	126024	5,432	18,134	15,104	20,431	20,289	21,058	4,974		**105,422**
300 SEL	126025	1,379	4,815	6,886	8,686	10,985	6,428	1,777		**40,956**
420 SE	126034	1,689	4,181	2,704	2,368	1,528	1,345	181		**13,996**
420 SEL	126035	6,102	19,238	18,623	9,467	9,181	8,324	3,082		**74,017**
500 SE	126036		2,351	1,722	1,895	2,676	2,308	718		**11,670**
500 SEL	126037		4,032	2,163	2,087	1,560	1,331	244	6	**11,423**
560 SE	126038				486	428	337	1		**1,252**
560 SEL	126039	2,097	16,559	13,494	12,832	12,990	13,728	3,339	32	**75,071**
420 SEC	126043	273	896	714	593	534	451	219		**3,680**
500 SEC	126044		2,020	1,107	1,056	1,062	1,067	499		**6,811**
560 SEC	126045	989	4,745	5,476	5,012	5,299	5,270	2,138		**28,929**
300 SDL	126120	47	8,274	5,509						**13,830**
350 SD	126134						1,181	885		**2,066**
350 SDL	126135					18	2,032	875		**2,925**
Total by Year		20,230	91,443	78,159	68,033	69,005	66,960	19,016	38	**412,884**

INDEX